Ghost Stories

Whit Taylor

Cover Design by Sean Ford

Published by Rosarium Publishing
P.O. Box 544
Greenbelt, MD 20768-0544
www.rosariumpublishing.com

Printed in Canada

Stories

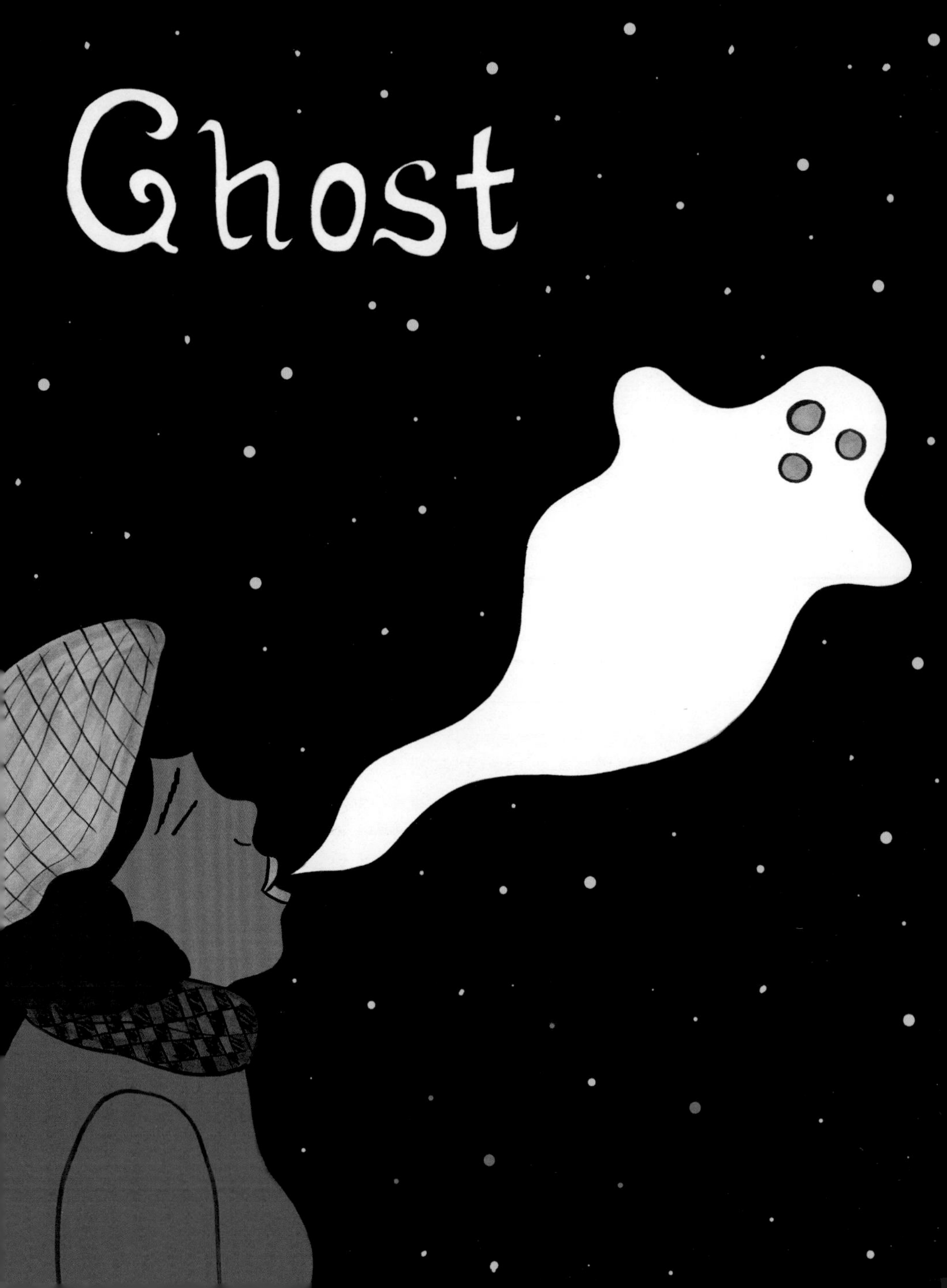
Ghost

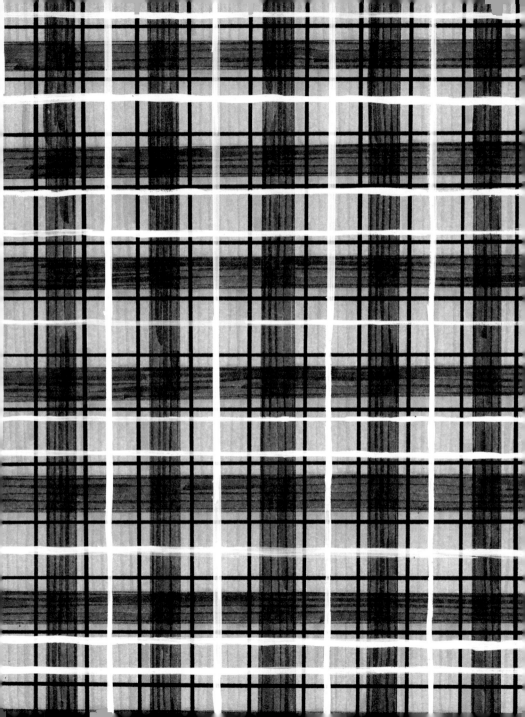

MEET YOUR IDOLS

THEY TOLD ME I COULD MEET MY IDOLS.

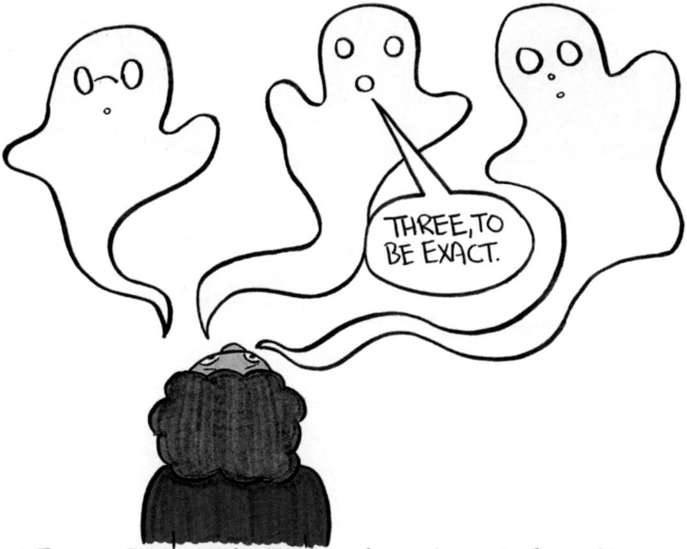
THREE, TO BE EXACT.

I SPENT MY DAY PONDERING WHO THEY WOULD BE.

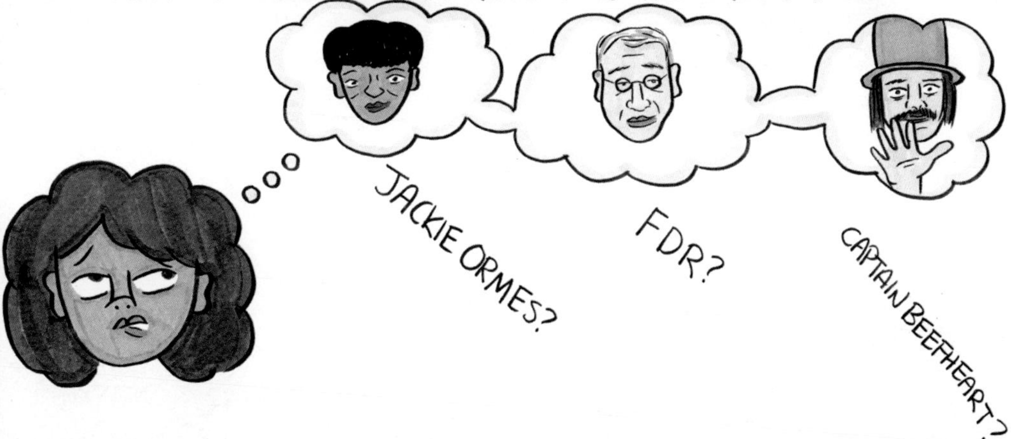
JACKIE ORMES?
FDR?
CAPTAIN BEEFHEART?

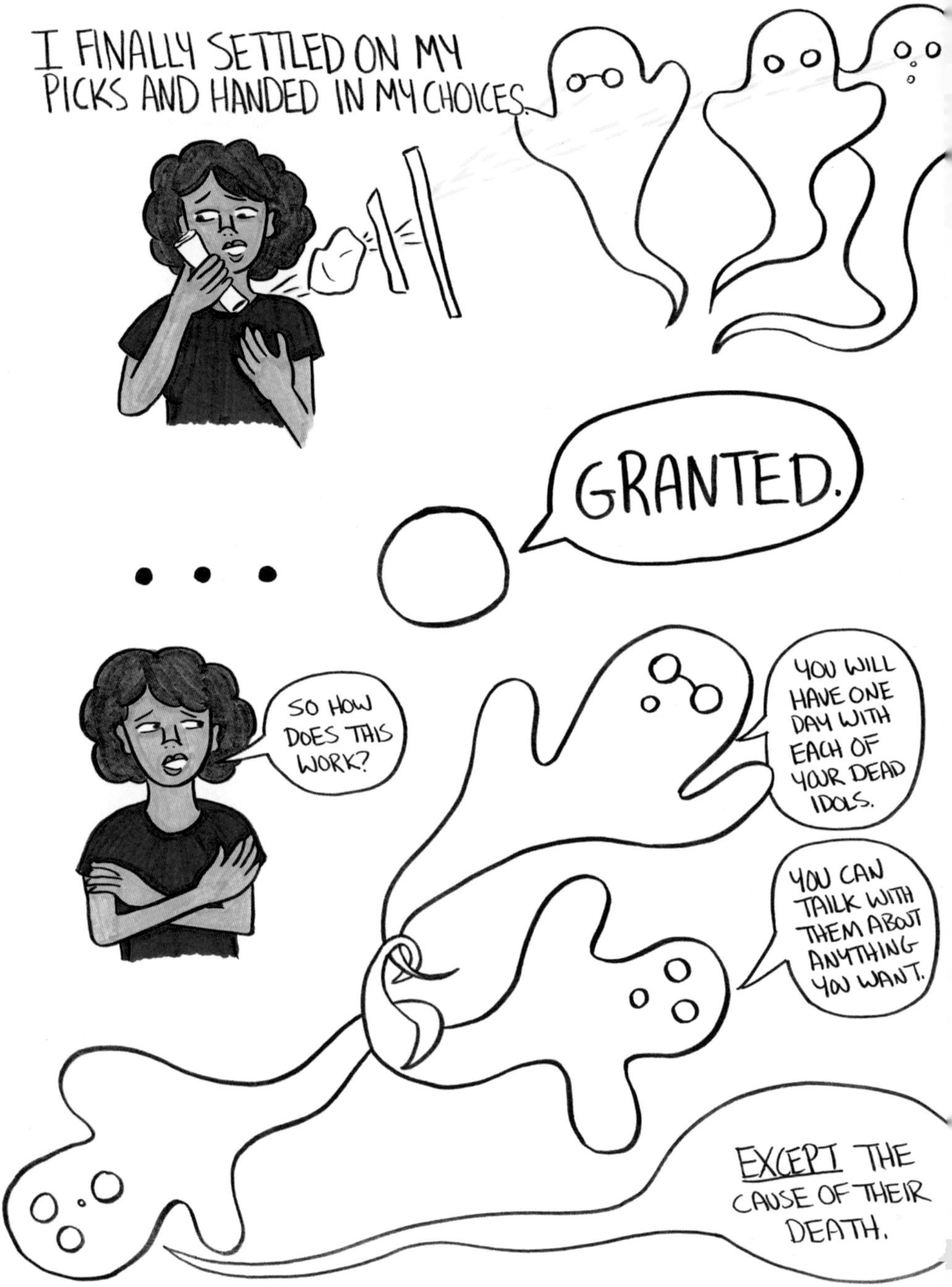
I FINALLY SETTLED ON MY PICKS AND HANDED IN MY CHOICES.
GRANTED.
. . .
SO HOW DOES THIS WORK?
YOU WILL HAVE ONE DAY WITH EACH OF YOUR DEAD IDOLS.
YOU CAN TALK WITH THEM ABOUT ANYTHING YOU WANT.
EXCEPT THE CAUSE OF THEIR DEATH.

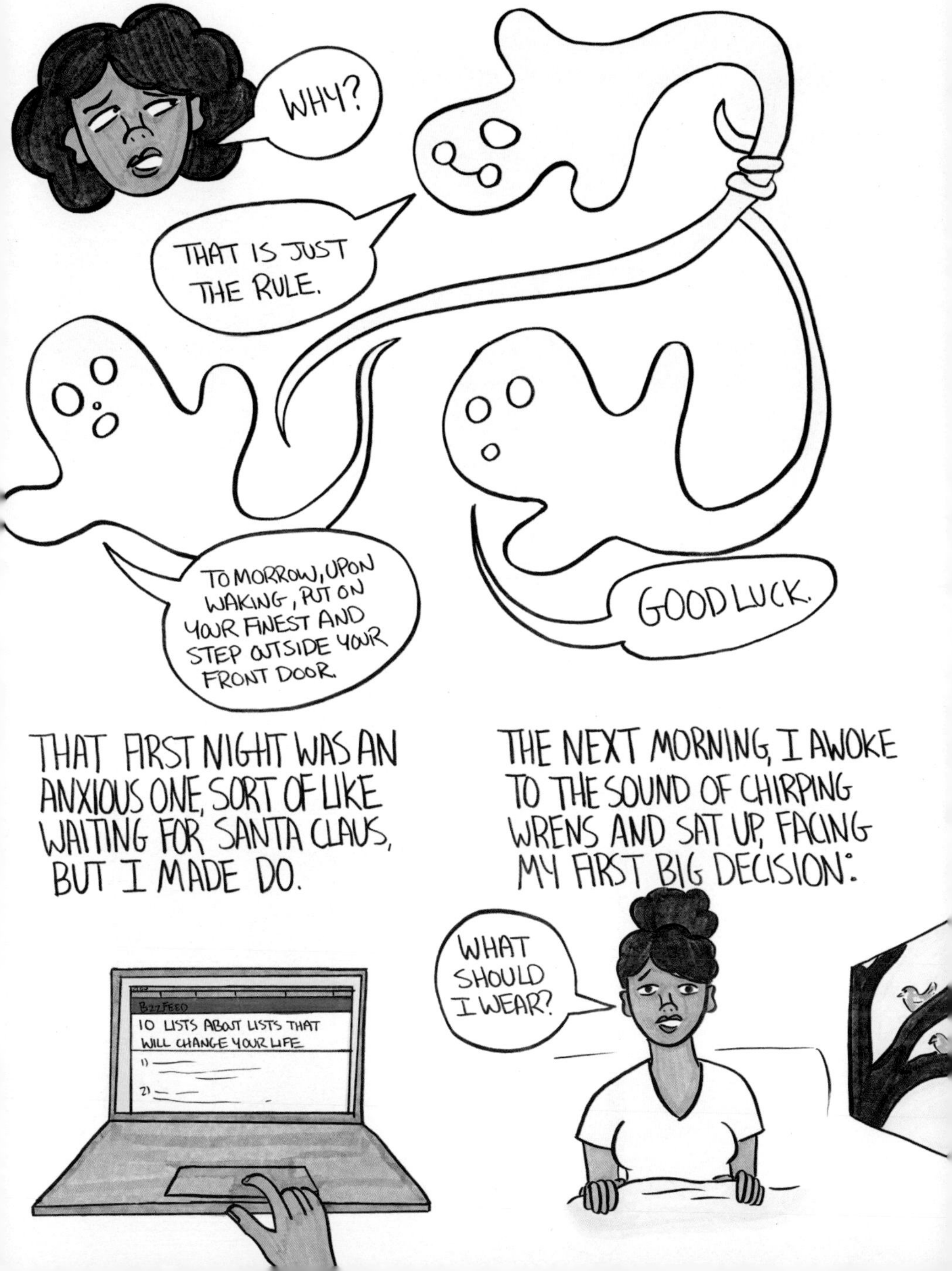
WHY?
THAT IS JUST THE RULE.
TOMORROW, UPON WAKING, PUT ON YOUR FINEST AND STEP OUTSIDE YOUR FRONT DOOR.
GOOD LUCK.
THAT FIRST NIGHT WAS AN ANXIOUS ONE, SORT OF LIKE WAITING FOR SANTA CLAUS, BUT I MADE DO.
10 LISTS ABOUT LISTS THAT WILL CHANGE YOUR LIFE
THE NEXT MORNING, I AWOKE TO THE SOUND OF CHIRPING WRENS AND SAT UP, FACING MY FIRST BIG DECISION:
WHAT SHOULD I WEAR?

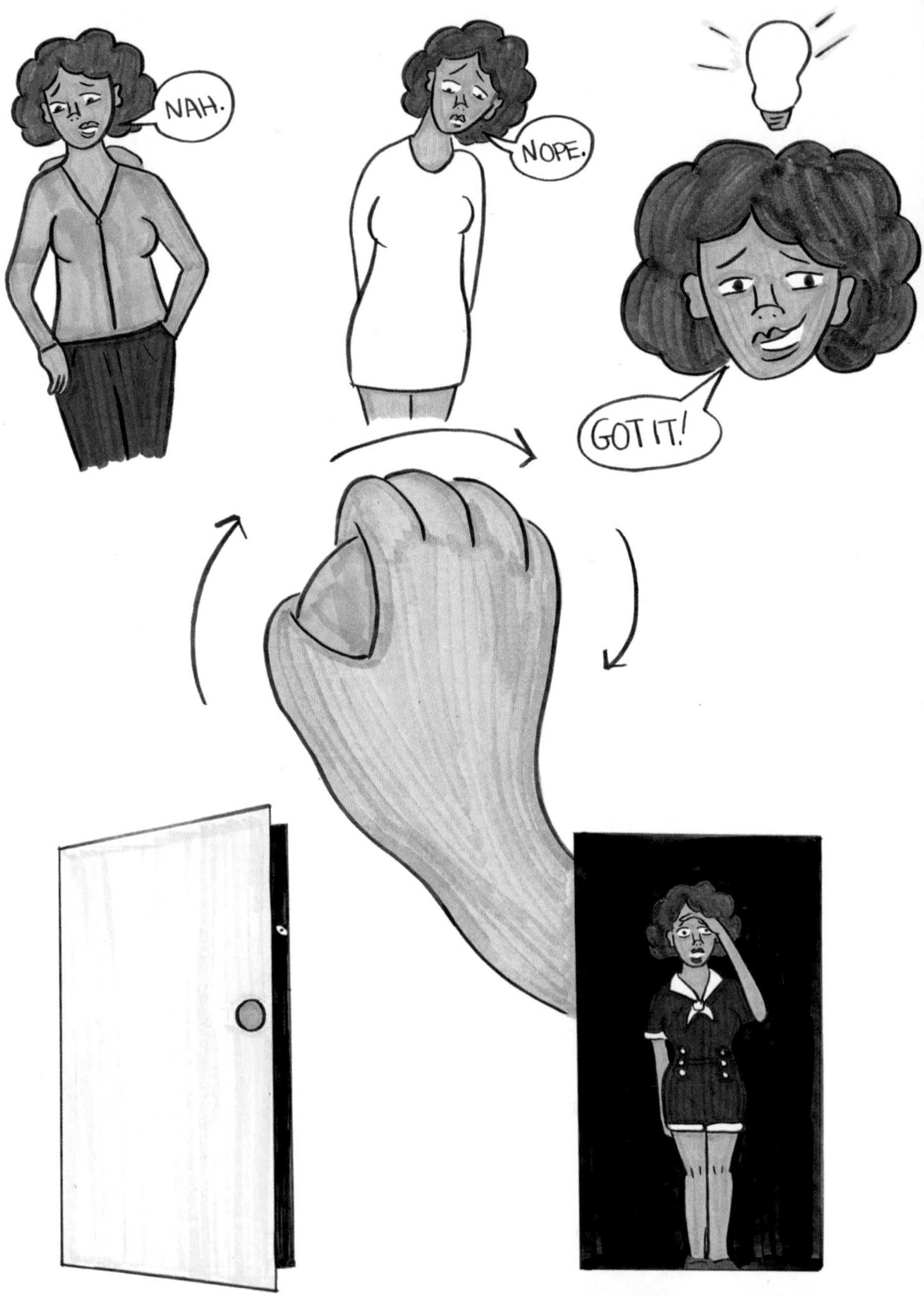
NAH.
NOPE.
GOT IT!

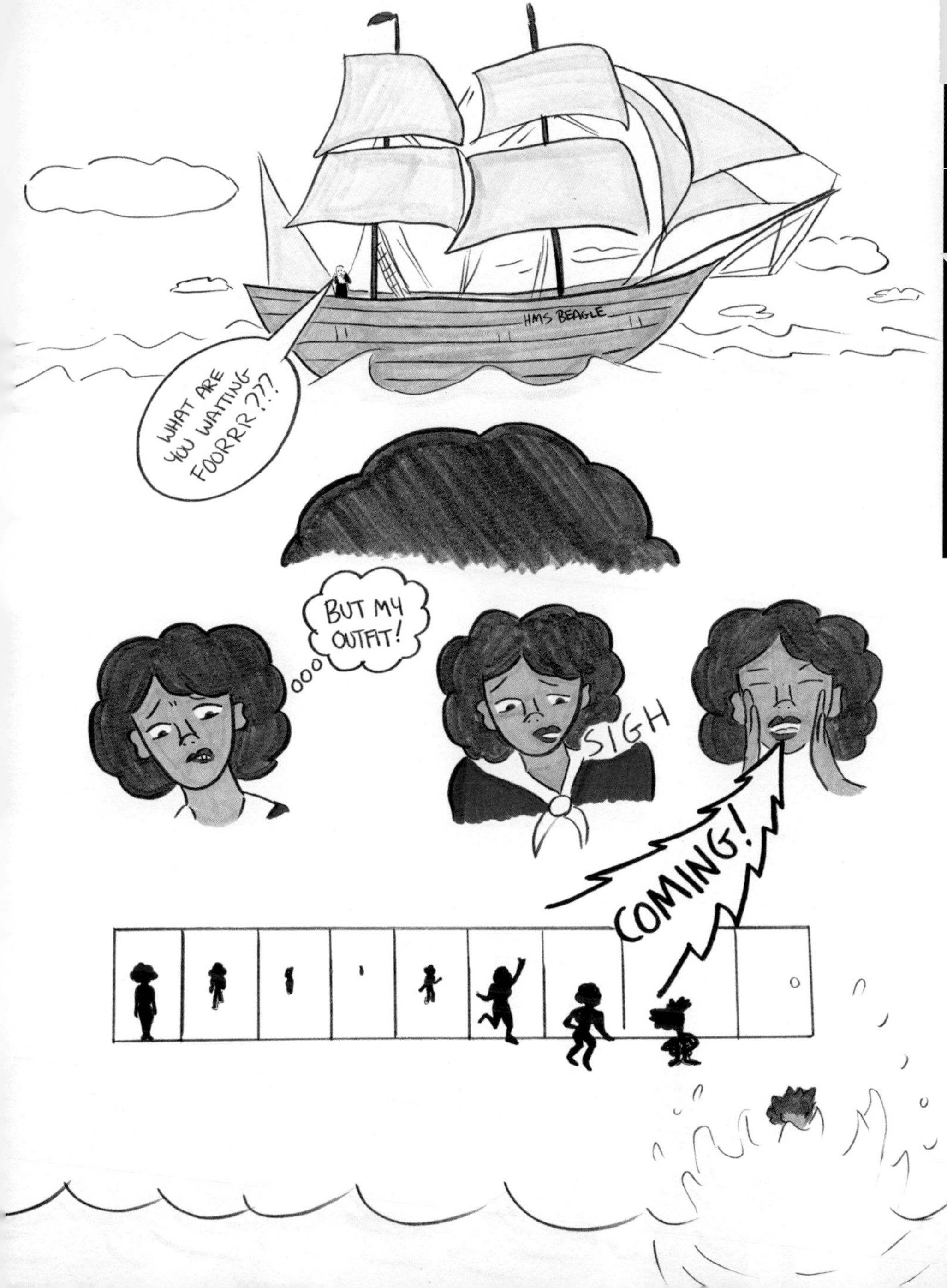
HMS BEAGLE
WHAT ARE YOU WAITING FOORRR???
BUT MY OUTFIT!
SIGH
COMING!

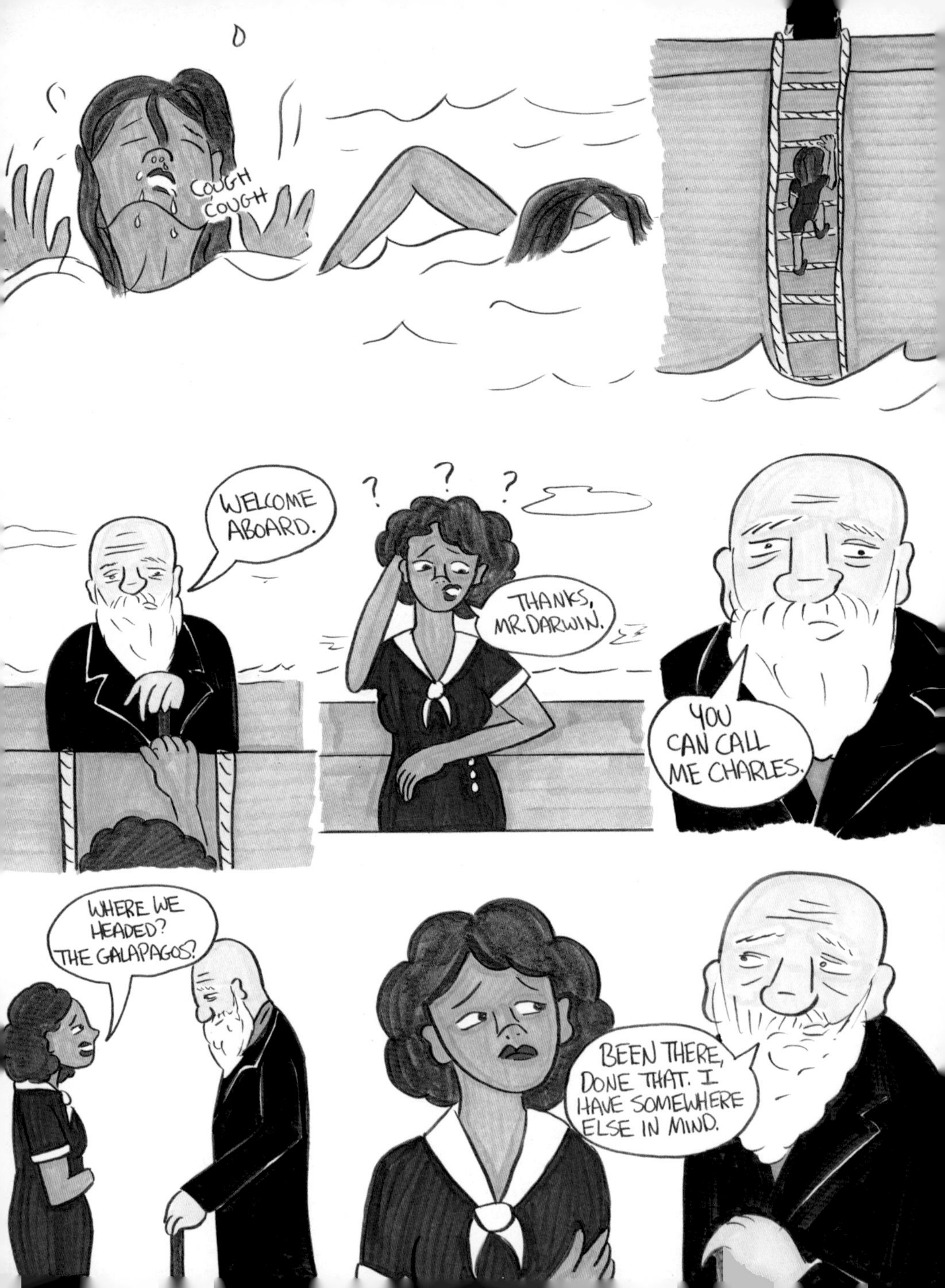
COUGH
COUGH
WELCOME ABOARD.
THANKS, MR. DARWIN.
YOU CAN CALL ME CHARLES.
WHERE WE HEADED? THE GALAPAGOS?
BEEN THERE, DONE THAT. I HAVE SOMEWHERE ELSE IN MIND.

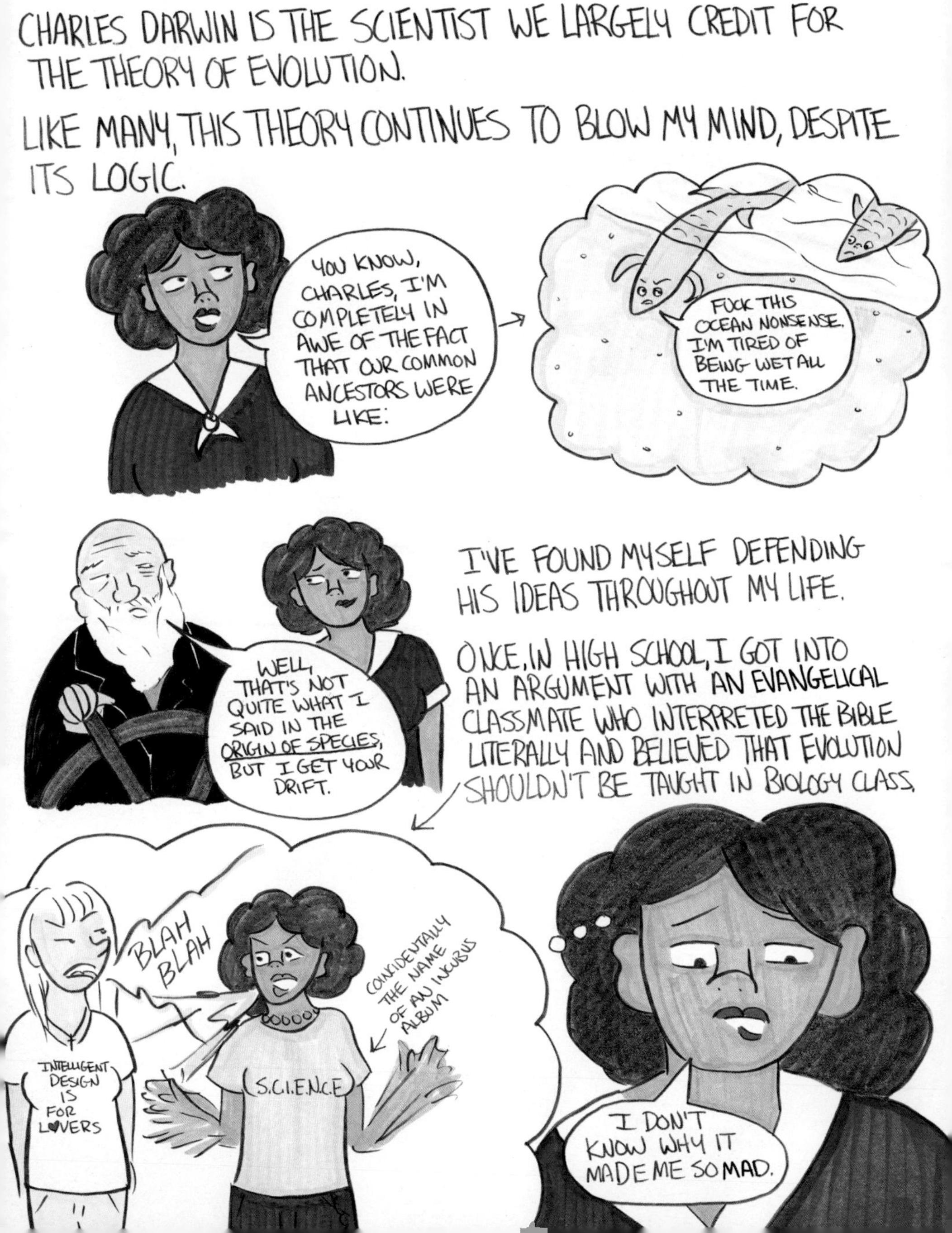
CHARLES DARWIN IS THE SCIENTIST WE LARGELY CREDIT FOR THE THEORY OF EVOLUTION.
LIKE MANY, THIS THEORY CONTINUES TO BLOW MY MIND, DESPITE ITS LOGIC.
YOU KNOW, CHARLES, I'M COMPLETELY IN AWE OF THE FACT THAT OUR COMMON ANCESTORS WERE LIKE:
FUCK THIS OCEAN NONSENSE. I'M TIRED OF BEING WET ALL THE TIME.
I'VE FOUND MYSELF DEFENDING HIS IDEAS THROUGHOUT MY LIFE.
WELL, THAT'S NOT QUITE WHAT I SAID IN THE ORIGIN OF SPECIES, BUT I GET YOUR DRIFT.
ONCE, IN HIGH SCHOOL, I GOT INTO AN ARGUMENT WITH AN EVANGELICAL CLASSMATE WHO INTERPRETED THE BIBLE LITERALLY AND BELIEVED THAT EVOLUTION SHOULDN'T BE TAUGHT IN BIOLOGY CLASS.
BLAH BLAH
INTELLIGENT DESIGN IS FOR LOVERS
COINCIDENTALLY THE NAME OF AN INCUBUS ALBUM
S.C.I.E.N.C.E
I DON'T KNOW WHY IT MADE ME SO MAD.

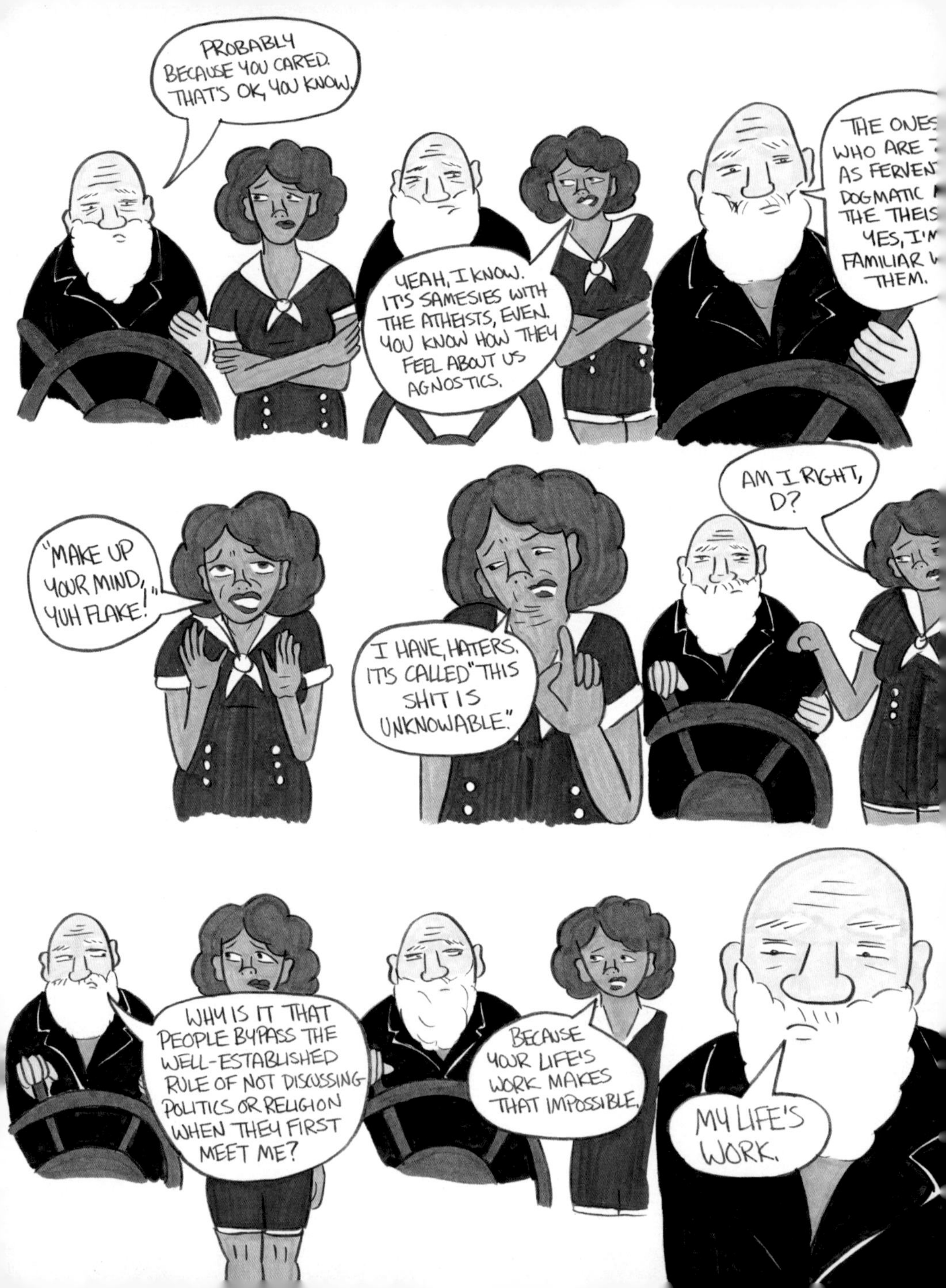
PROBABLY BECAUSE YOU CARED. THAT'S OK, YOU KNOW.
YEAH, I KNOW. IT'S SAMESIES WITH THE ATHEISTS, EVEN. YOU KNOW HOW THEY FEEL ABOUT US AGNOSTICS.
THE ONES WHO ARE AS FERVENT DOGMATIC THE THEIS YES, I'M FAMILIAR THEM.
"MAKE UP YOUR MIND, YUH FLAKE!"
I HAVE, HATERS. IT'S CALLED "THIS SHIT IS UNKNOWABLE."
AM I RIGHT, D?
WHY IS IT THAT PEOPLE BYPASS THE WELL-ESTABLISHED RULE OF NOT DISCUSSING POLITICS OR RELIGION WHEN THEY FIRST MEET ME?
BECAUSE YOUR LIFE'S WORK MAKES THAT IMPOSSIBLE.
MY LIFE'S WORK.

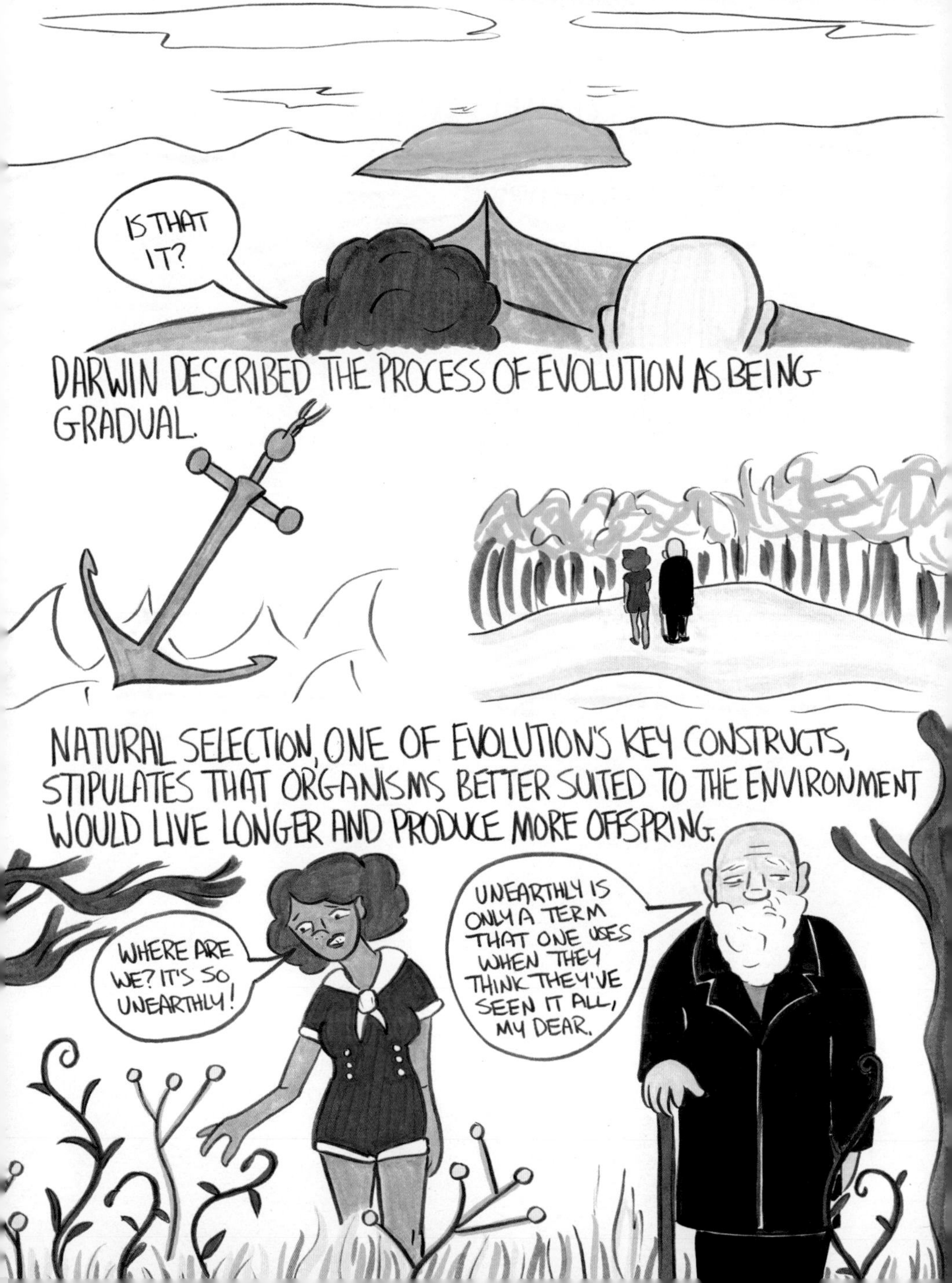
IS THAT IT?
DARWIN DESCRIBED THE PROCESS OF EVOLUTION AS BEING GRADUAL.
NATURAL SELECTION, ONE OF EVOLUTION'S KEY CONSTRUCTS, STIPULATES THAT ORGANISMS BETTER SUITED TO THE ENVIRONMENT WOULD LIVE LONGER AND PRODUCE MORE OFFSPRING.
WHERE ARE WE? IT'S SO UNEARTHLY!
UNEARTHLY IS ONLY A TERM THAT ONE USES WHEN THEY THINK THEY'VE SEEN IT ALL, MY DEAR.

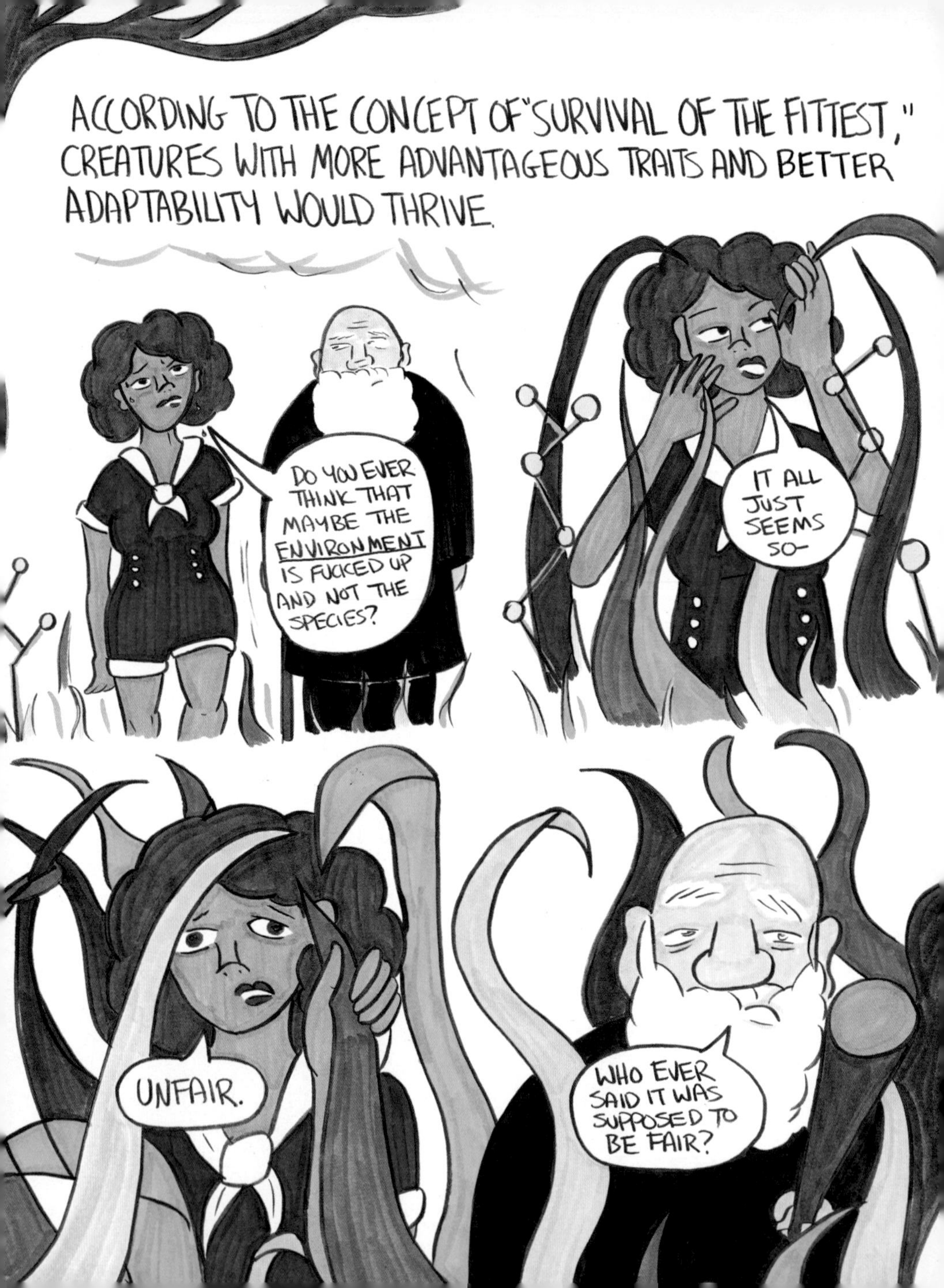
ACCORDING TO THE CONCEPT OF "SURVIVAL OF THE FITTEST," CREATURES WITH MORE ADVANTAGEOUS TRAITS AND BETTER ADAPTABILITY WOULD THRIVE.
DO YOU EVER THINK THAT MAYBE THE ENVIRONMENT IS FUCKED UP AND NOT THE SPECIES?
IT ALL JUST SEEMS SO—
UNFAIR.
WHO EVER SAID IT WAS SUPPOSED TO BE FAIR?

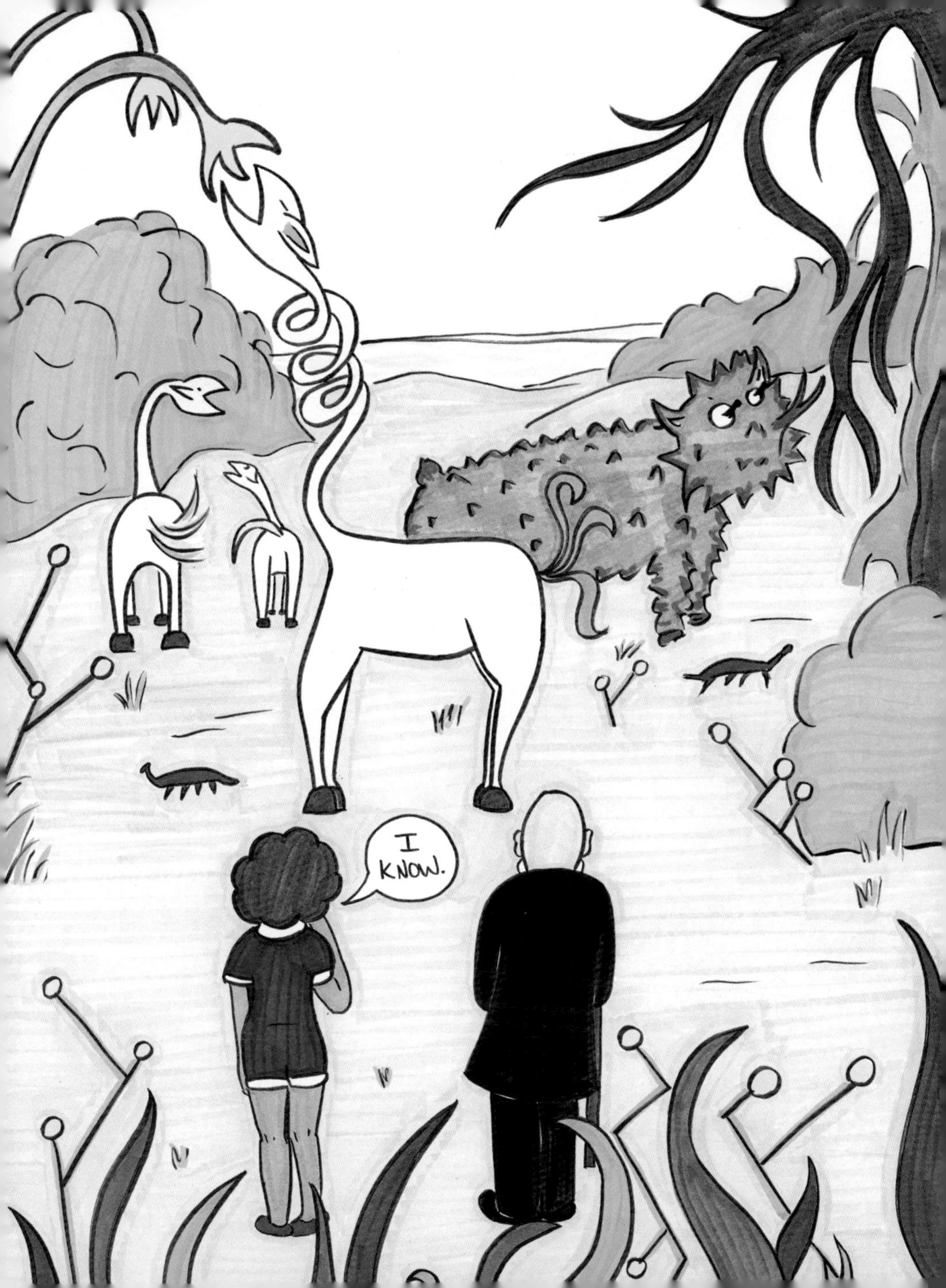
I KNOW.

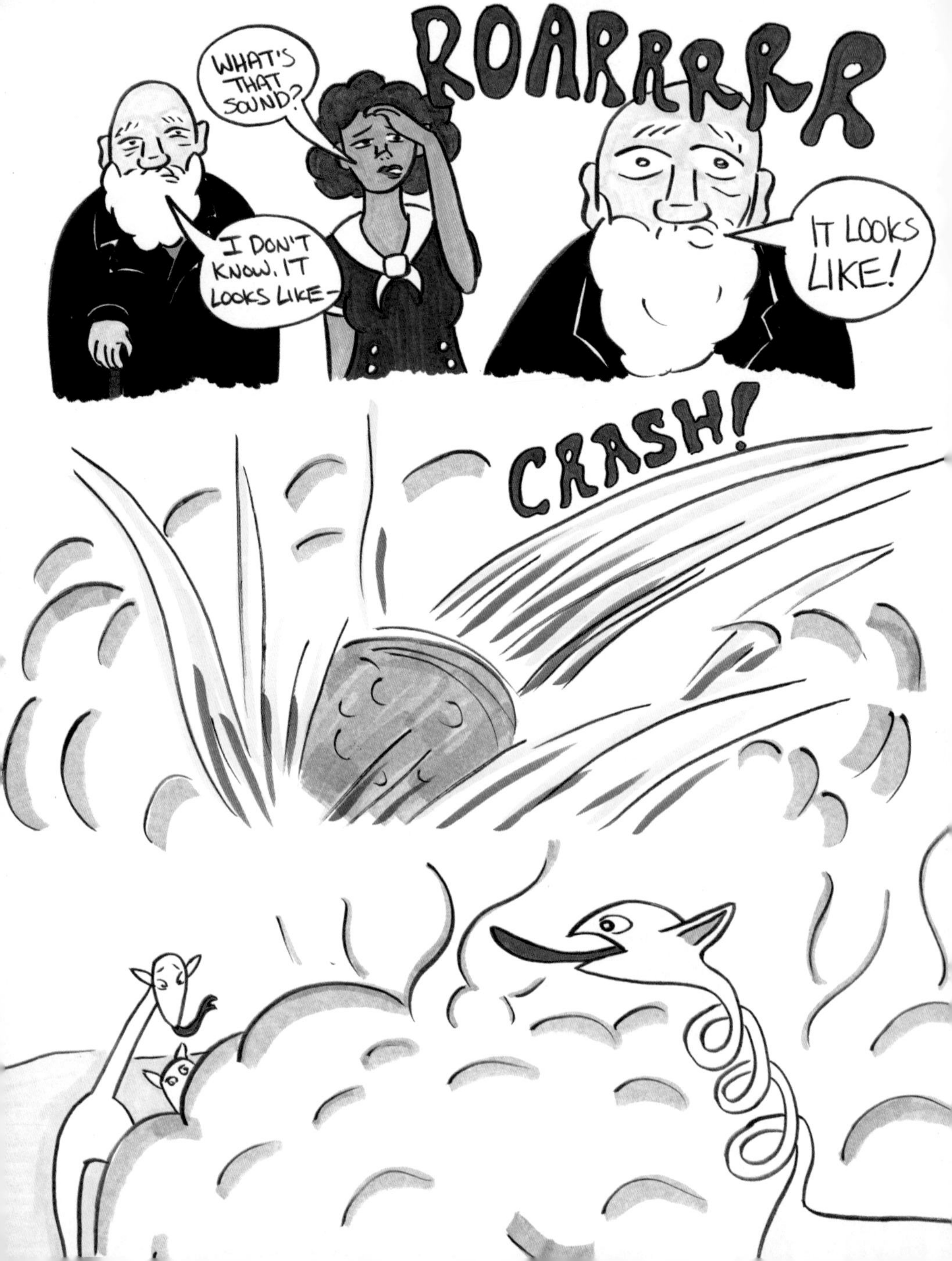
WHAT'S THAT SOUND?
I DON'T KNOW. IT LOOKS LIKE-
ROARRRRRR
IT LOOKS LIKE!
CRASH!

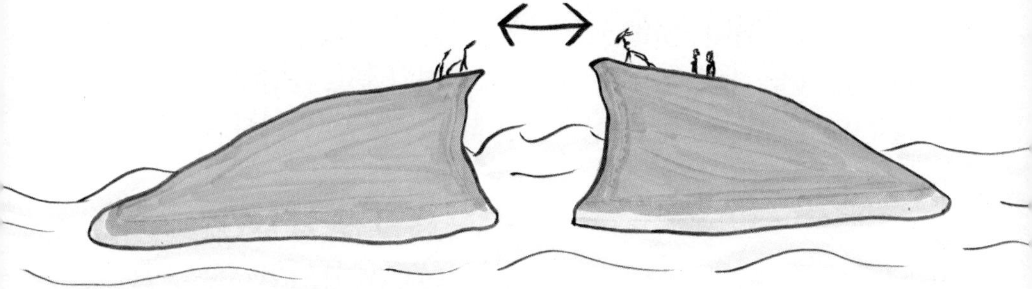

DARWIN WAS ALWAYS HAUNTED BY GHOSTS OF THE INTERMEDIATE SPECIES, OR "MISSING LINKS," ABSENT FROM THE FOSSIL RECORD.

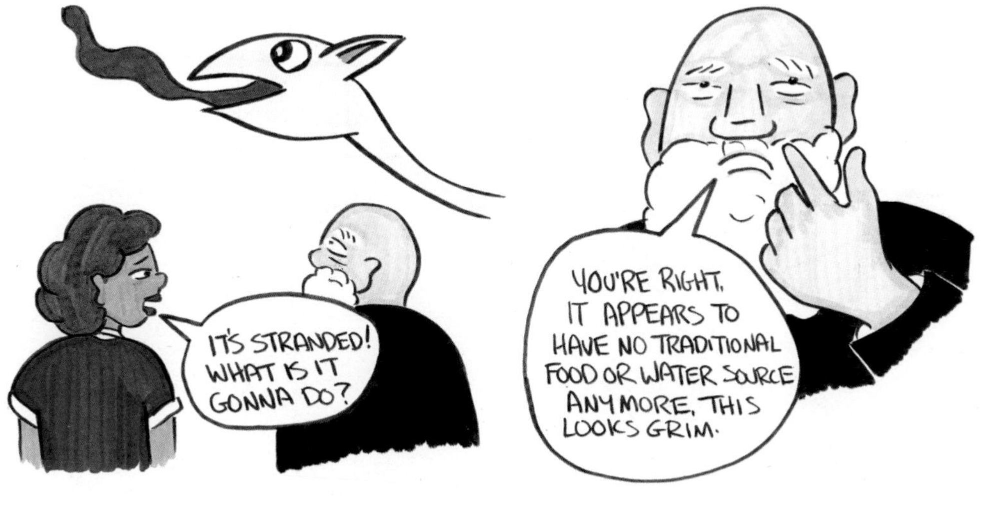
IT'S STRANDED! WHAT IS IT GONNA DO?
YOU'RE RIGHT. IT APPEARS TO HAVE NO TRADITIONAL FOOD OR WATER SOURCE ANYMORE. THIS LOOKS GRIM.

IN THE EARLY 1970s, EVOLUTIONARY BIOLOGISTS STEPHEN JAY GOULD AND NILES ELDREDGE PROPOSED THE HYPOTHESIS OF

"PUNCTUATED EQUILIBRIUM."

IT POSITS THAT SPECIES ARE GENERALLY STABLE FOR MILLIONS OF YEARS UNTIL THEY BECOME "PUNCTUATED" BY A RAPID PERIOD OF CHANGE, WHICH RESULTS IN A NEW SPECIES.

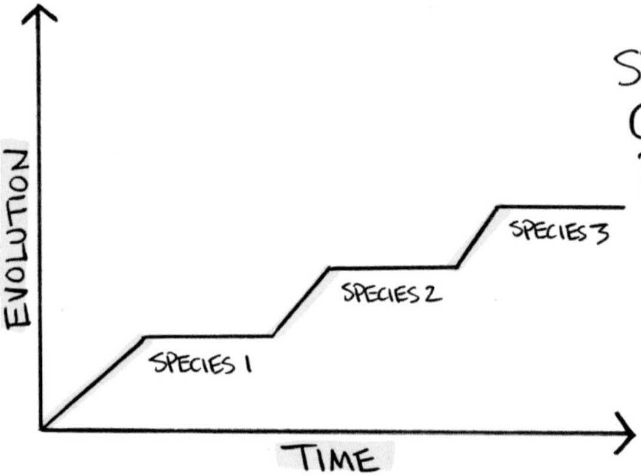
EVOLUTION
TIME
SPECIES 1
SPECIES 2
SPECIES 3

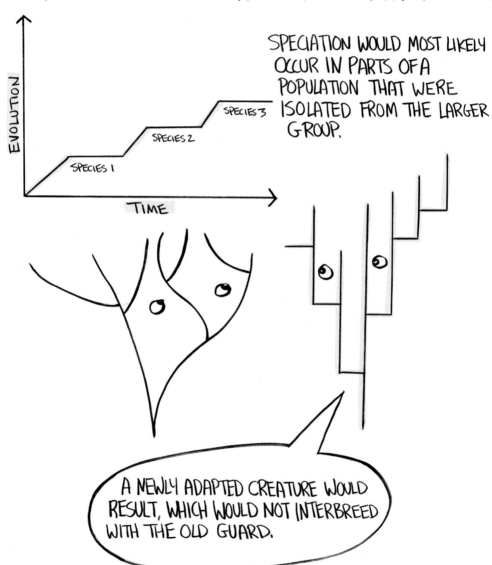

SPECIATION WOULD MOST LIKELY OCCUR IN PARTS OF A POPULATION THAT WERE ISOLATED FROM THE LARGER GROUP.

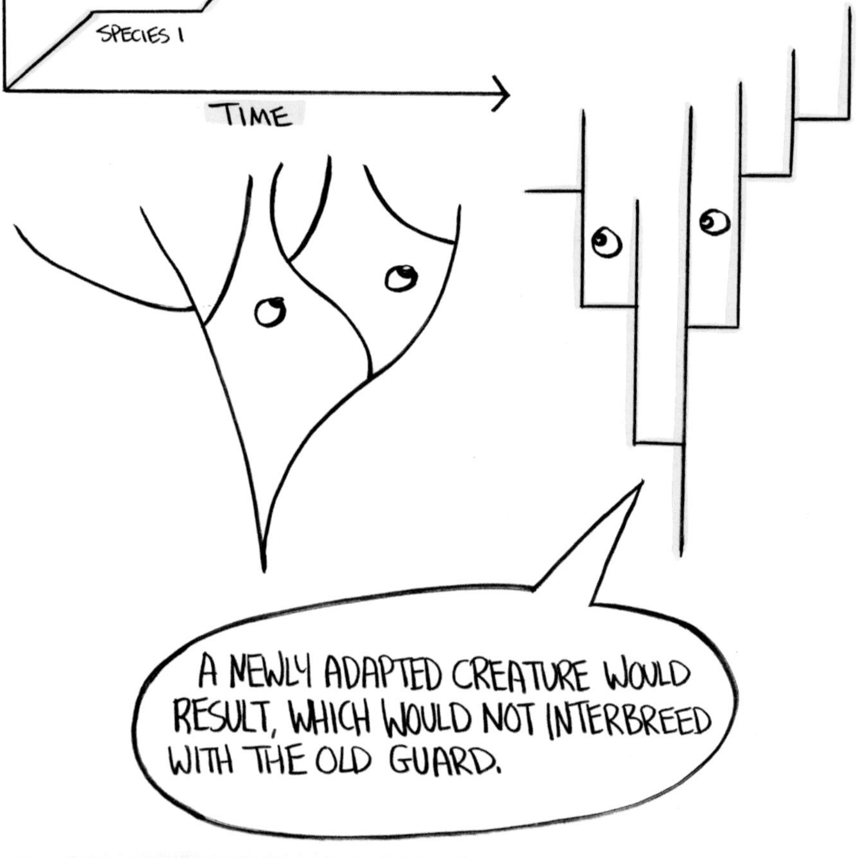
A NEWLY ADAPTED CREATURE WOULD RESULT, WHICH WOULD NOT INTERBREED WITH THE OLD GUARD.

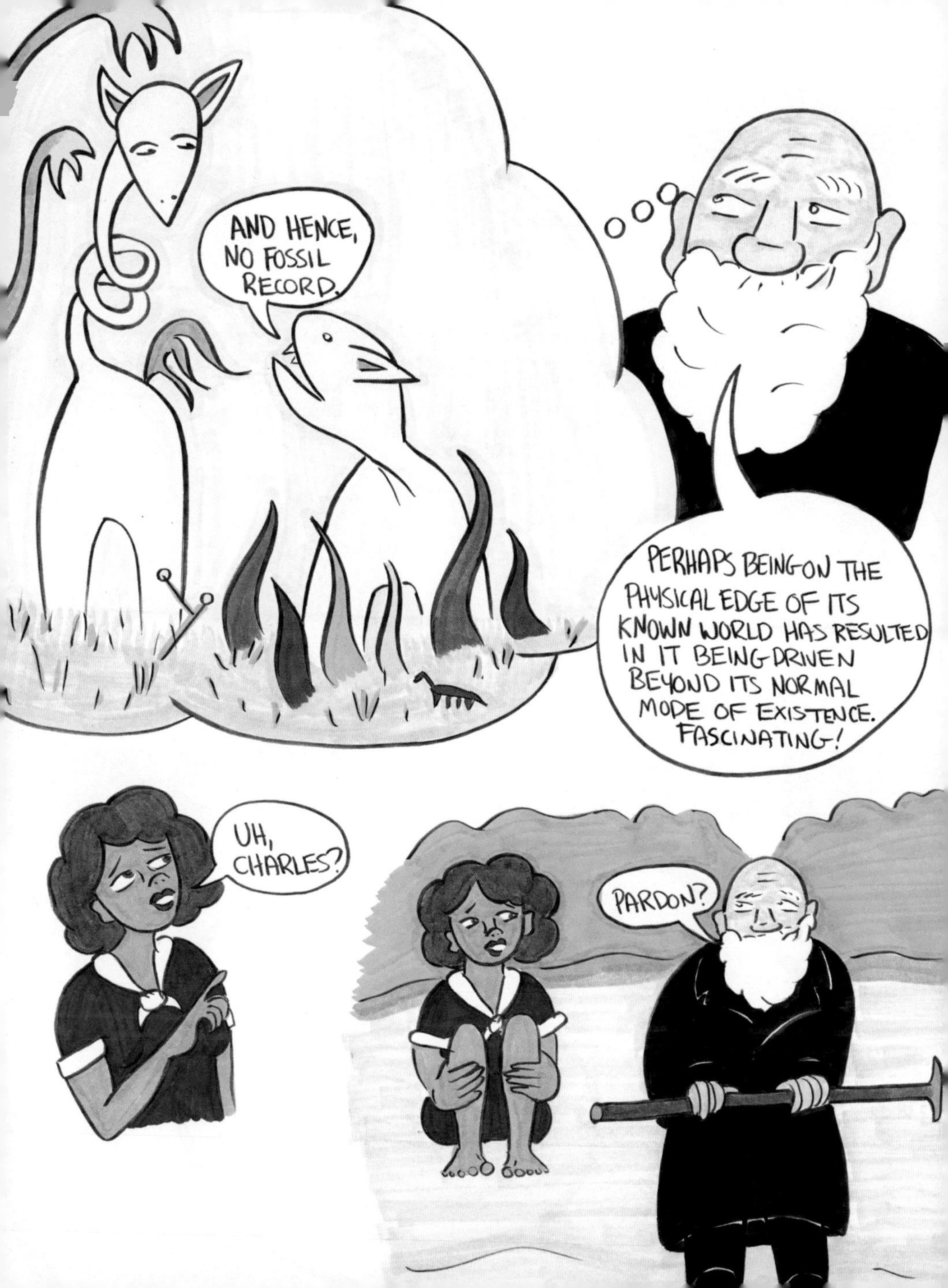
AND HENCE, NO FOSSIL RECORD.
PERHAPS BEING ON THE PHYSICAL EDGE OF ITS KNOWN WORLD HAS RESULTED IN IT BEING DRIVEN BEYOND ITS NORMAL MODE OF EXISTENCE. FASCINATING!
UH, CHARLES?
PARDON?

IT MAKES ME THINK ABOUT MYSELF, YOU KNOW.

I'VE CHANGED SLOWLY OVER TIME IN SOME WAYS, BUT THERE HAVE BEEN EVENTS IN MY LIFE WHICH HAVE ACCELERATED THAT.

SORRY IF I'M BEING SELF-CENTERED.

NOT AT ALL. AND THIS, MY DEAR, IS AT THE HEART OF IT. EVOLUTION MAKES PEOPLE FEEL FUNNY BECAUSE IT'S ABOUT THEM.

WHAT IF THE HISTORY OF LIFE PARALLELS OUR LIFE HISTORY?

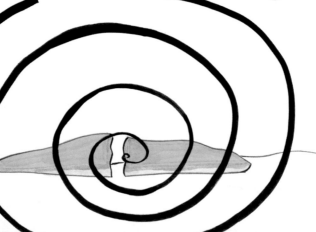

SWEET WILLIAM

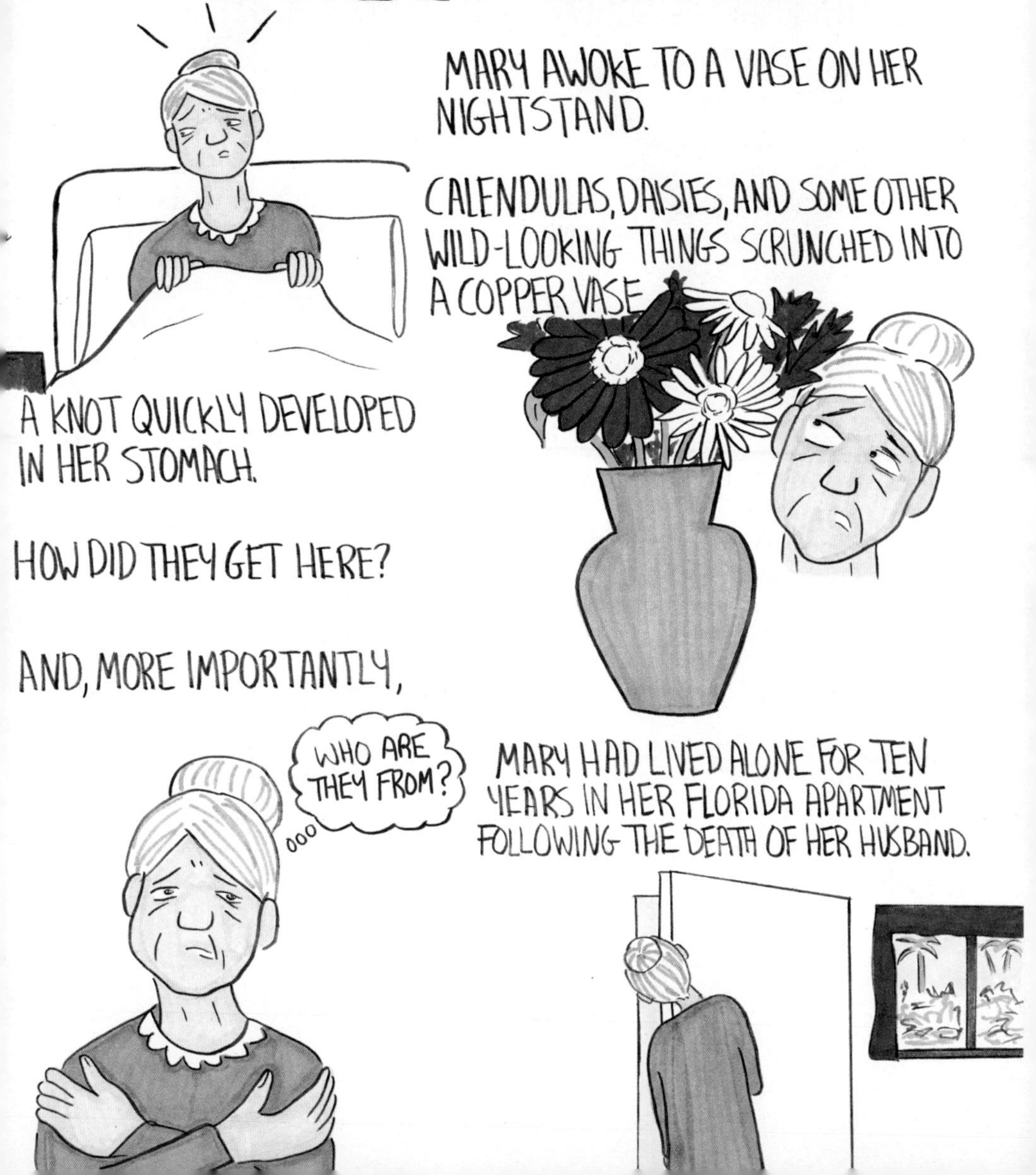
MARY AWOKE TO A VASE ON HER NIGHTSTAND.
CALENDULAS, DAISIES, AND SOME OTHER WILD-LOOKING THINGS SCRUNCHED INTO A COPPER VASE.
A KNOT QUICKLY DEVELOPED IN HER STOMACH.
HOW DID THEY GET HERE?
AND, MORE IMPORTANTLY,
WHO ARE THEY FROM?
MARY HAD LIVED ALONE FOR TEN YEARS IN HER FLORIDA APARTMENT FOLLOWING THE DEATH OF HER HUSBAND.

BEING ALONE HAD PROGRESSED FROM ANGUISH, TO LONELINESS, TO A SOLITUDE SHE HAD NOT EXPECTED.

AFTER CHECKING THE BACK DOORS, MARY PICKED UP THE VASE CAUTIOUSLY.

IT WAS HEAVIER THAN SHE ASSUMED, AND SHE FELT THE UNEASY SWAY OF WATER WITHIN.

DIGGING THROUGH THE BOUQET TO REMOVE THE UNWANTED FERNS, SHE JERKED BACK.

HER FINGER WAS BLOODY AND NICKED.

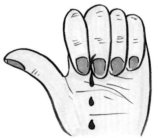

BUT NOT FROM A THORN OR NETTLE.

IT WAS A PAPERCUT.

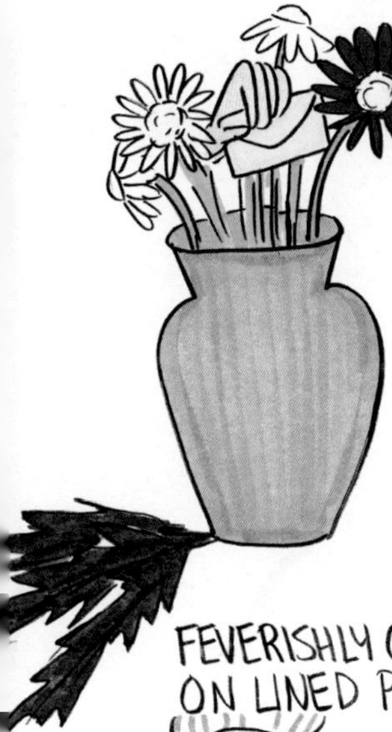

SHE SLOWLY EXTRACTED A TINY SEALED ENVELOPE.

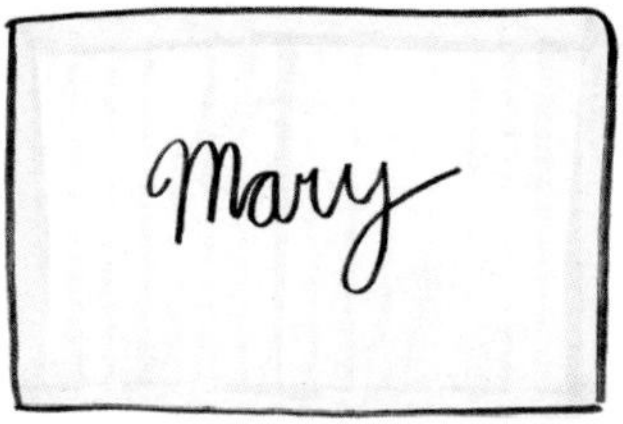
Mary

FEVERISHLY OPENING IT, SHE PULLED OUT A LETTER WRITTEN ON LINED PAPER.

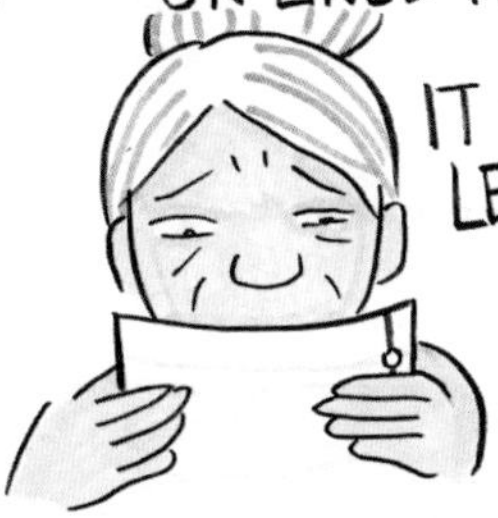

IT SEEMED AS IF THE WORLD HAD STOPPED WRITING LETTERS, SAVE FOR SPECIAL OCCASIONS.

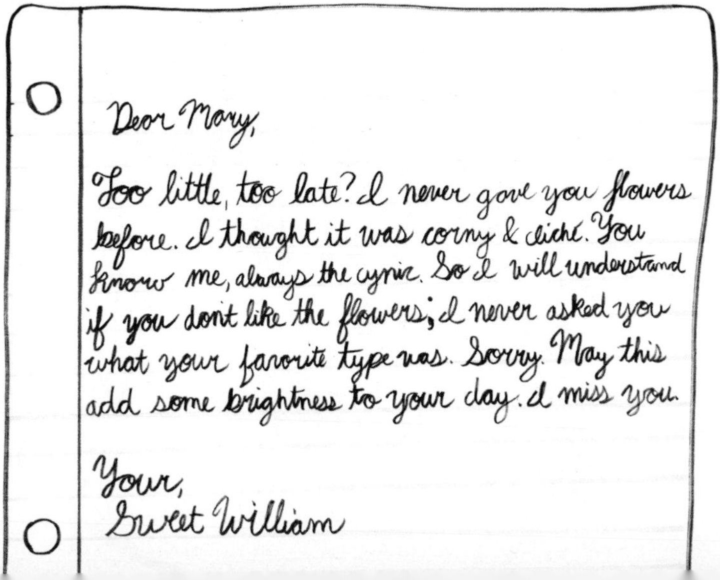

Dear Mary,

Too little, too late? I never gave you flowers before. I thought it was corny & cliché. You know me, always the cynic. So I will understand if you don't like the flowers; I never asked you what your favorite type was. Sorry. May this add some brightness to your day. I miss you.

Your,
Sweet William

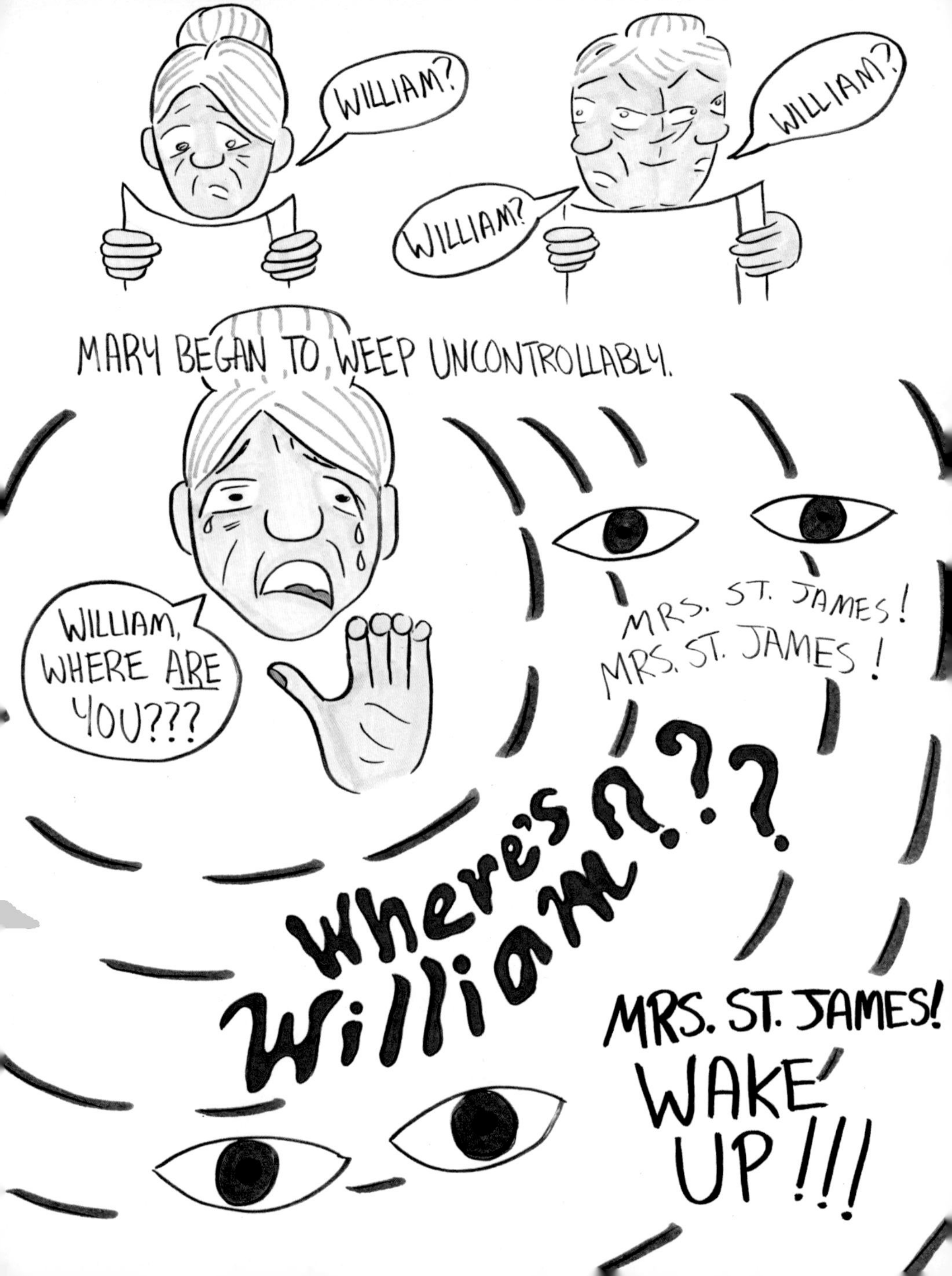
WILLIAM?
WILLIAM?
WILLIAM?
MARY BEGAN TO WEEP UNCONTROLLABLY.
WILLIAM, WHERE ARE YOU???
MRS. ST. JAMES!
MRS. ST. JAMES!
Where's William???
MRS. ST. JAMES! WAKE UP!!!

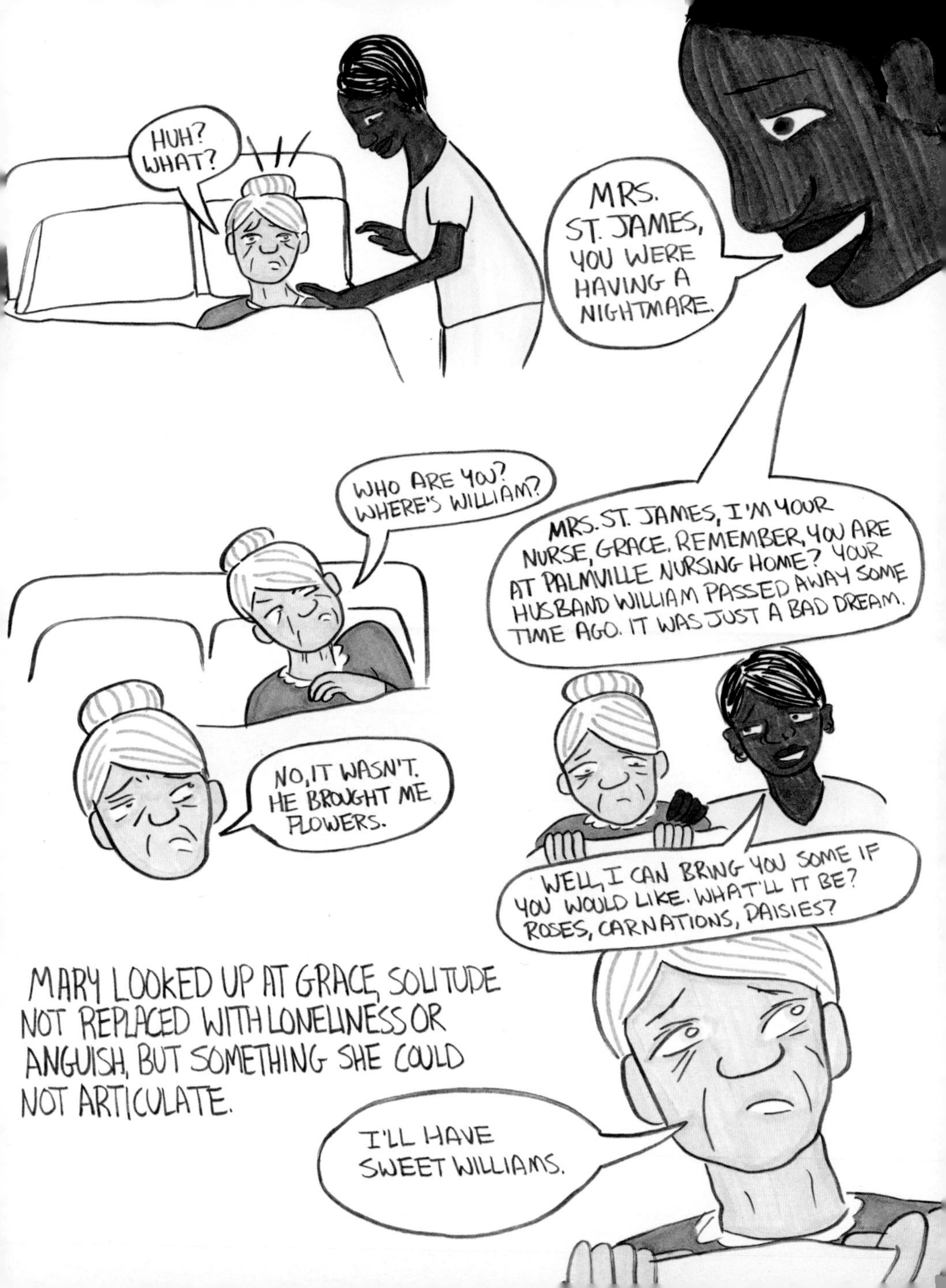
HUH? WHAT?
MRS. ST. JAMES, YOU WERE HAVING A NIGHTMARE.
WHO ARE YOU? WHERE'S WILLIAM?
MRS. ST. JAMES, I'M YOUR NURSE, GRACE. REMEMBER, YOU ARE AT PALMVILLE NURSING HOME? YOUR HUSBAND WILLIAM PASSED AWAY SOME TIME AGO. IT WAS JUST A BAD DREAM.
NO, IT WASN'T. HE BROUGHT ME FLOWERS.
WELL, I CAN BRING YOU SOME IF YOU WOULD LIKE. WHAT'LL IT BE? ROSES, CARNATIONS, DAISIES?
MARY LOOKED UP AT GRACE, SOLITUDE NOT REPLACED WITH LONELINESS OR ANGUISH, BUT SOMETHING SHE COULD NOT ARTICULATE.
I'LL HAVE SWEET WILLIAMS.

Dianthus barbatus
(Sweet William)

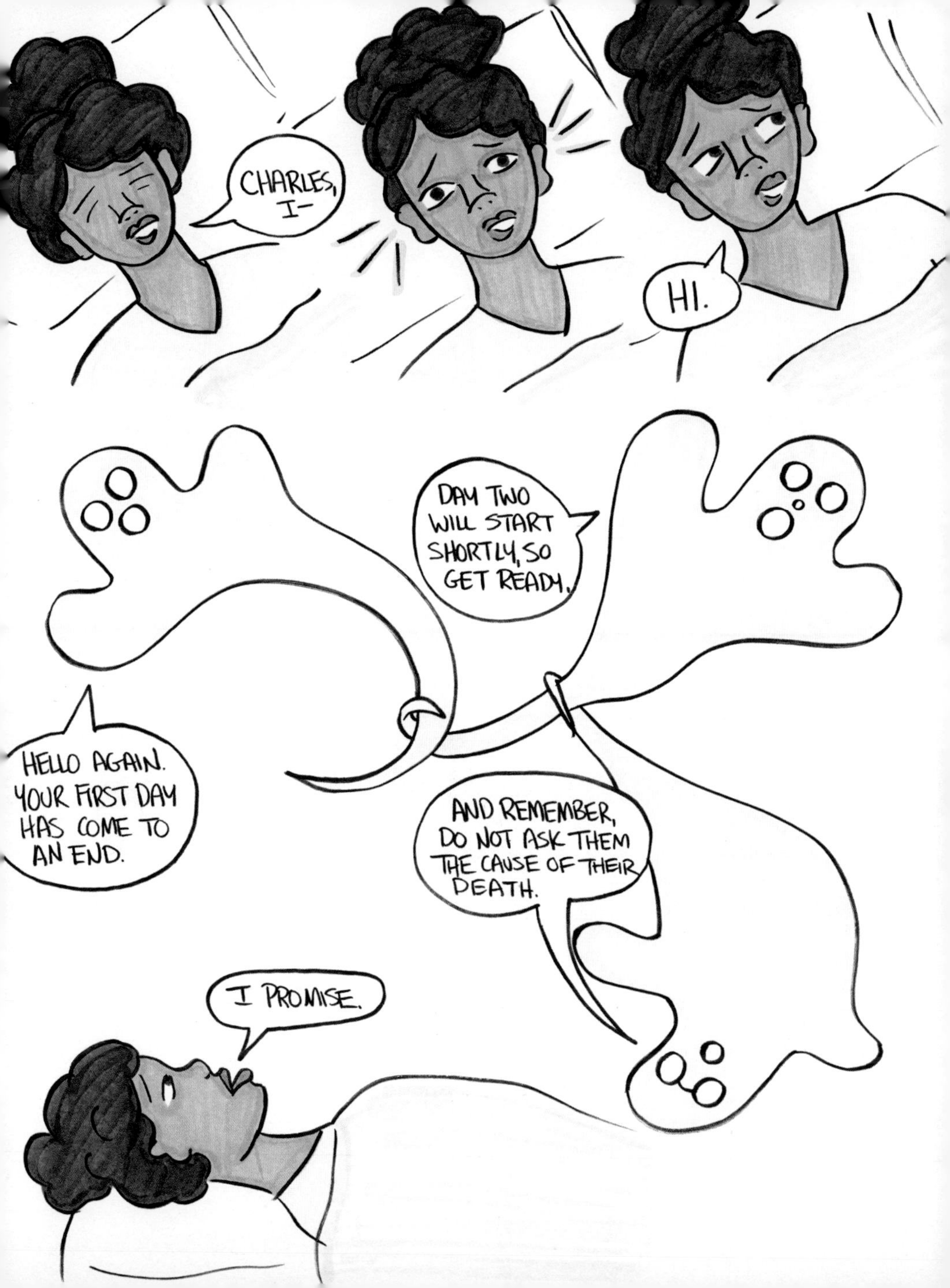
CHARLES, I–
HI.
HELLO AGAIN. YOUR FIRST DAY HAS COME TO AN END.
DAY TWO WILL START SHORTLY, SO GET READY.
AND REMEMBER, DO NOT ASK THEM THE CAUSE OF THEIR DEATH.
I PROMISE.

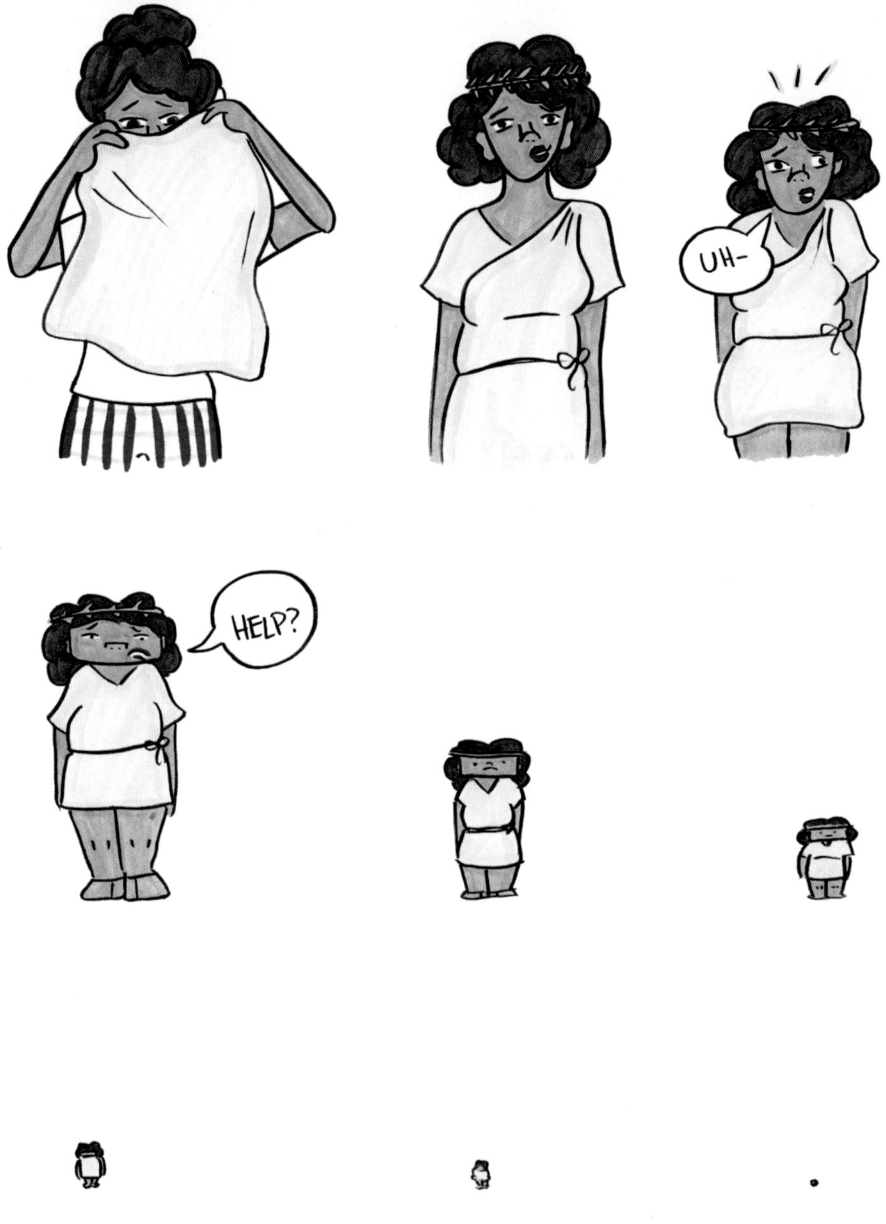
UH-
HELP?

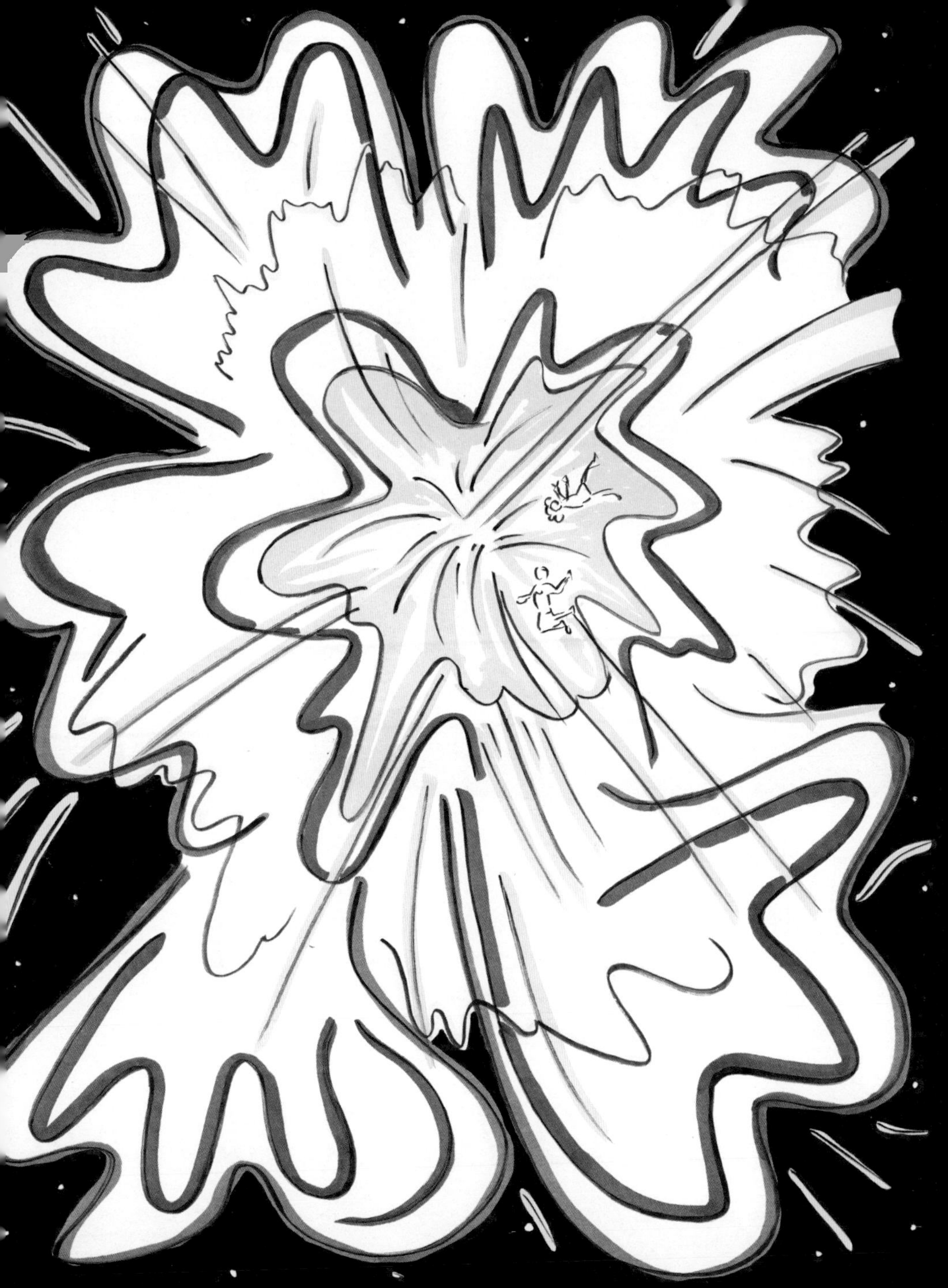

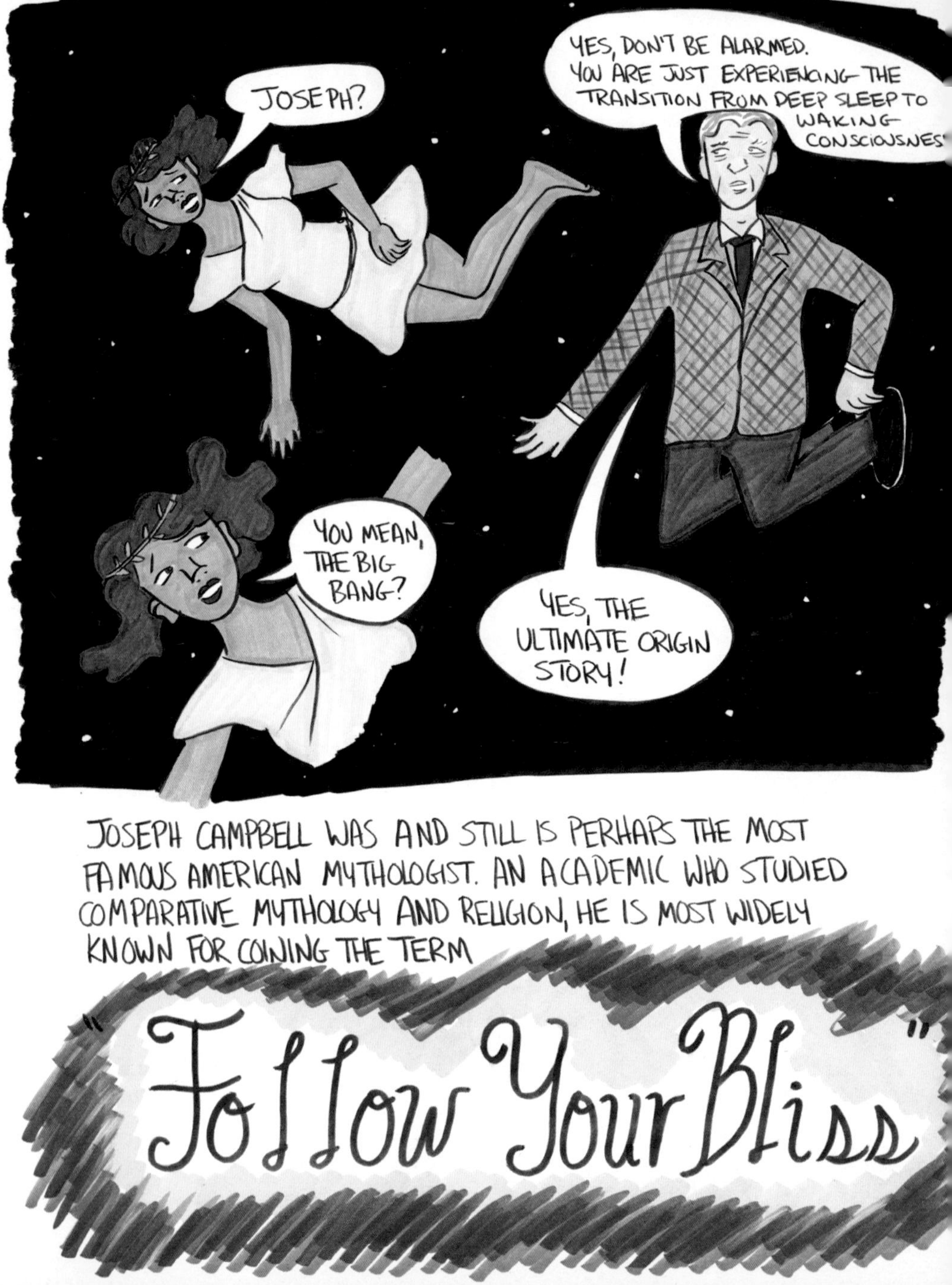
JOSEPH?
YES, DON'T BE ALARMED. YOU ARE JUST EXPERIENCING THE TRANSITION FROM DEEP SLEEP TO WAKING CONSCIOUSNES
YOU MEAN, THE BIG BANG?
YES, THE ULTIMATE ORIGIN STORY!

JOSEPH CAMPBELL WAS AND STILL IS PERHAPS THE MOST FAMOUS AMERICAN MYTHOLOGIST. AN ACADEMIC WHO STUDIED COMPARATIVE MYTHOLOGY AND RELIGION, HE IS MOST WIDELY KNOWN FOR COINING THE TERM

"Follow Your Bliss"

EVER SINCE WATCHING BILL MOYERS INTERVIEW CAMPBELL IN HIS 1988 PBS DOCUMENTARY, "THE POWER OF MYTH," I WAS HOOKED ON HIS WORK.

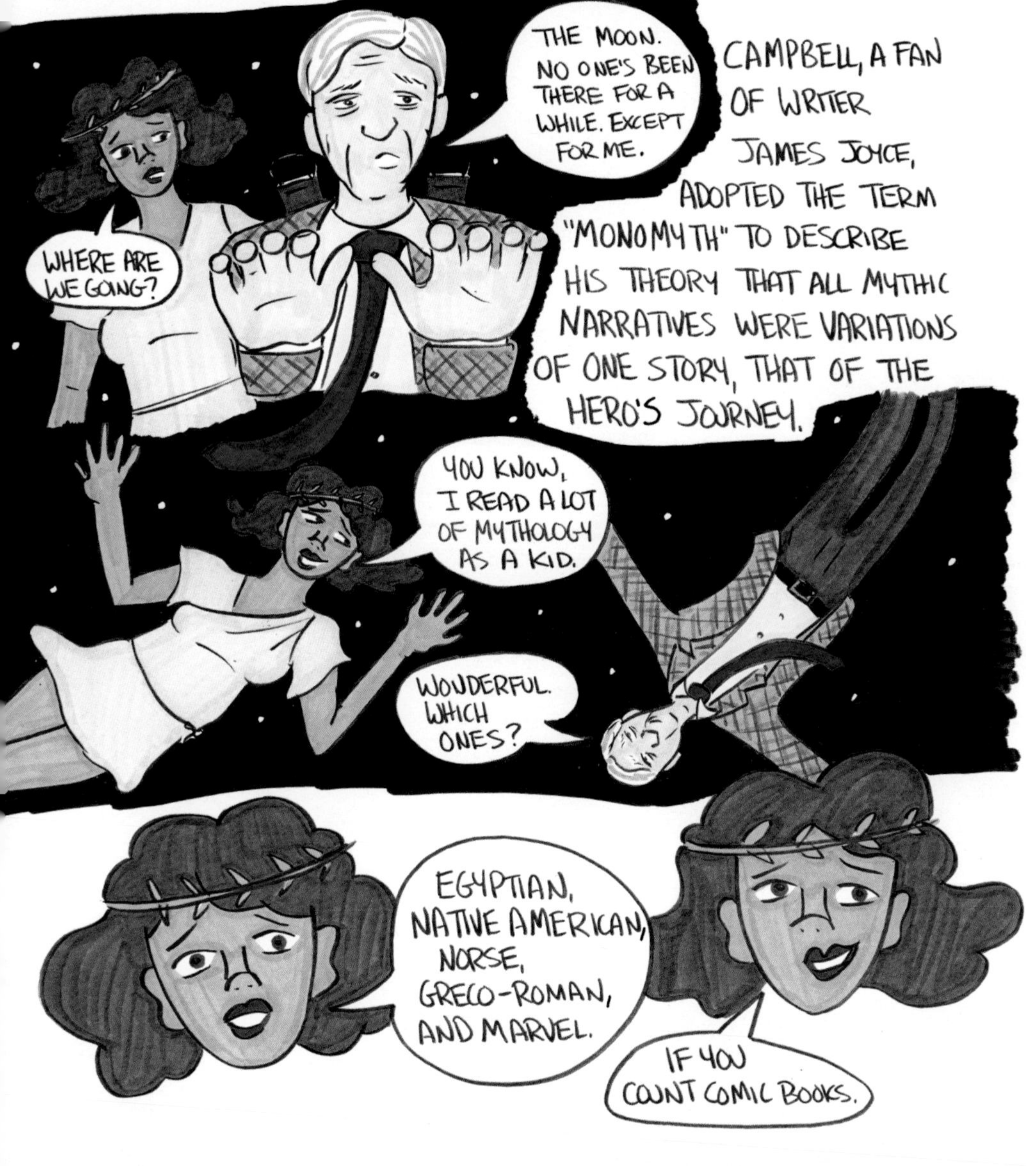
THE MOON. NO ONE'S BEEN THERE FOR A WHILE. EXCEPT FOR ME.
WHERE ARE WE GOING?
CAMPBELL, A FAN OF WRITER JAMES JOYCE, ADOPTED THE TERM "MONOMYTH" TO DESCRIBE HIS THEORY THAT ALL MYTHIC NARRATIVES WERE VARIATIONS OF ONE STORY, THAT OF THE HERO'S JOURNEY.
YOU KNOW, I READ A LOT OF MYTHOLOGY AS A KID.
WONDERFUL. WHICH ONES?
EGYPTIAN, NATIVE AMERICAN, NORSE, GRECO-ROMAN, AND MARVEL.
IF YOU COUNT COMIC BOOKS.

MYTHS WERE EXHILARATING, MYSTICAL, AND OFTEN CRUEL, BUT ALWAYS HAD A GREATER MESSAGE.

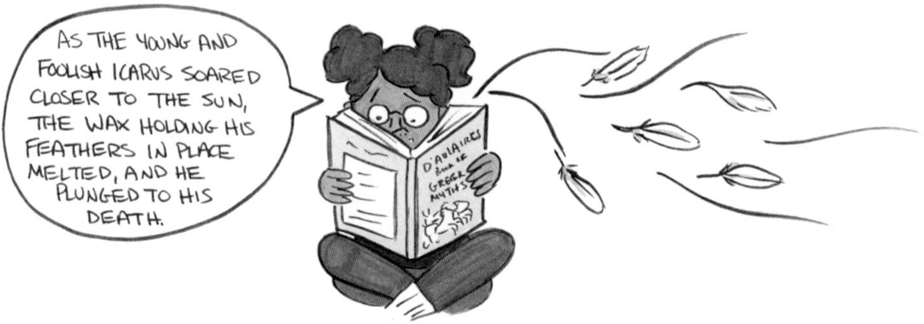
AS THE YOUNG AND FOOLISH ICARUS SOARED CLOSER TO THE SUN, THE WAX HOLDING HIS FEATHERS IN PLACE MELTED, AND HE PLUNGED TO HIS DEATH.
D'AULAIRES BOOK OF GREEK MYTHS

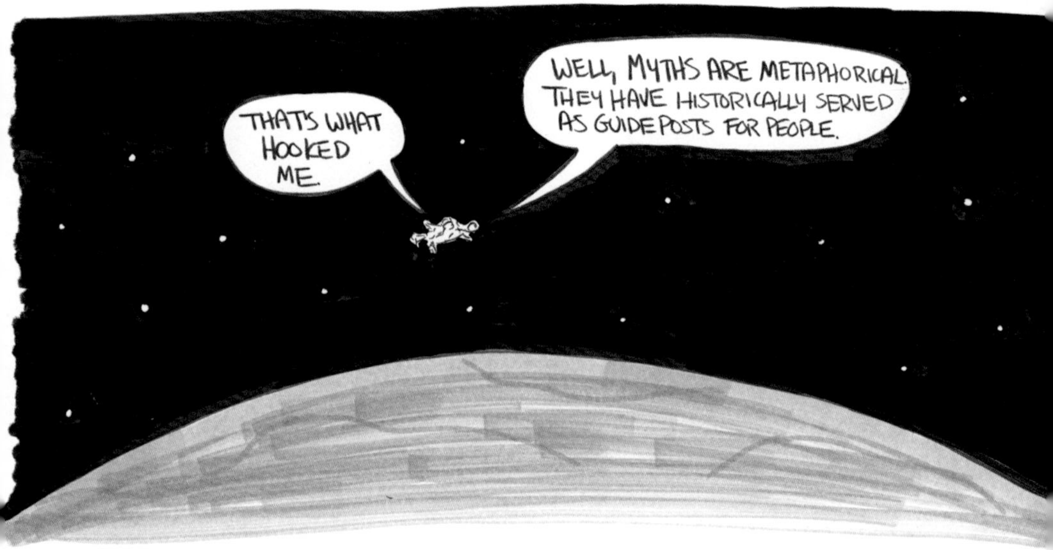
THAT'S WHAT HOOKED ME.
WELL, MYTHS ARE METAPHORICAL. THEY HAVE HISTORICALLY SERVED AS GUIDEPOSTS FOR PEOPLE.

CAMPBELL BELIEVED THAT THE MONOMYTH REFLECTED A PERSON WHO, THROUGH TRIALS AND SUFFERING, EVENTUALLY REACHED AN ETERNAL SOURCE AND COMPLETED THEIR JOURNEY BY USING THEIR NEWFOUND GIFTS TO HELP SOCIETY.

THE HERO'S JOURNEY CONSISTS OF THREE "ACTS" AND MULTIPLE STAGES WHICH REFLECT THE COURSE OF LIFE.

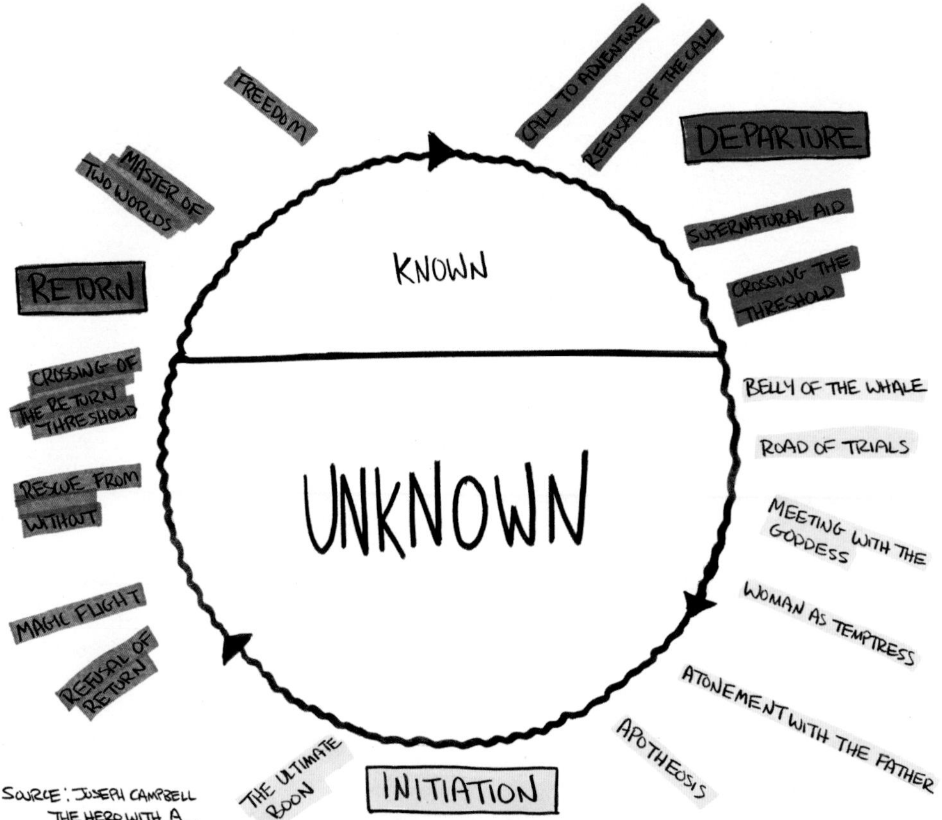
DEPARTURE
CALL TO ADVENTURE
REFUSAL OF THE CALL
SUPERNATURAL AID
CROSSING THE THRESHOLD
BELLY OF THE WHALE
INITIATION
ROAD OF TRIALS
MEETING WITH THE GODDESS
WOMAN AS TEMPTRESS
ATONEMENT WITH THE FATHER
APOTHEOSIS
THE ULTIMATE BOON
RETURN
REFUSAL OF RETURN
MAGIC FLIGHT
RESCUE FROM WITHOUT
CROSSING OF THE RETURN THRESHOLD
MASTER OF TWO WORLDS
FREEDOM
KNOWN
UNKNOWN

SOURCE: JOSEPH CAMPBELL
<u>THE HERO WITH A THOUSAND FACES</u> (1949)

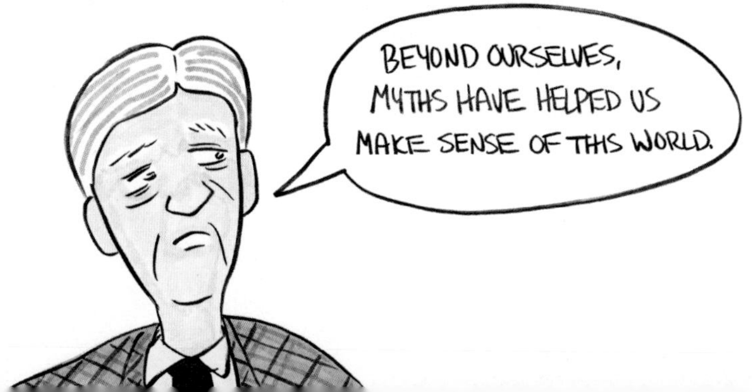
BEYOND OURSELVES, MYTHS HAVE HELPED US MAKE SENSE OF THIS WORLD.

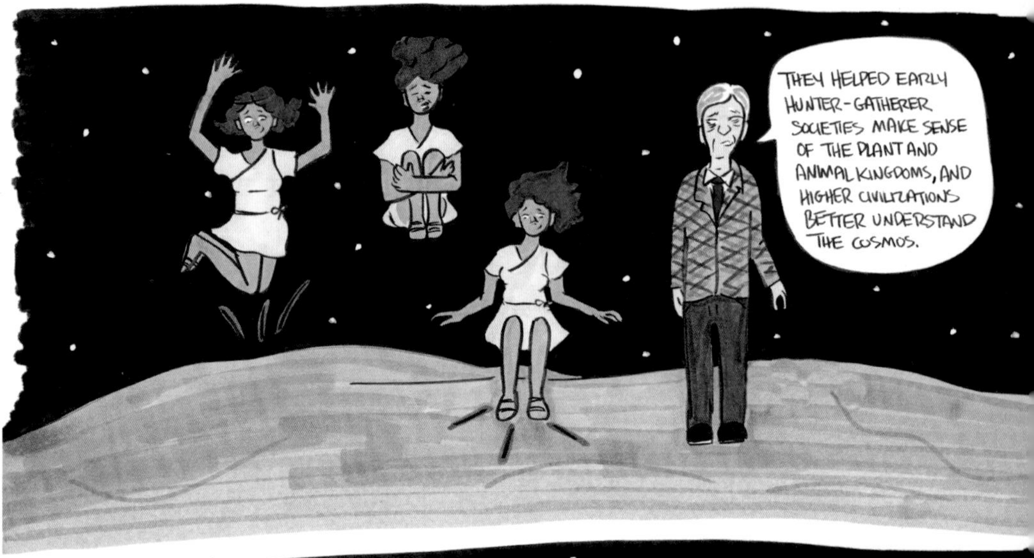
THEY HELPED EARLY HUNTER-GATHERER SOCIETIES MAKE SENSE OF THE PLANT AND ANIMAL KINGDOMS, AND HIGHER CIVILIZATIONS BETTER UNDERSTAND THE COSMOS.

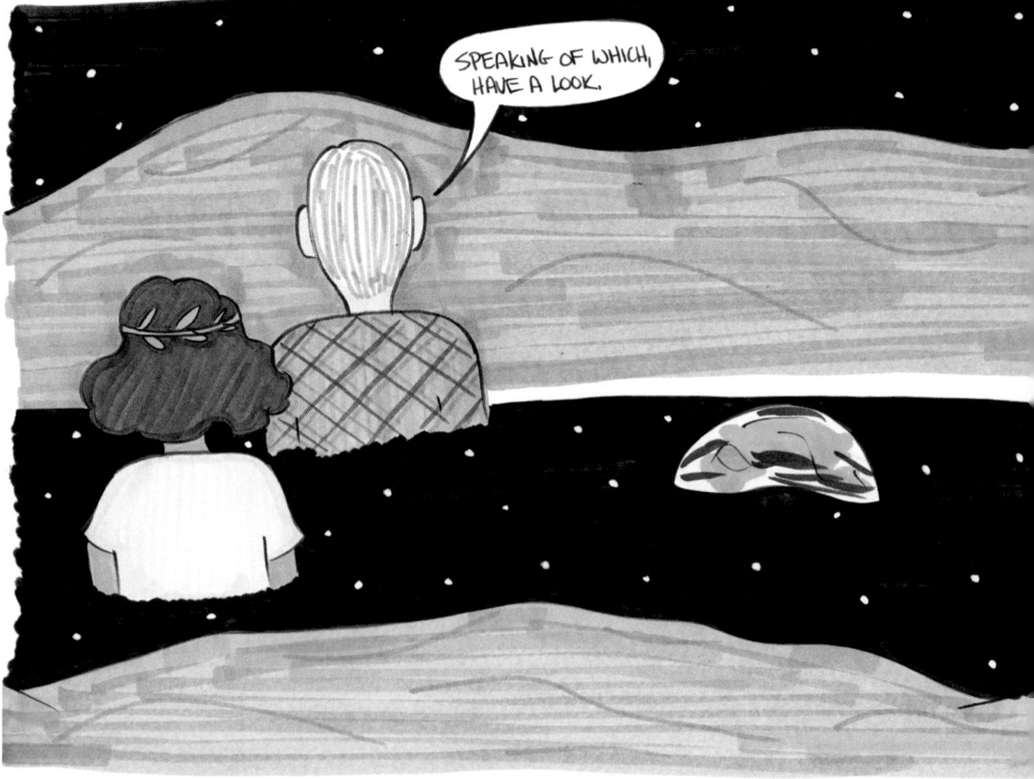
SPEAKING OF WHICH, HAVE A LOOK.

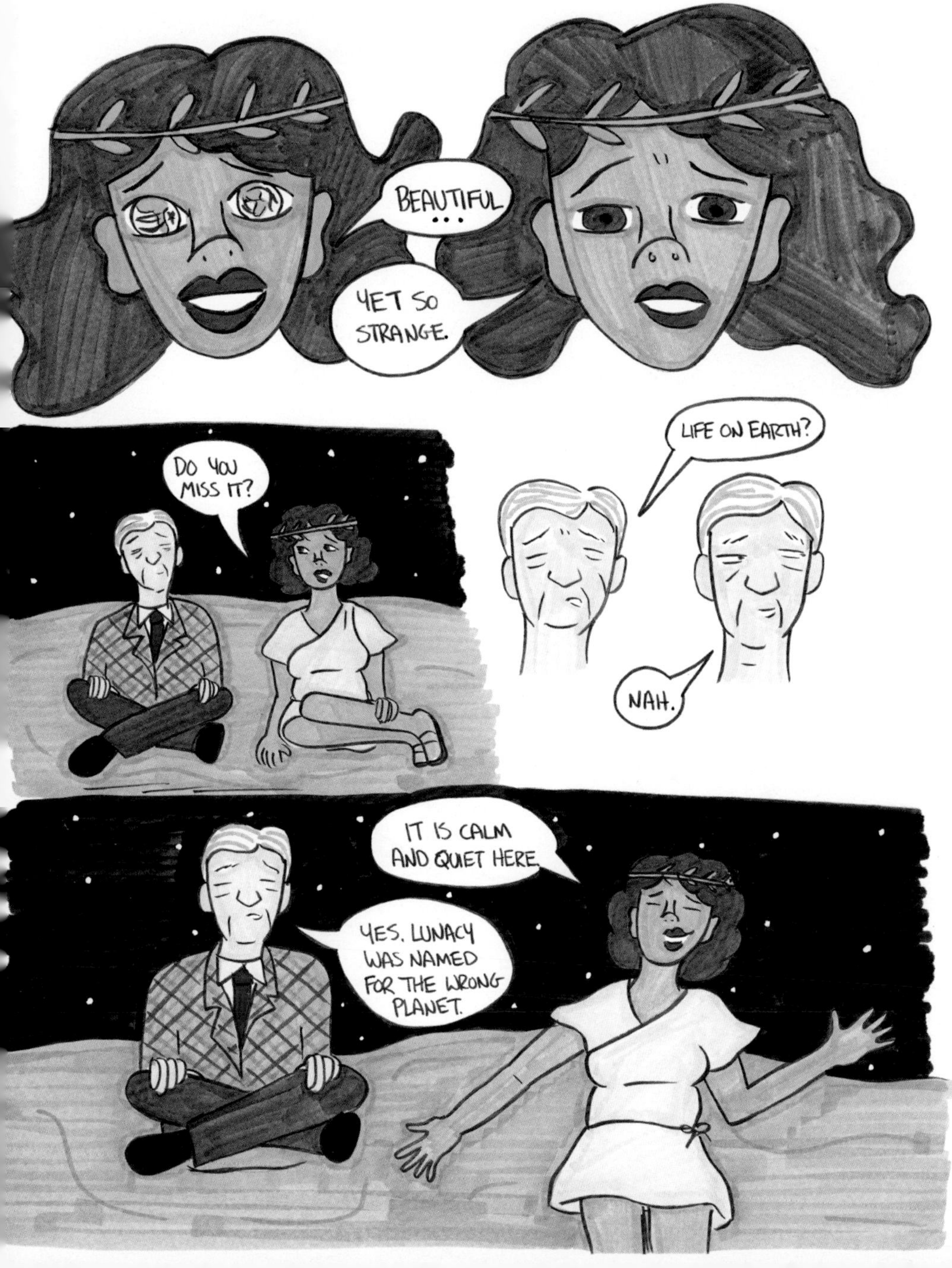
BEAUTIFUL . . .
YET SO STRANGE.
DO YOU MISS IT?
LIFE ON EARTH?
NAH.
IT IS CALM AND QUIET HERE.
YES. LUNACY WAS NAMED FOR THE WRONG PLANET.

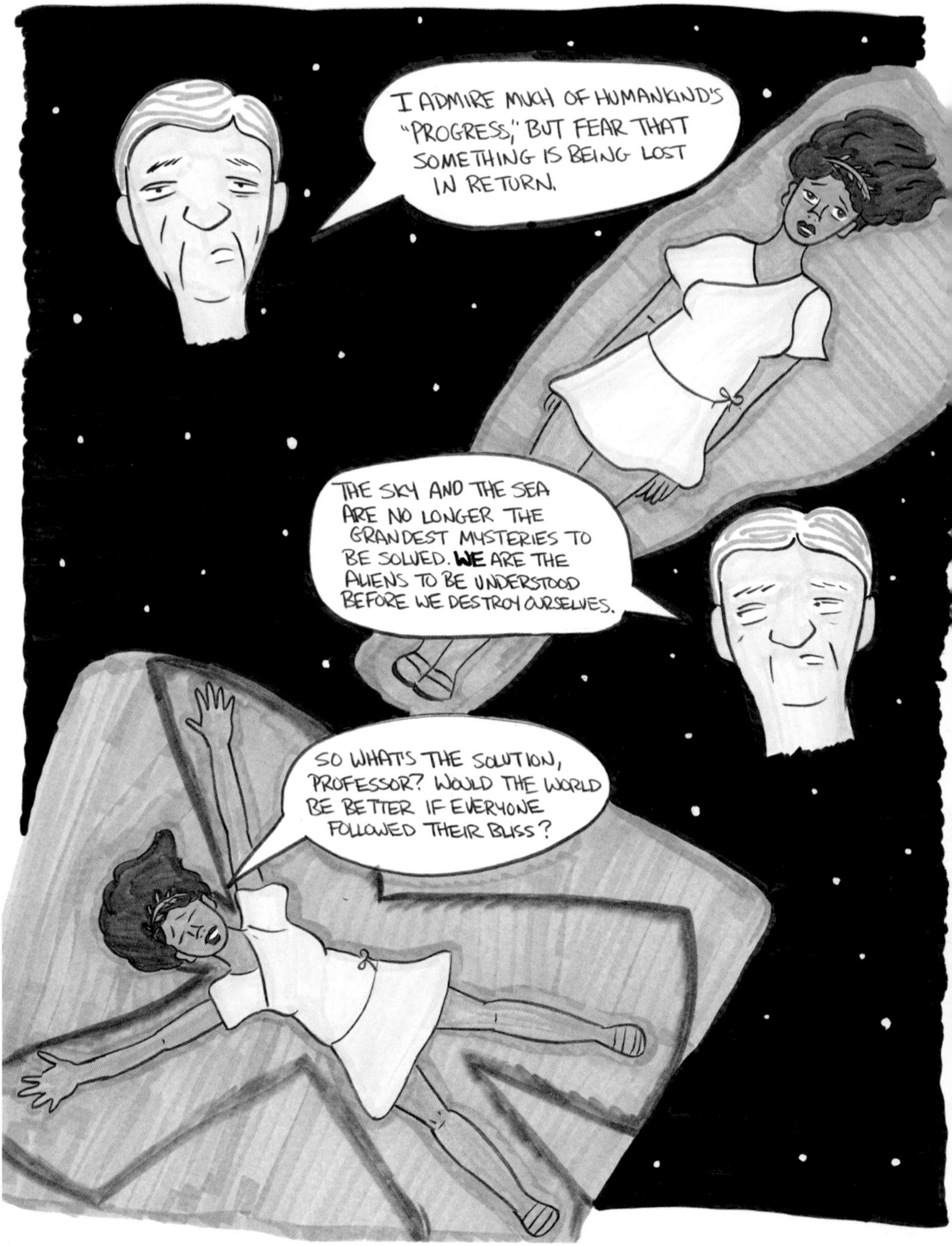
I ADMIRE MUCH OF HUMANKIND'S "PROGRESS," BUT FEAR THAT SOMETHING IS BEING LOST IN RETURN.
THE SKY AND THE SEA ARE NO LONGER THE GRANDEST MYSTERIES TO BE SOLVED. WE ARE THE ALIENS TO BE UNDERSTOOD BEFORE WE DESTROY OURSELVES.
SO WHAT'S THE SOLUTION, PROFESSOR? WOULD THE WORLD BE BETTER IF EVERYONE FOLLOWED THEIR BLISS?

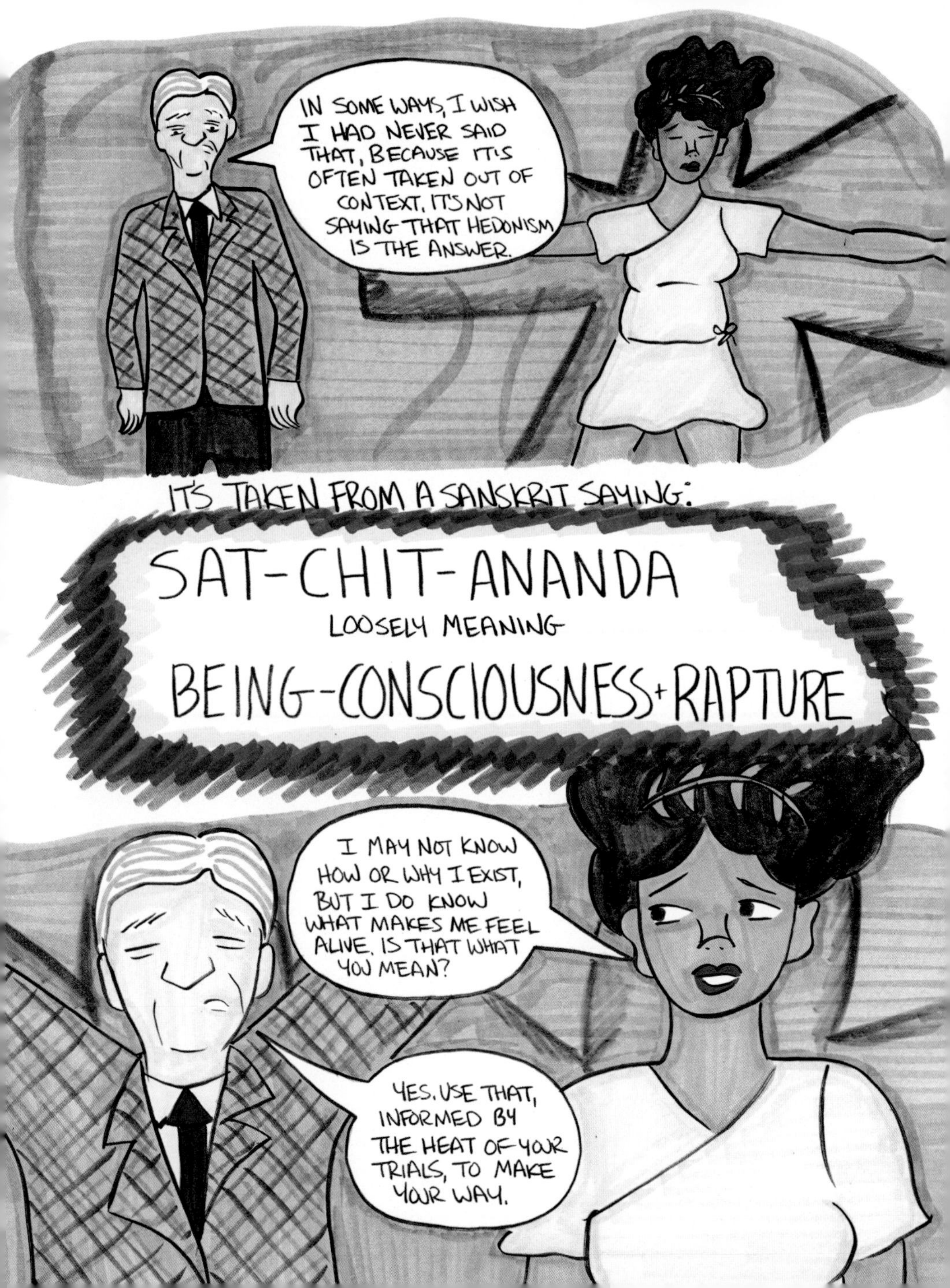
IN SOME WAYS, I WISH I HAD NEVER SAID THAT, BECAUSE IT'S OFTEN TAKEN OUT OF CONTEXT. IT'S NOT SAYING THAT HEDONISM IS THE ANSWER.
IT'S TAKEN FROM A SANSKRIT SAYING:
SAT-CHIT-ANANDA
LOOSELY MEANING
BEING--CONSCIOUSNESS+RAPTURE
I MAY NOT KNOW HOW OR WHY I EXIST, BUT I DO KNOW WHAT MAKES ME FEEL ALIVE. IS THAT WHAT YOU MEAN?
YES. USE THAT, INFORMED BY THE HEAT OF YOUR TRIALS, TO MAKE YOUR WAY.

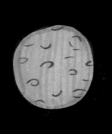

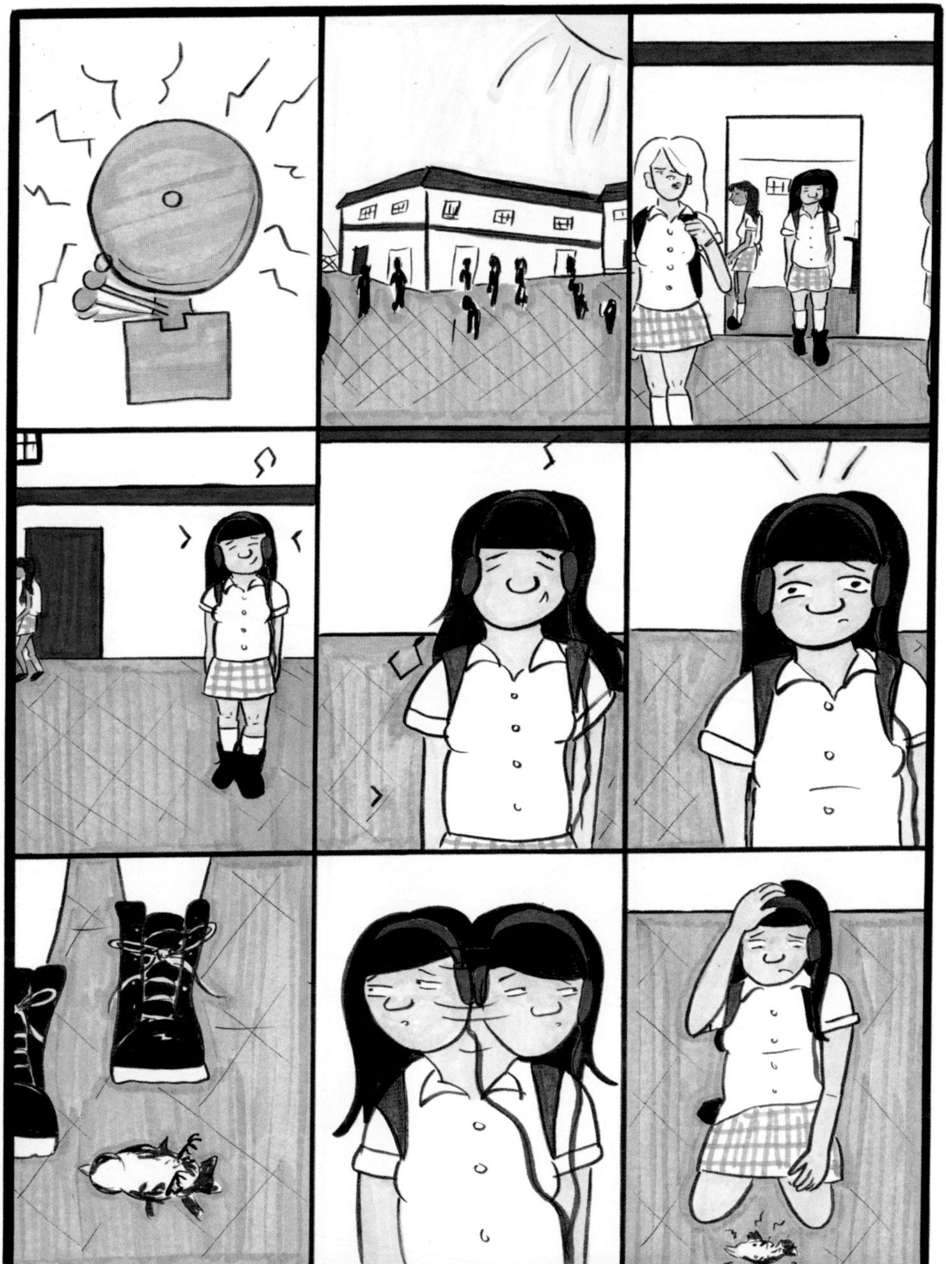

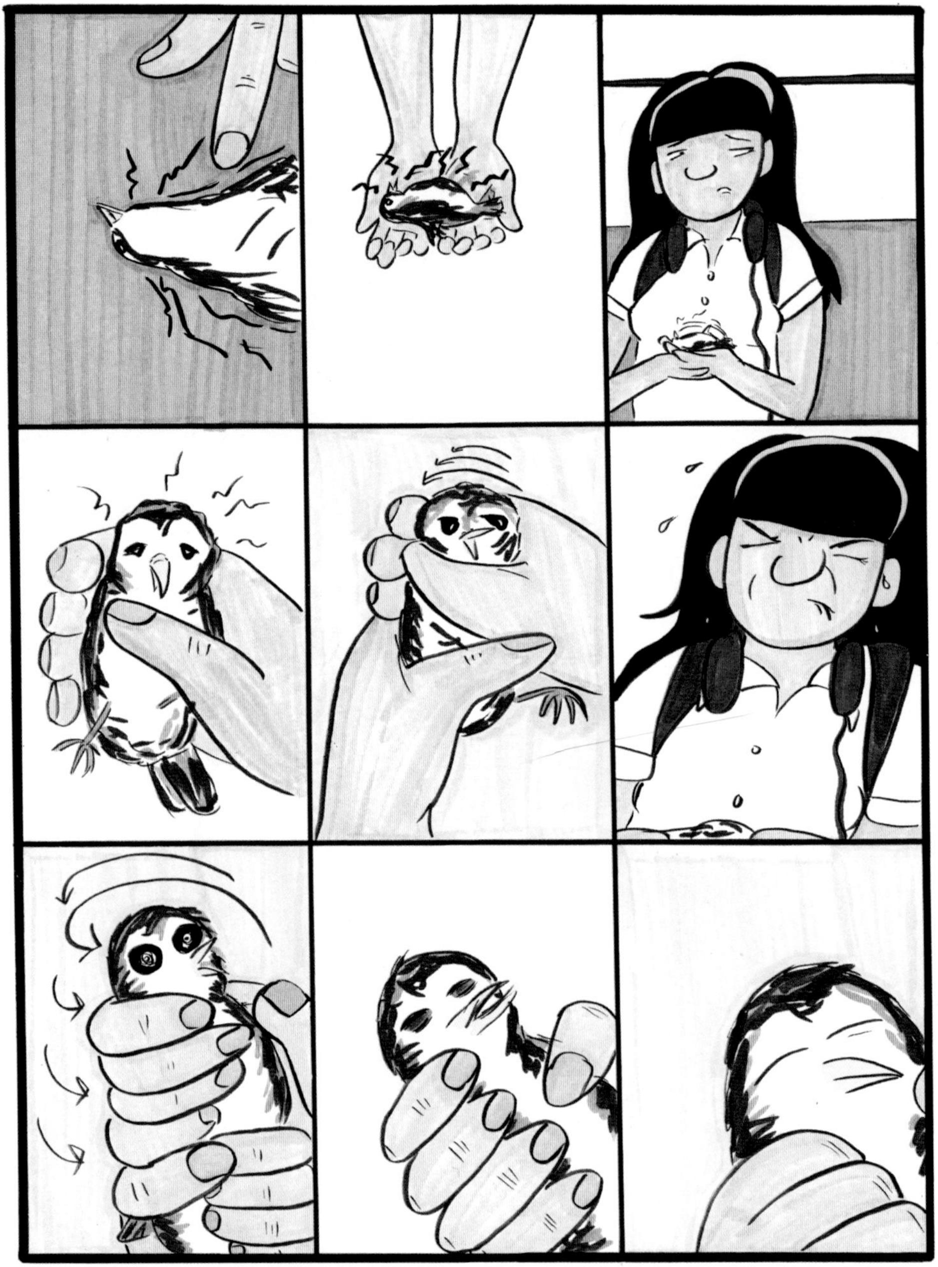

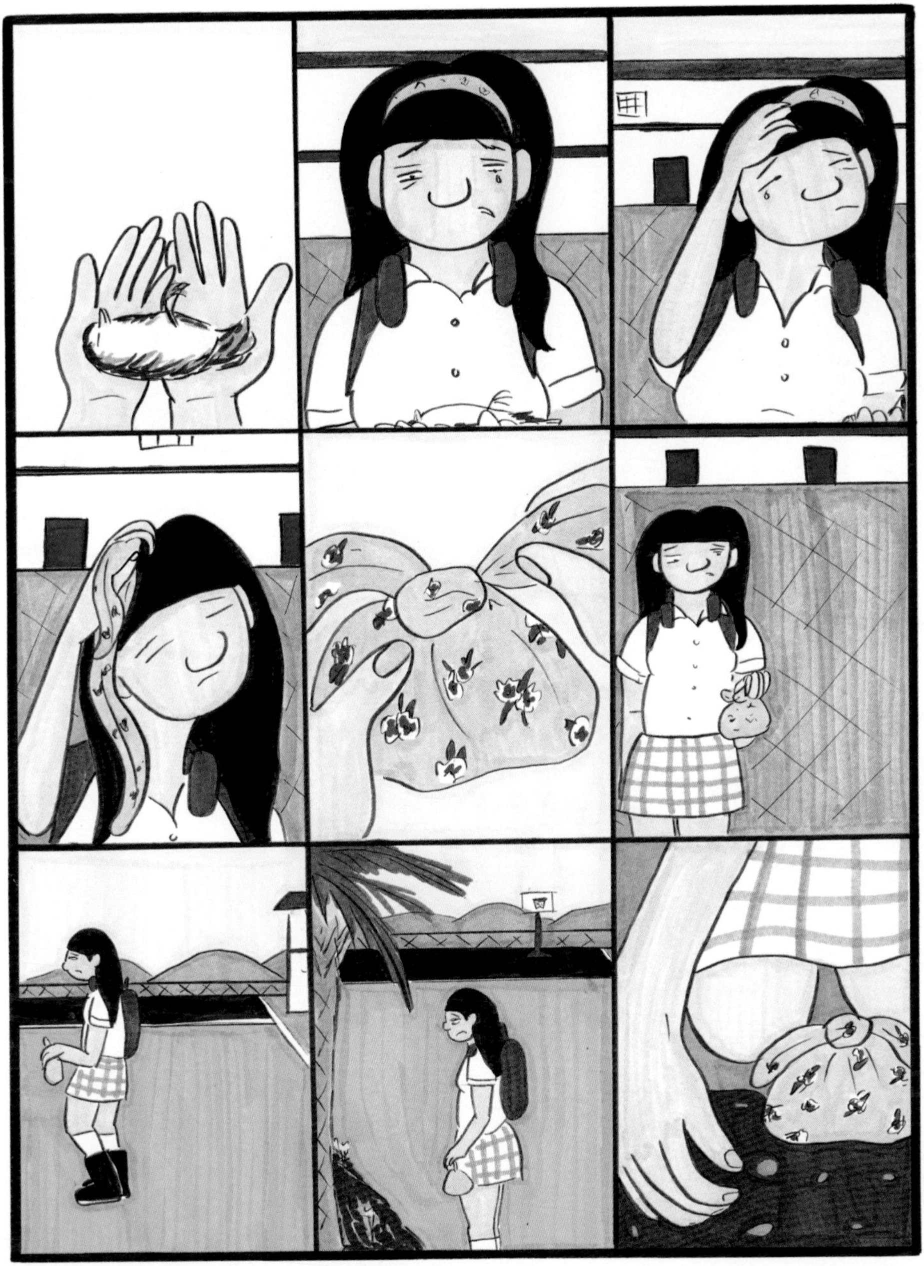

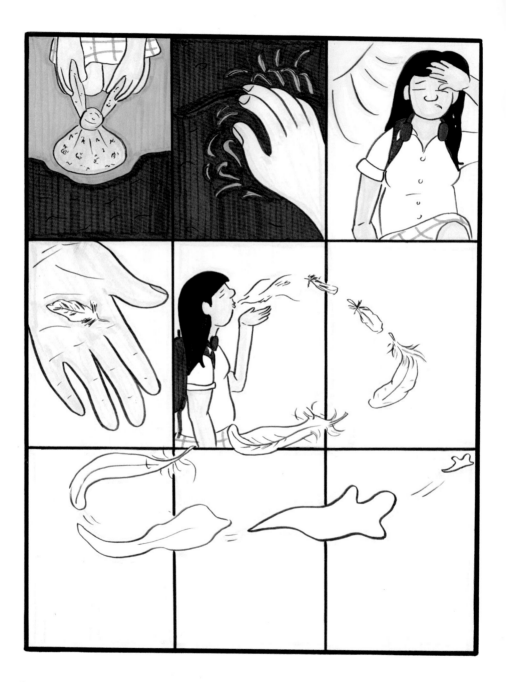

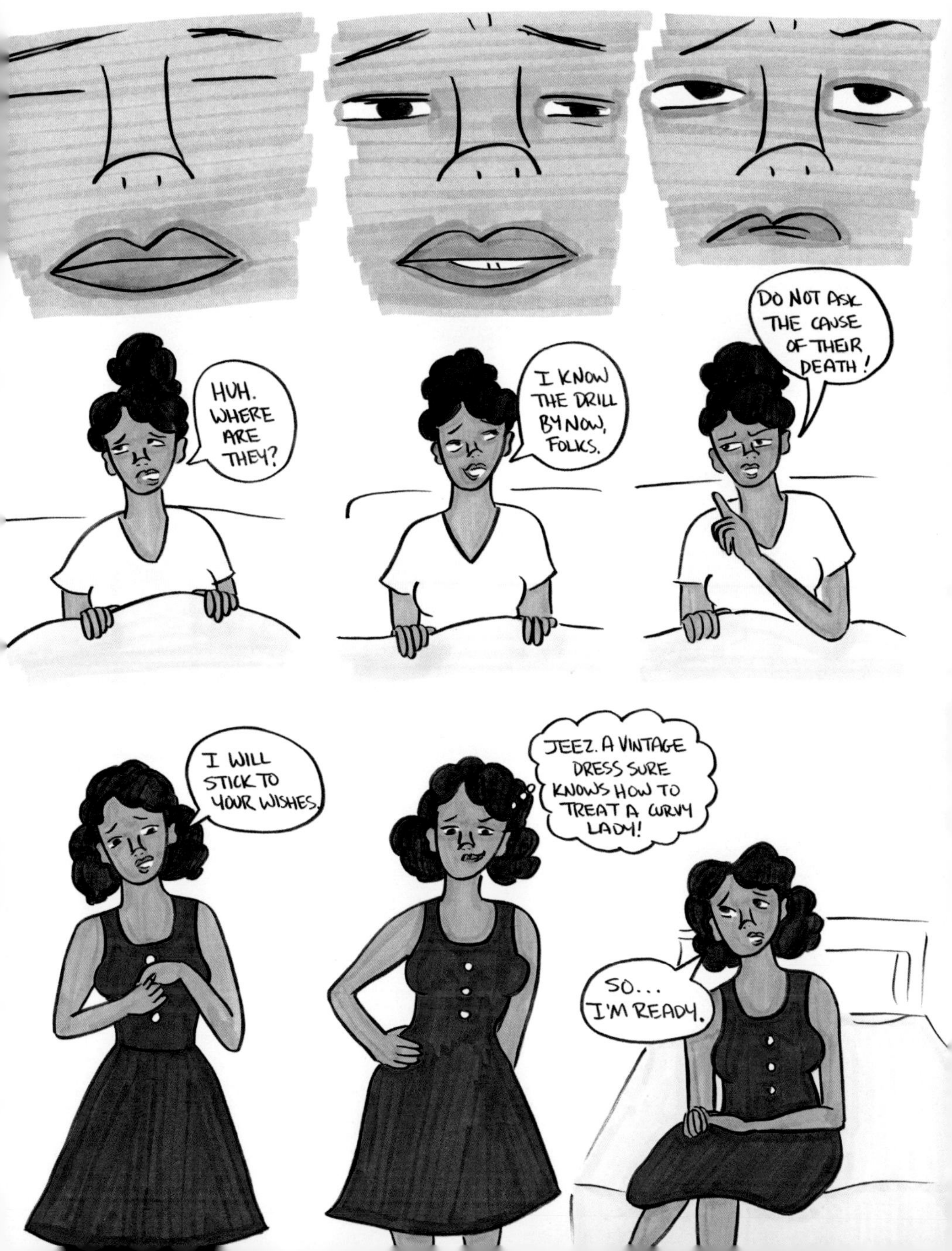
HUH. WHERE ARE THEY?
I KNOW THE DRILL BY NOW, FOLKS.
DO NOT ASK THE CAUSE OF THEIR DEATH!
I WILL STICK TO YOUR WISHES.
JEEZ. A VINTAGE DRESS SURE KNOWS HOW TO TREAT A CURVY LADY!
SO... I'M READY.

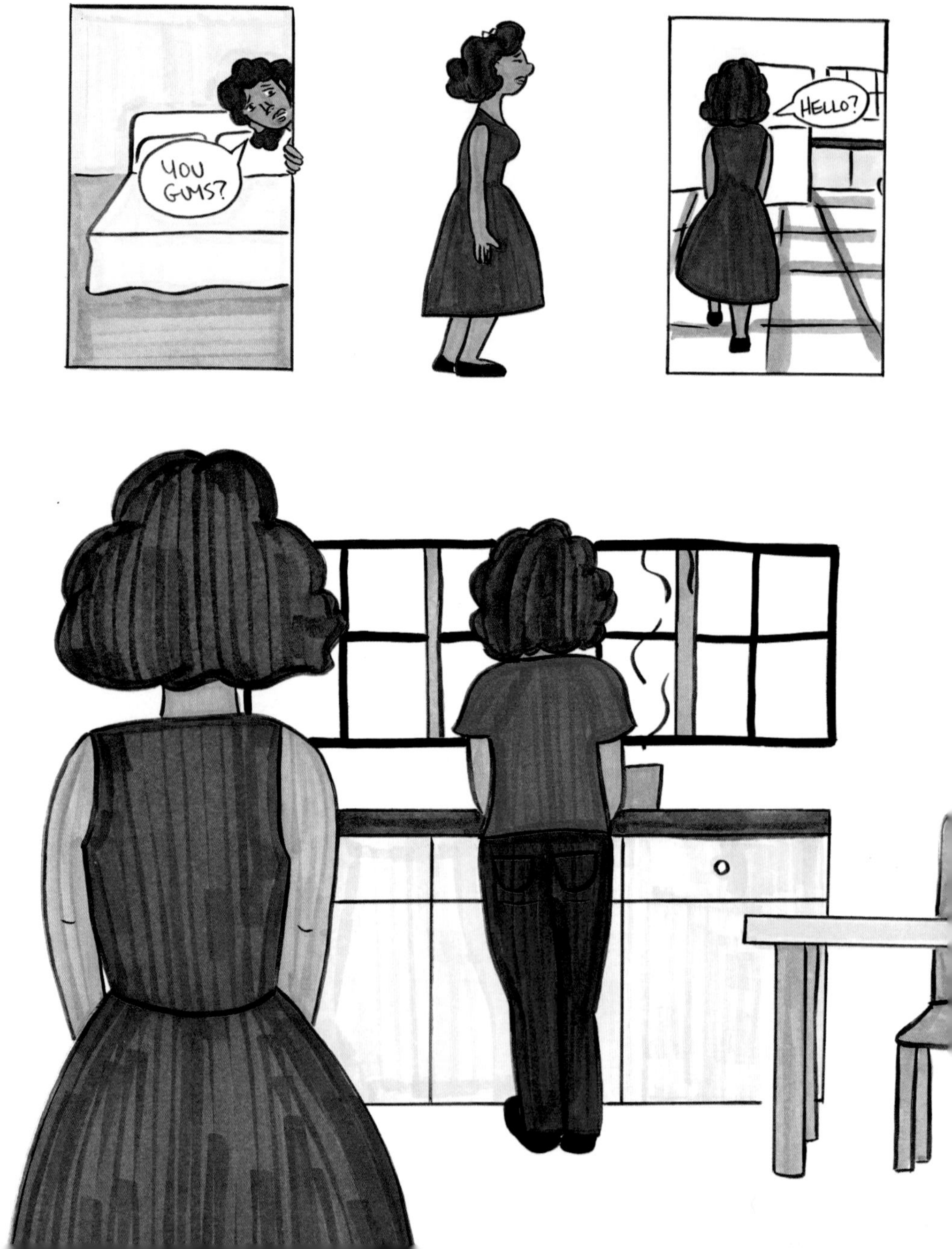
YOU GUMS?
HELLO?

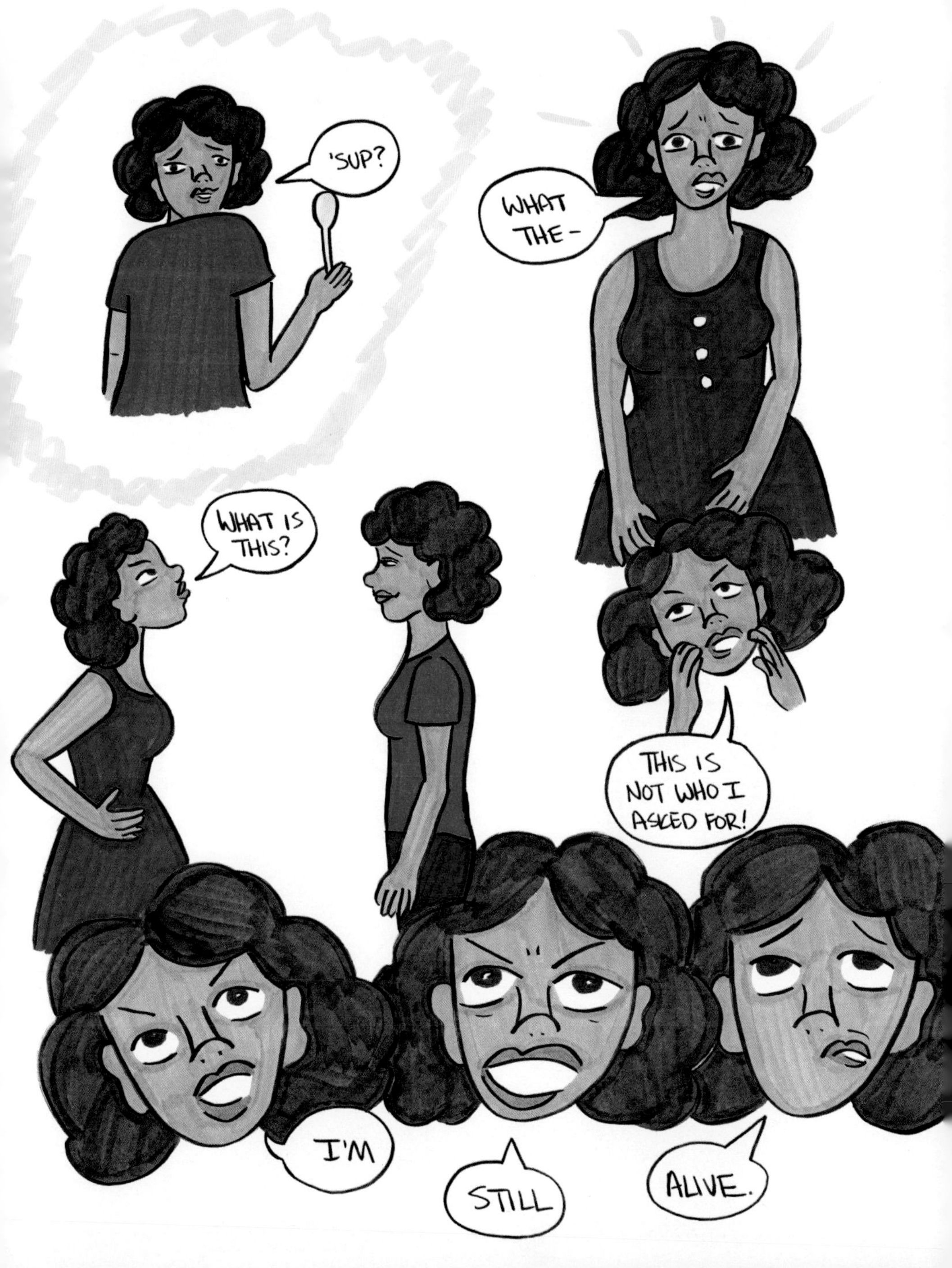
'SUP?
WHAT THE-
WHAT IS THIS?
THIS IS NOT WHO I ASKED FOR!
I'M
STILL
ALIVE.

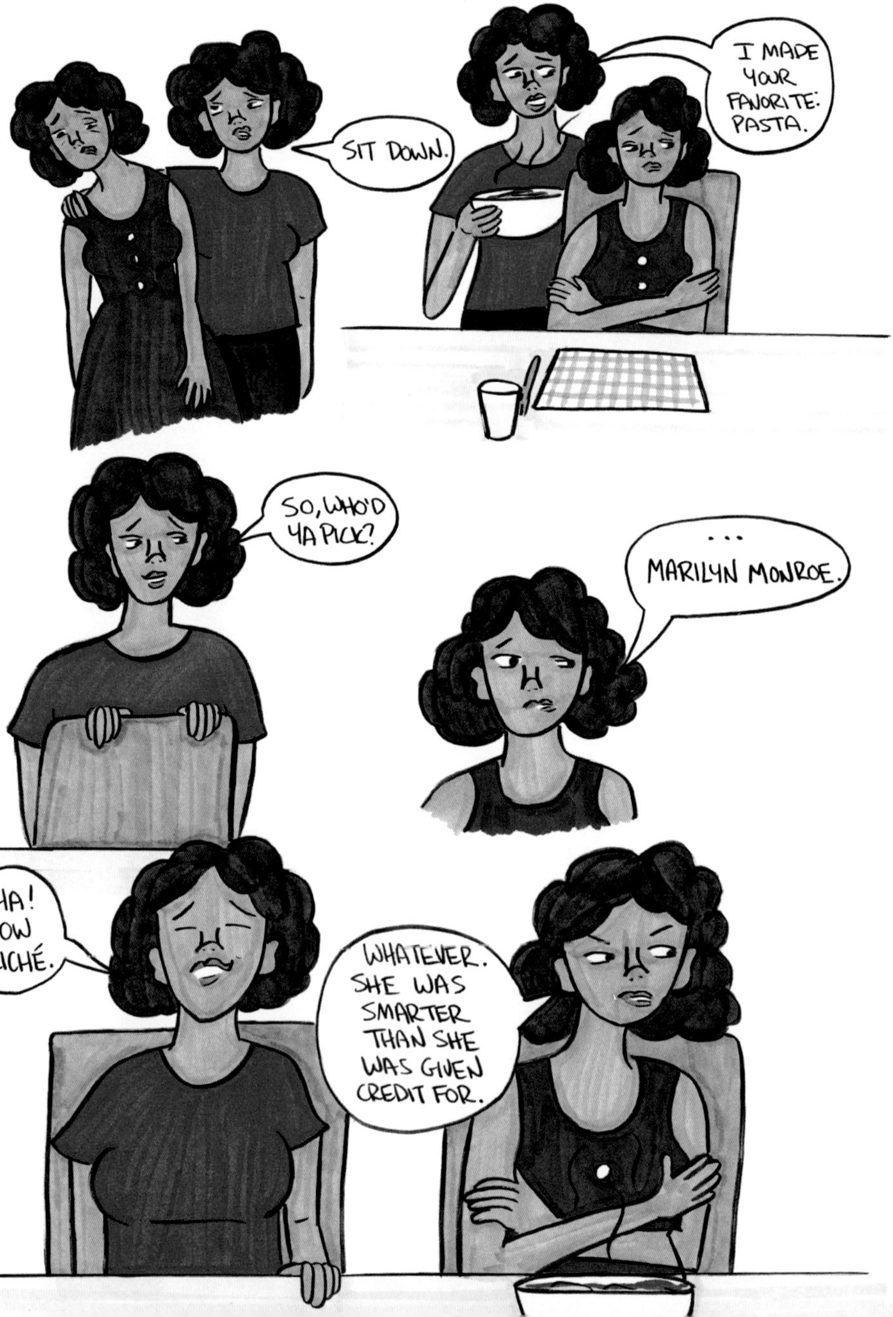
SIT DOWN.
I MADE YOUR FAVORITE: PASTA.
SO, WHO'D YA PICK?
...
MARILYN MONROE.
HA! HOW CLICHÉ.
WHATEVER. SHE WAS SMARTER THAN SHE WAS GIVEN CREDIT FOR.

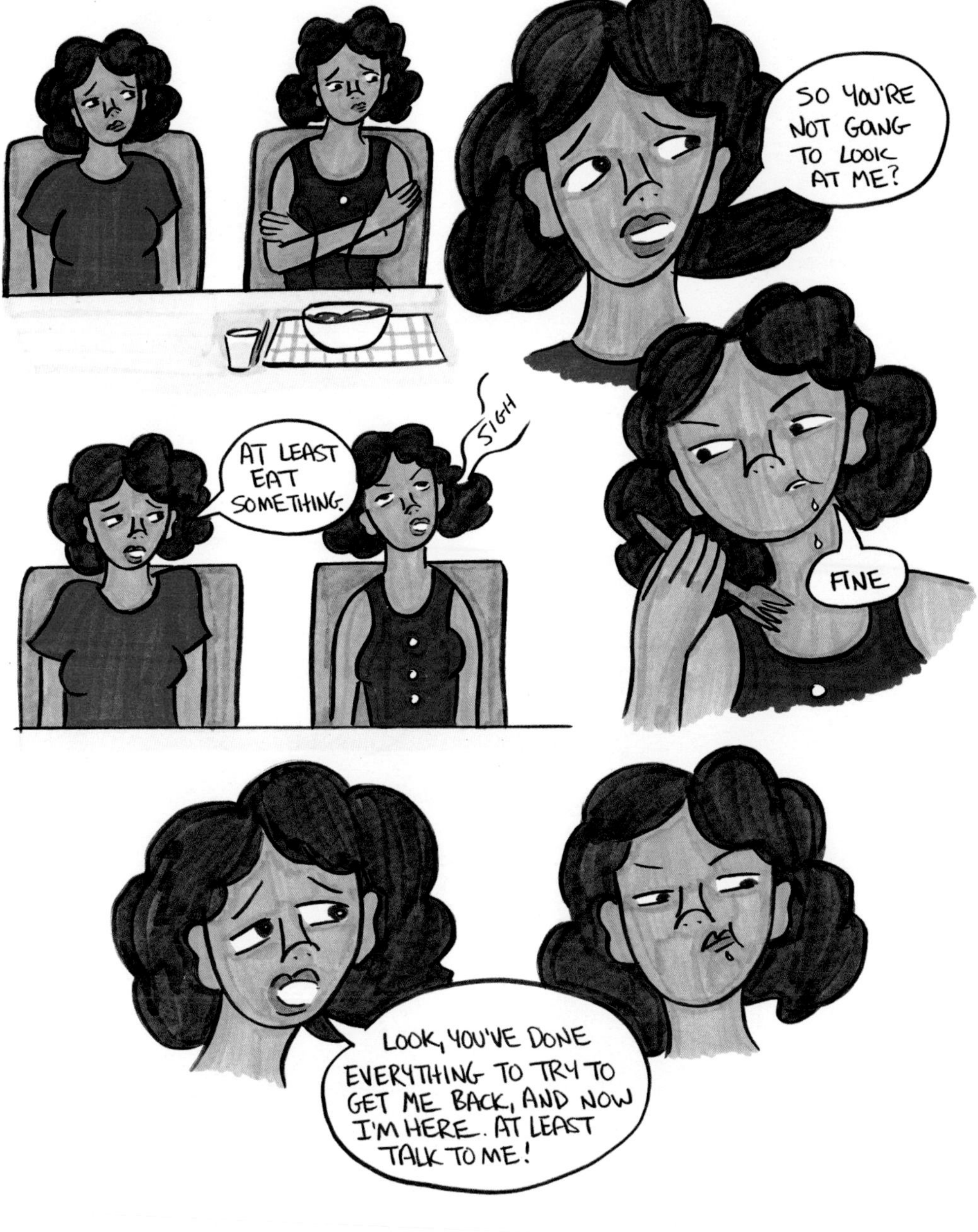
SO YOU'RE NOT GOING TO LOOK AT ME?
AT LEAST EAT SOMETHING.
SIGH
FINE
LOOK, YOU'VE DONE EVERYTHING TO TRY TO GET ME BACK, AND NOW I'M HERE. AT LEAST TALK TO ME!

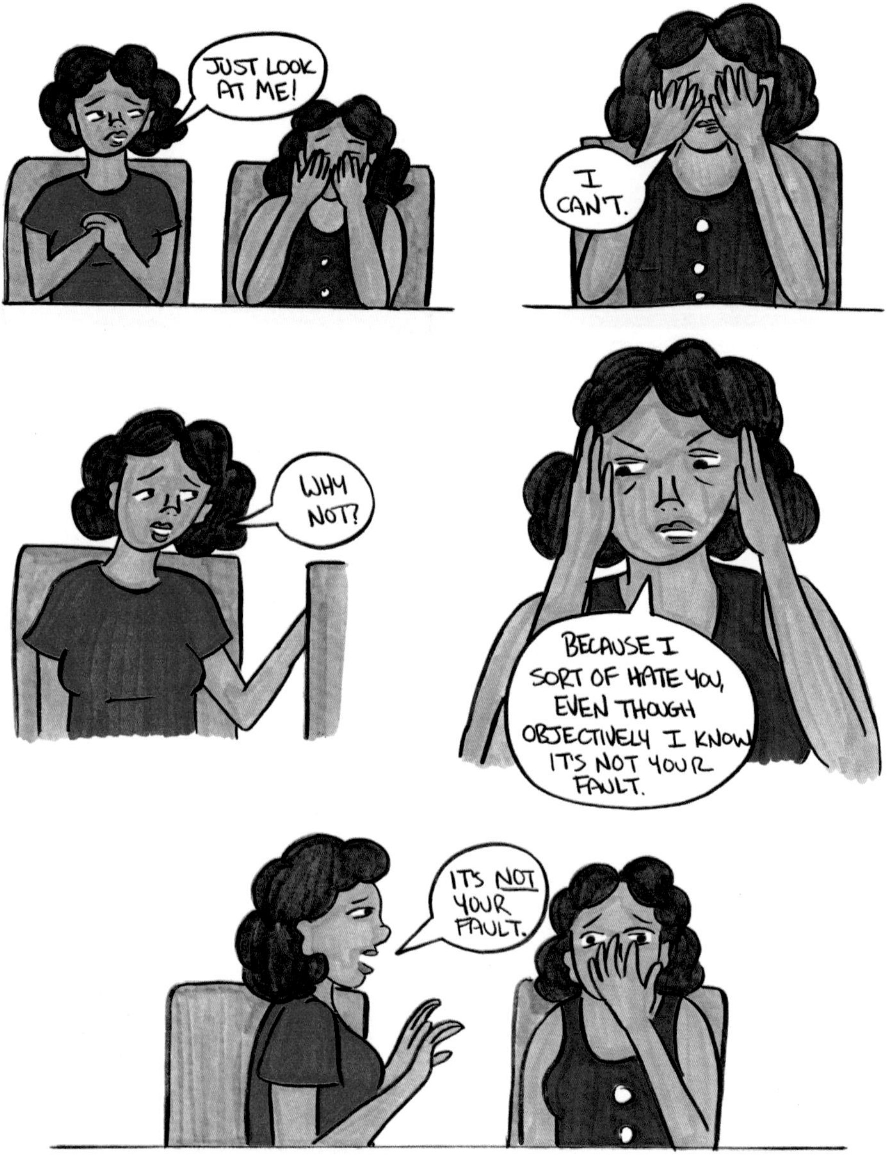
JUST LOOK AT ME!
I CAN'T.
WHY NOT?
BECAUSE I SORT OF HATE YOU, EVEN THOUGH OBJECTIVELY I KNOW IT'S NOT YOUR FAULT.
IT'S NOT YOUR FAULT.

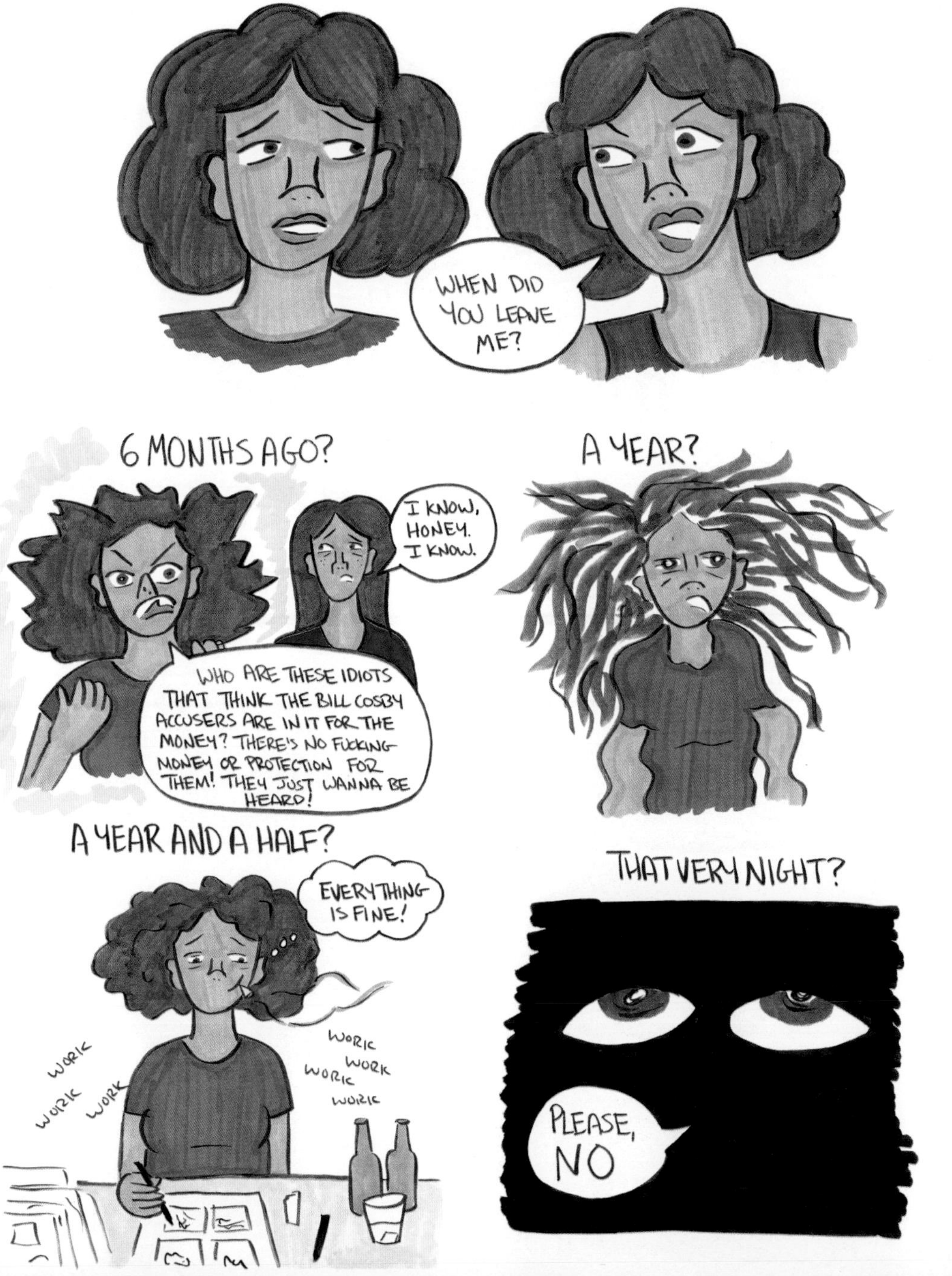

WHEN DID YOU LEAVE ME?
6 MONTHS AGO?
I KNOW, HONEY. I KNOW.
WHO ARE THESE IDIOTS THAT THINK THE BILL COSBY ACCUSERS ARE IN IT FOR THE MONEY? THERE'S NO FUCKING MONEY OR PROTECTION FOR THEM! THEY JUST WANNA BE HEARD!
A YEAR?
A YEAR AND A HALF?
EVERYTHING IS FINE!
WORK
WORK
WORK
WORK
WORK
WORK
WORK
THAT VERY NIGHT?
PLEASE, NO

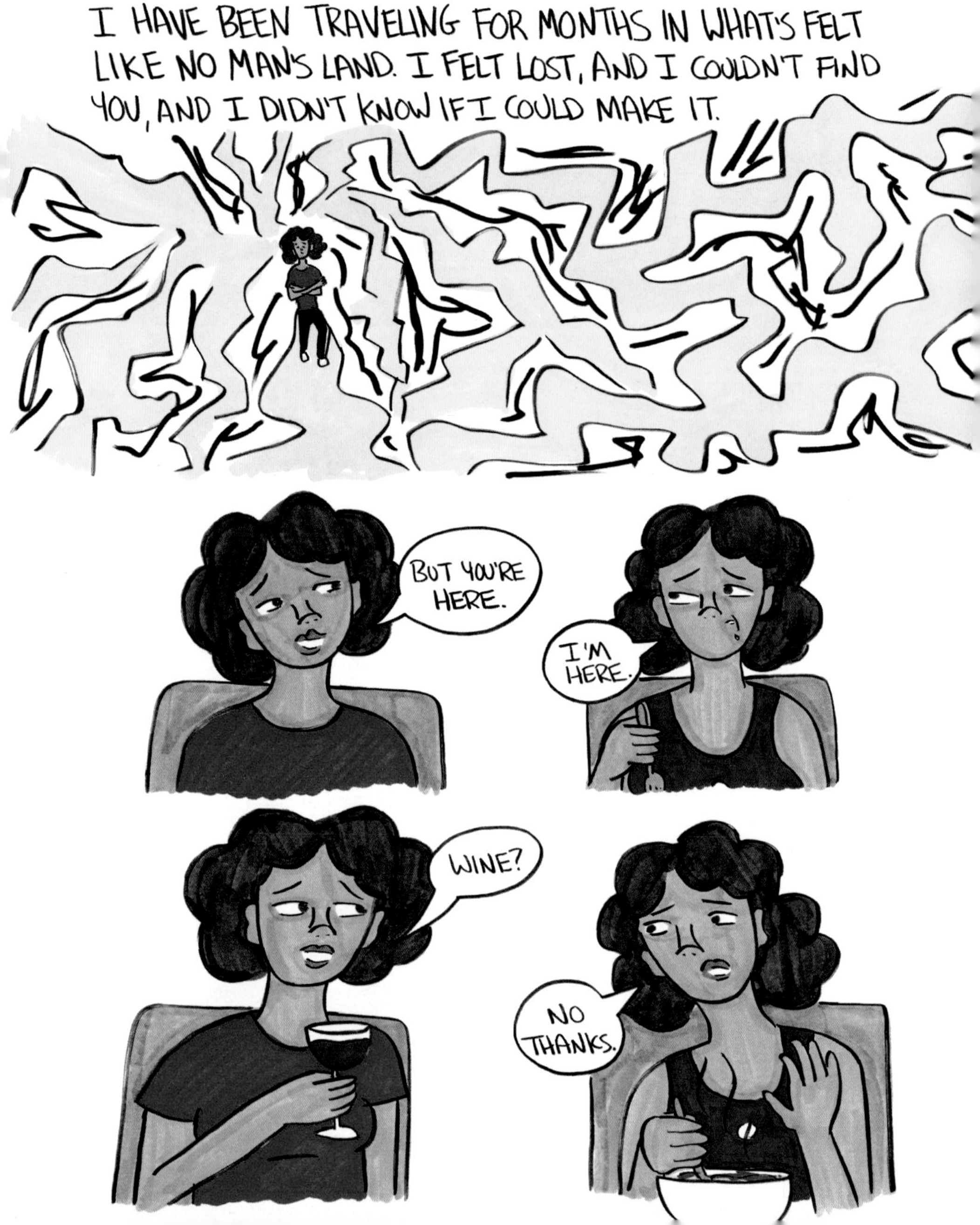
I HAVE BEEN TRAVELING FOR MONTHS IN WHAT'S FELT LIKE NO MAN'S LAND. I FELT LOST, AND I COULDN'T FIND YOU, AND I DIDN'T KNOW IF I COULD MAKE IT.
BUT YOU'RE HERE.
I'M HERE.
WINE?
NO THANKS.

UP UNTIL MY ASSAULT, MUCH OF MY SENSE OF SELF WAS BASED ON WHAT I DID OR HAD ACHIEVED.

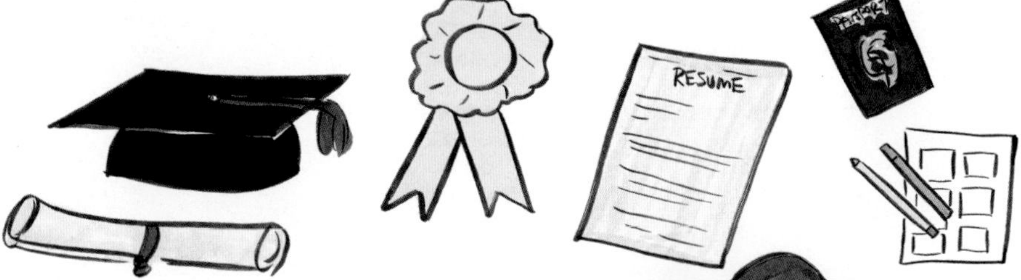
RESUME

A FEW MONTHS AFTER, PAST THE INITIAL SHOCK AND THE BURYING OF FEELINGS, LIFE SUDDENLY FELT UNMANAGEABLE.

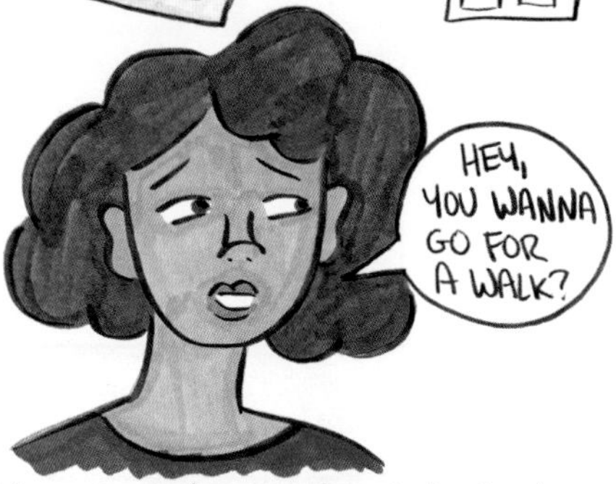
HEY, YOU WANNA GO FOR A WALK?

ON MY 30TH BIRTHDAY, I LEFT MY JOB AND MOVED IN WITH MY PARENTS.

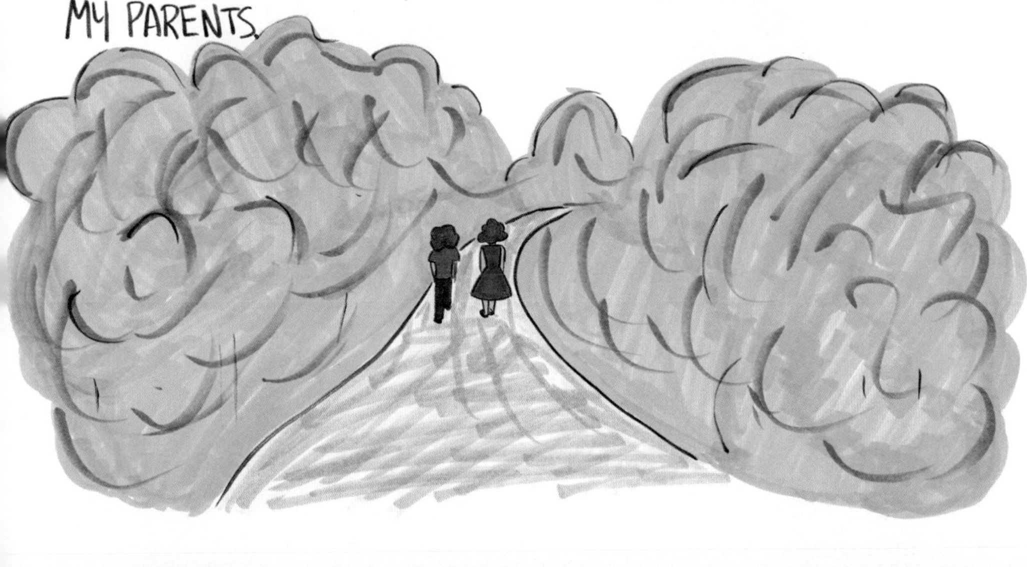

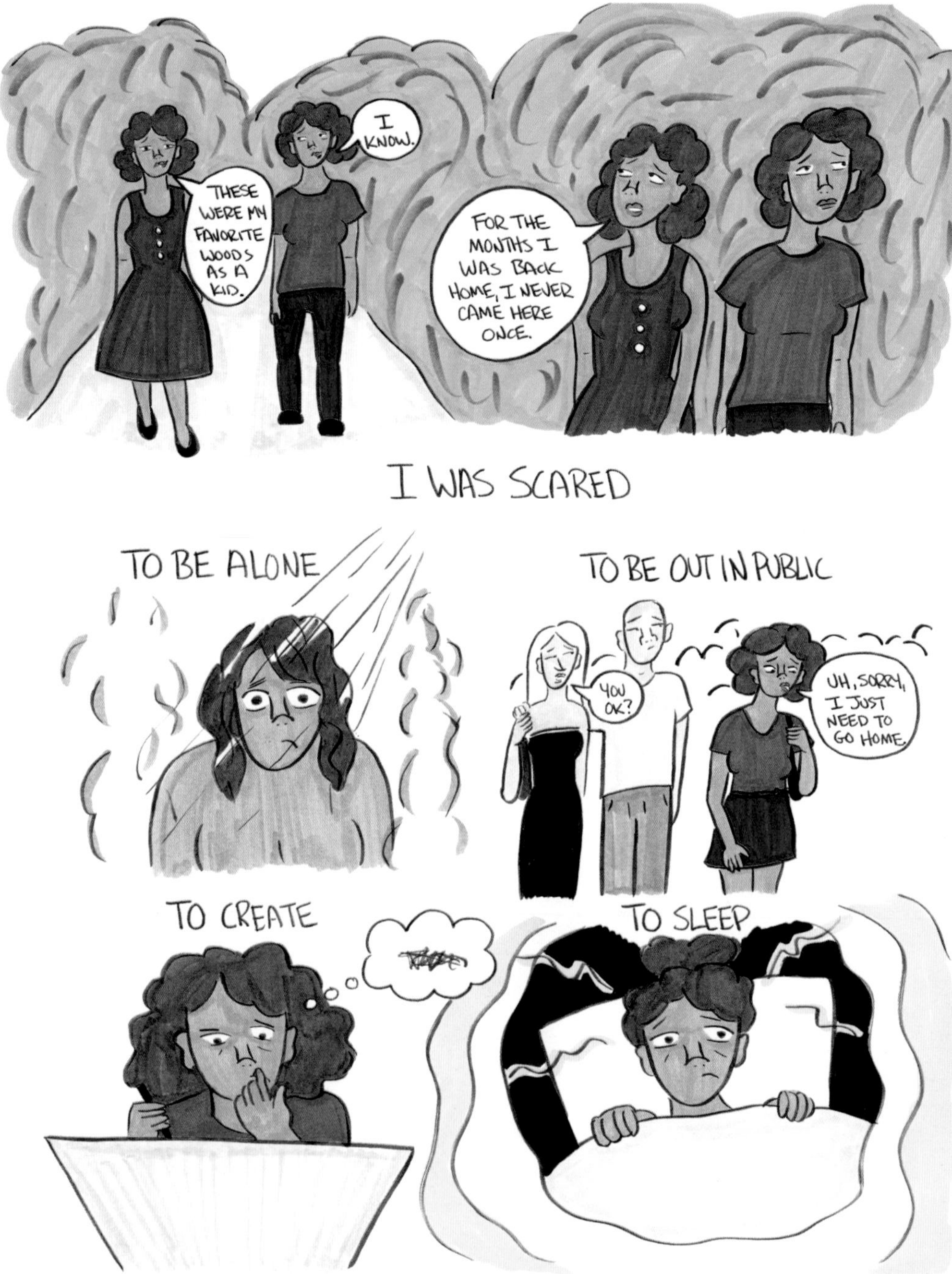
THESE WERE MY FAVORITE WOODS AS A KID.
I KNOW.
FOR THE MONTHS I WAS BACK HOME, I NEVER CAME HERE ONCE.
I WAS SCARED
TO BE ALONE
TO BE OUT IN PUBLIC
YOU OK?
UH, SORRY, I JUST NEED TO GO HOME.
TO CREATE
TO SLEEP

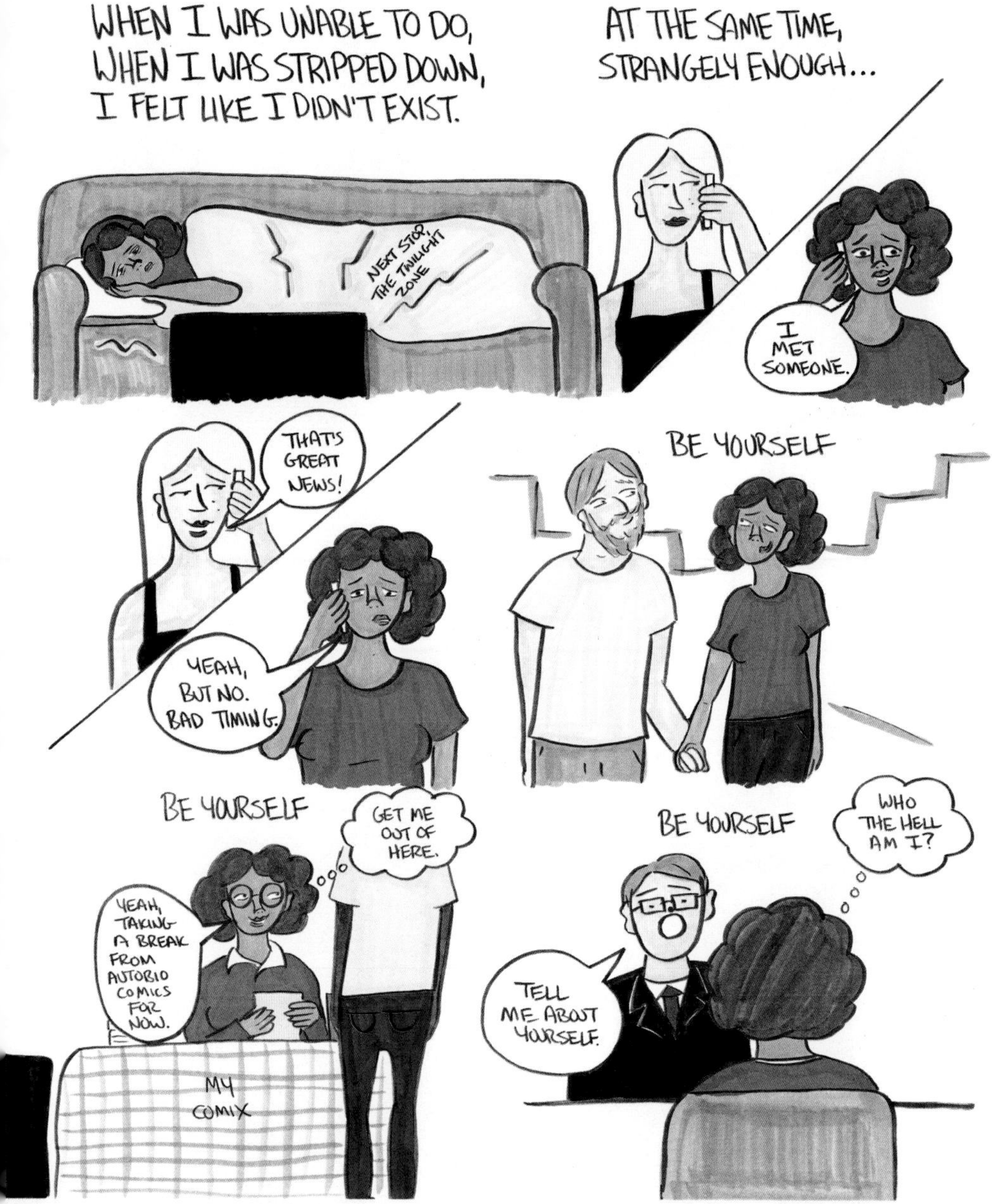
WHEN I WAS UNABLE TO DO,
WHEN I WAS STRIPPED DOWN,
I FELT LIKE I DIDN'T EXIST.
NEXT STOP, THE TWILIGHT ZONE
AT THE SAME TIME,
STRANGELY ENOUGH...
I MET SOMEONE.
THAT'S GREAT NEWS!
YEAH, BUT NO. BAD TIMING.
BE YOURSELF
BE YOURSELF
GET ME OUT OF HERE.
YEAH, TAKING A BREAK FROM AUTOBIO COMICS FOR NOW.
MY COMIX
BE YOURSELF
WHO THE HELL AM I?
TELL ME ABOUT YOURSELF.

WINTER, FRIEND'S WEDDING
I LOVE YOUR DRESS! WHERE'S IT FROM?
IT'S VINTAGE.
WELL, YOU LOOK GLOWING!
HA, THANKS.
LATER
WHAT'S UP, BABE?
I NEED HELP.

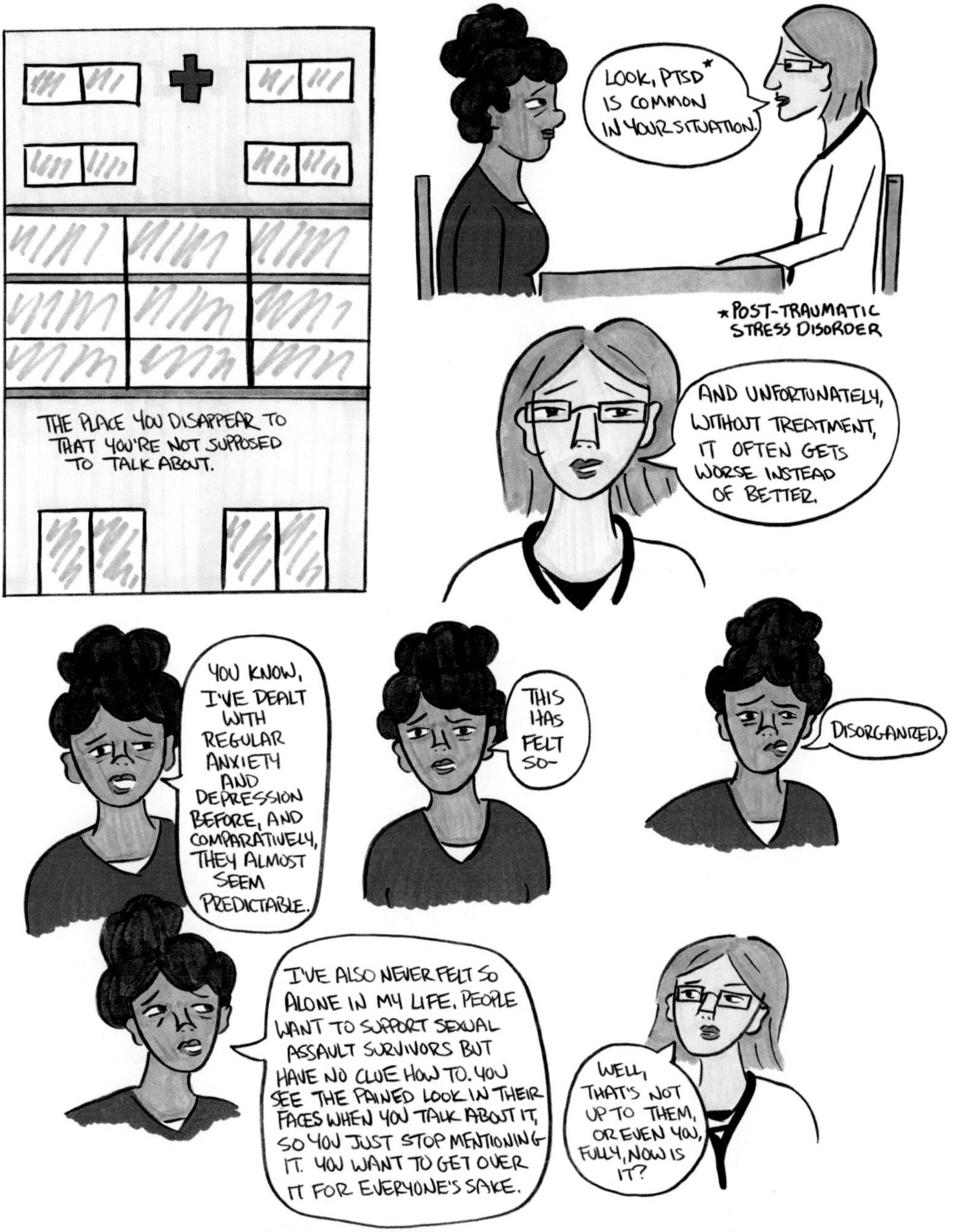
THE PLACE YOU DISAPPEAR TO THAT YOU'RE NOT SUPPOSED TO TALK ABOUT.
LOOK, PTSD* IS COMMON IN YOUR SITUATION.
*POST-TRAUMATIC STRESS DISORDER
AND UNFORTUNATELY, WITHOUT TREATMENT, IT OFTEN GETS WORSE INSTEAD OF BETTER.
YOU KNOW, I'VE DEALT WITH REGULAR ANXIETY AND DEPRESSION BEFORE, AND COMPARATIVELY, THEY ALMOST SEEM PREDICTABLE.
THIS HAS FELT SO-
DISORGANIZED.
I'VE ALSO NEVER FELT SO ALONE IN MY LIFE. PEOPLE WANT TO SUPPORT SEXUAL ASSAULT SURVIVORS BUT HAVE NO CLUE HOW TO. YOU SEE THE PAINED LOOK IN THEIR FACES WHEN YOU TALK ABOUT IT, SO YOU JUST STOP MENTIONING IT. YOU WANT TO GET OVER IT FOR EVERYONE'S SAKE.
WELL, THAT'S NOT UP TO THEM, OR EVEN YOU, FULLY, NOW IS IT?

THROUGH GROUPS, THROUGH MEALS, AND THROUGH IMPROMPTU CHATS, I HEARD STORIES AND SHARED MY OWN.

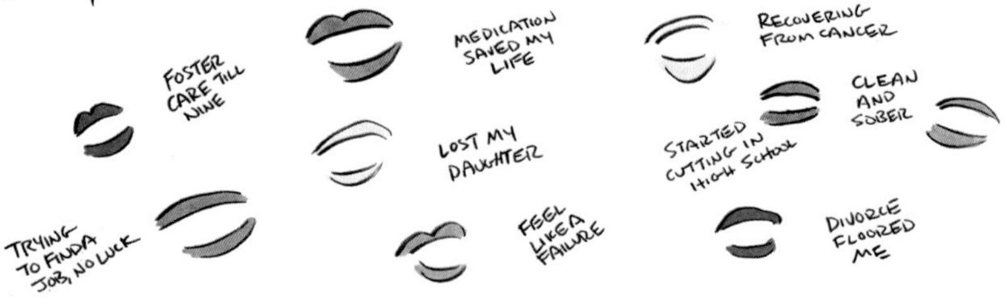
FOSTER CARE TILL NINE
MEDICATION SAVED MY LIFE
RECOVERING FROM CANCER
CLEAN AND SOBER
LOST MY DAUGHTER
STARTED CUTTING IN HIGH SCHOOL
TRYING TO FIND A JOB, NO LUCK
FEEL LIKE A FAILURE
DIVORCE FLOORED ME

BECAUSE REGARDLESS OF WHAT YOU ASSUME, EVERYONE HAS A STORY.

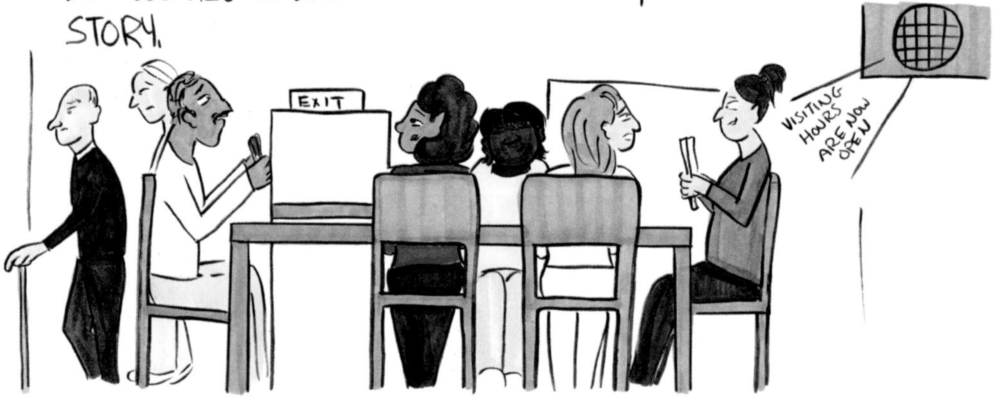
EXIT
VISITING HOURS ARE NOW OPEN

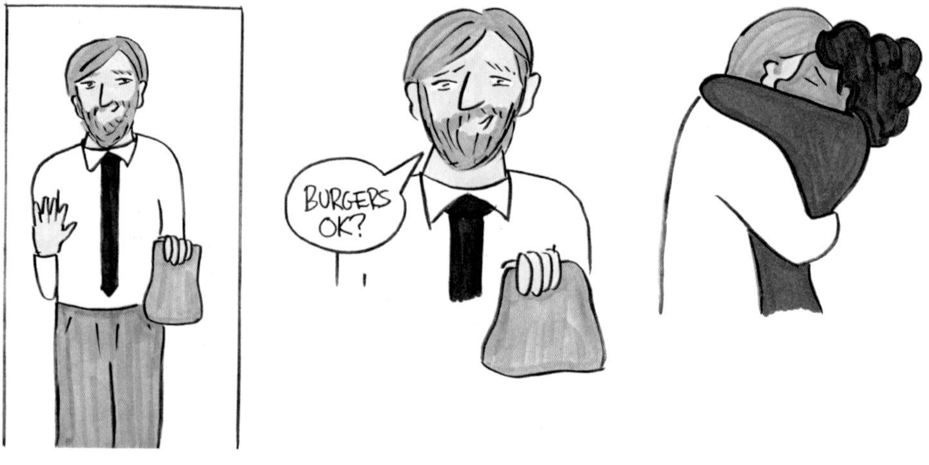
BURGERS OK?

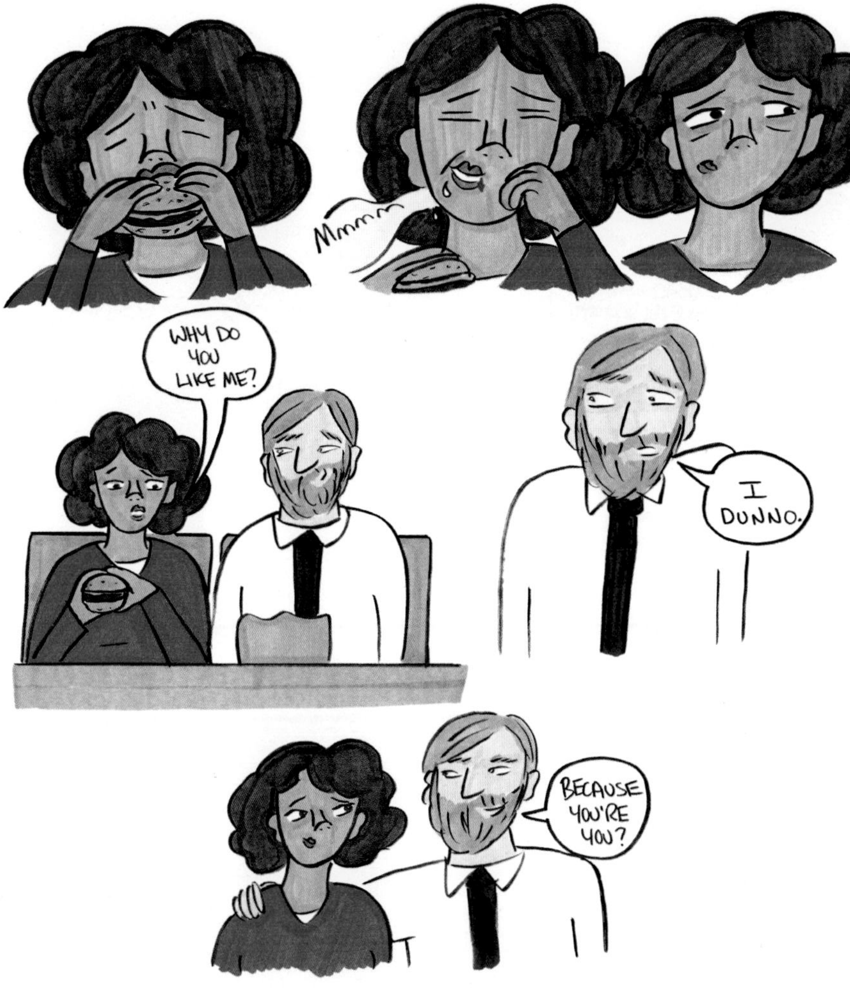
Mmmm
WHY DO YOU LIKE ME?
I DUNNO.
BECAUSE YOU'RE YOU?

THAT WAS BEING PROVEN TO ME. I WAS MEETING PEOPLE FROM ALL WALKS OF LIFE, WHO DIDN'T CARE WHERE I WAS FROM OR WHAT I DID.

THERE WAS ONLY ONE PERSON LEFT TO CONVINCE.

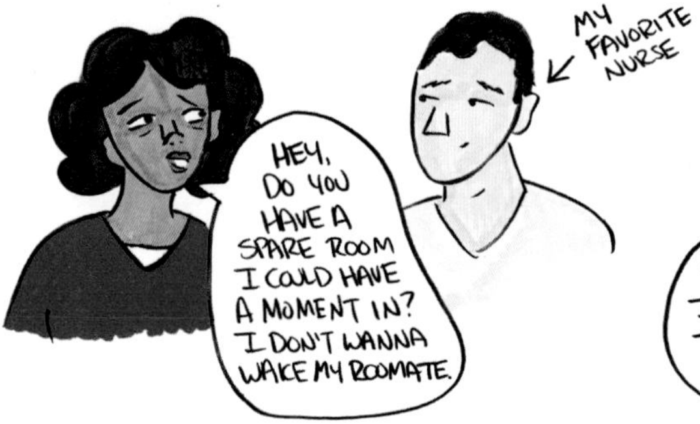
MY FAVORITE NURSE
HEY, DO YOU HAVE A SPARE ROOM I COULD HAVE A MOMENT IN? I DON'T WANNA WAKE MY ROOMATE.

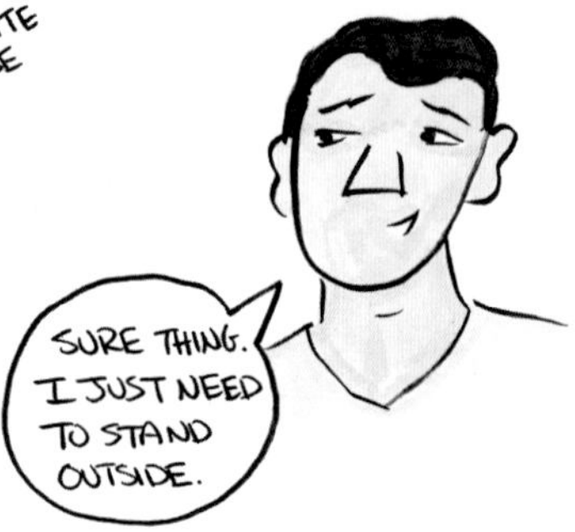
SURE THING. I JUST NEED TO STAND OUTSIDE.

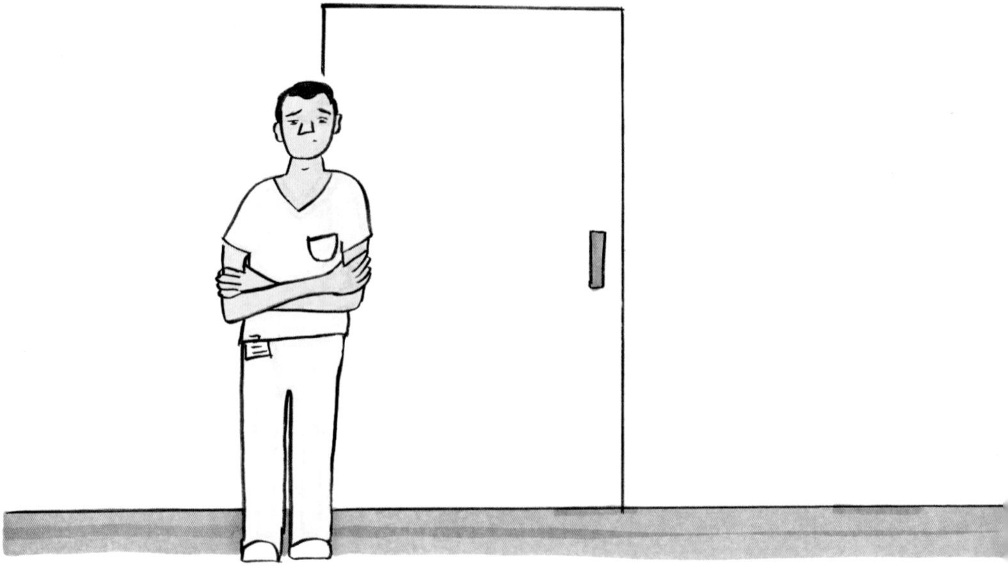

IT WAS THE FIRST TIME I FELT SAFE CRYING IN MONTHS.

I CAN'T SAY THAT IT COMPLETELY FIXED EVERYTHING, BUT PERHAPS IT MADE ME REALIZE, AT THE END OF THE DAY, WHAT MATTERED MOST WAS MY HUMANITY.

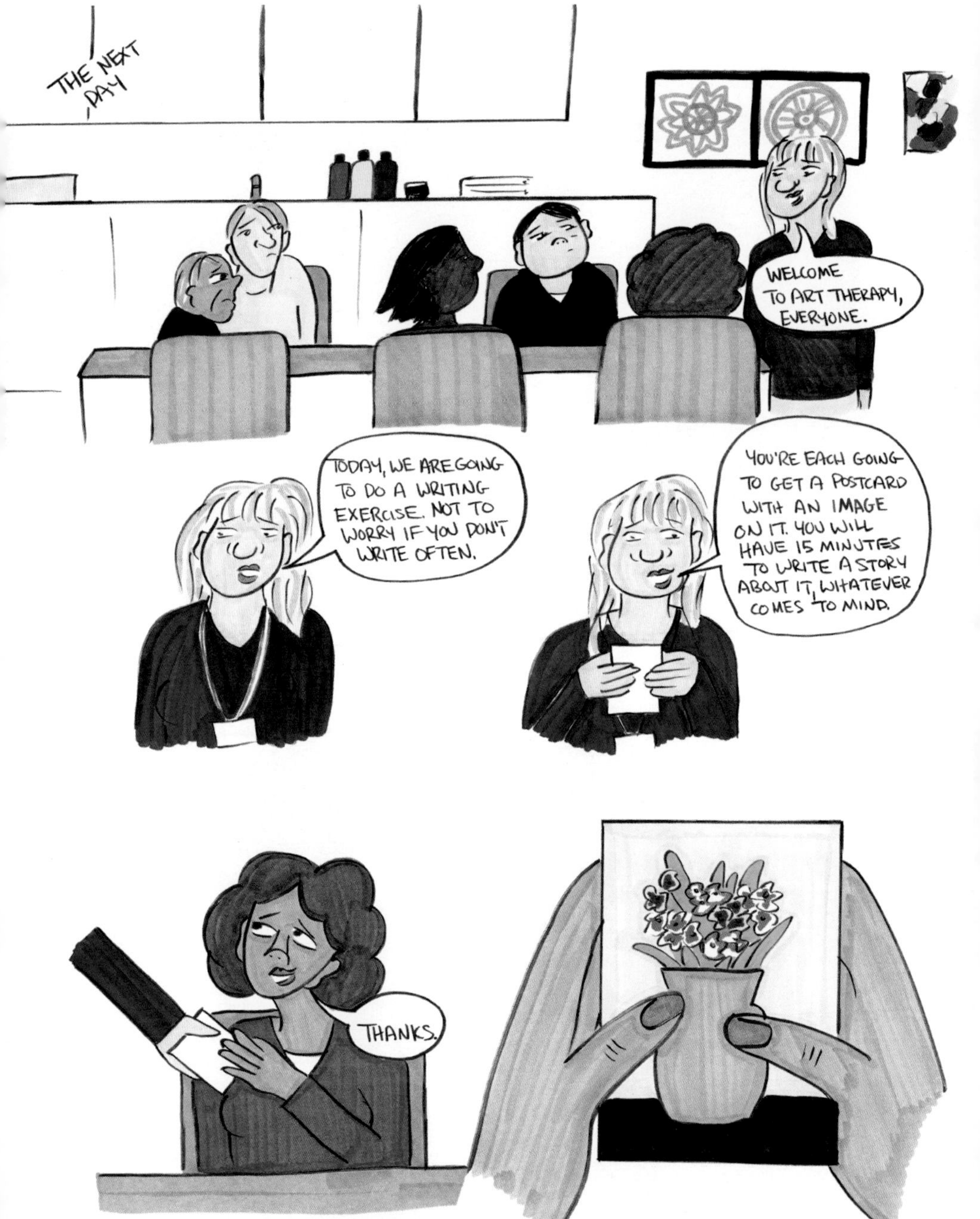
THE NEXT DAY
WELCOME TO ART THERAPY, EVERYONE.
TODAY, WE ARE GOING TO DO A WRITING EXERCISE. NOT TO WORRY IF YOU DON'T WRITE OFTEN.
YOU'RE EACH GOING TO GET A POSTCARD WITH AN IMAGE ON IT. YOU WILL HAVE 15 MINUTES TO WRITE A STORY ABOUT IT, WHATEVER COMES TO MIND.
THANKS.

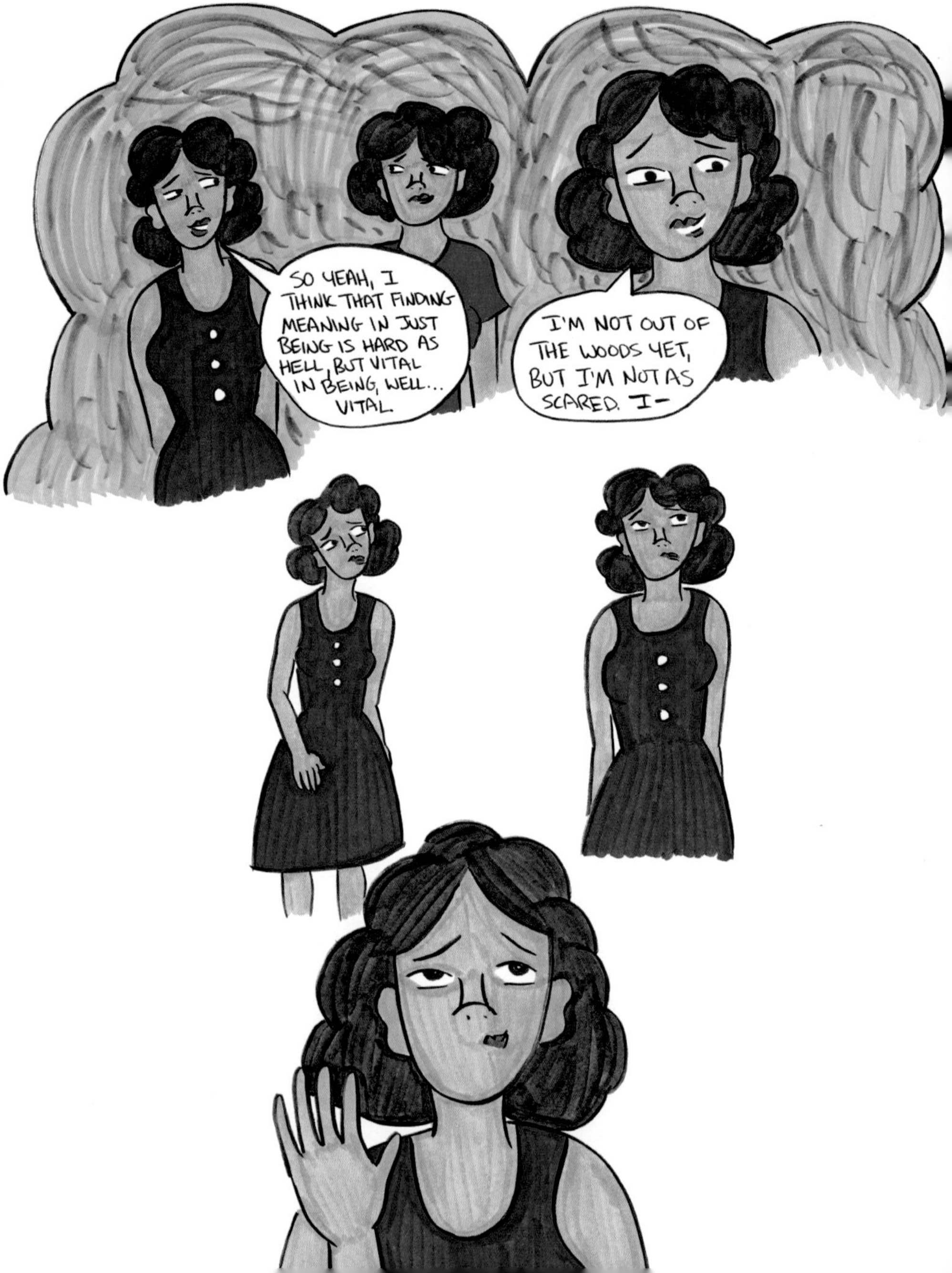
SO YEAH, I THINK THAT FINDING MEANING IN JUST BEING IS HARD AS HELL, BUT VITAL IN BEING, WELL... VITAL.
I'M NOT OUT OF THE WOODS YET, BUT I'M NOT AS SCARED. I-

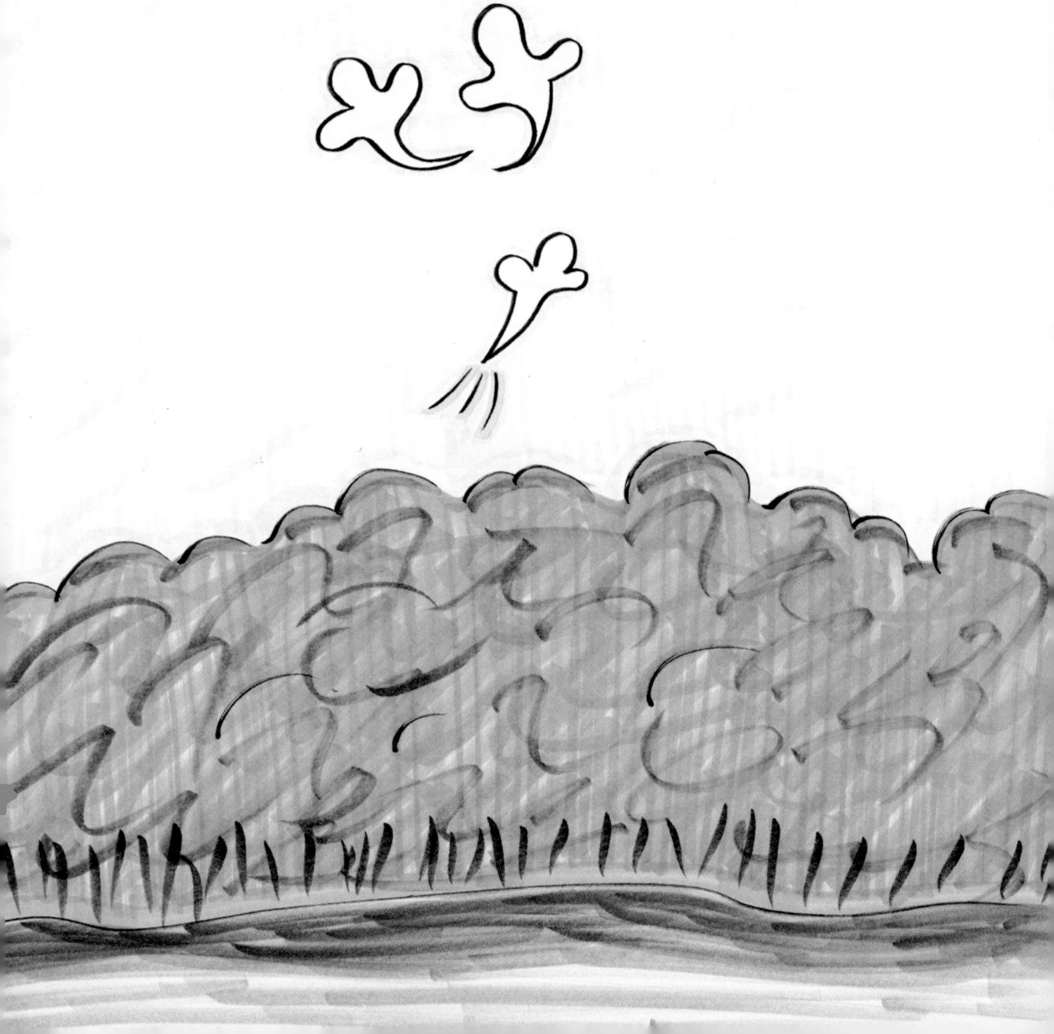

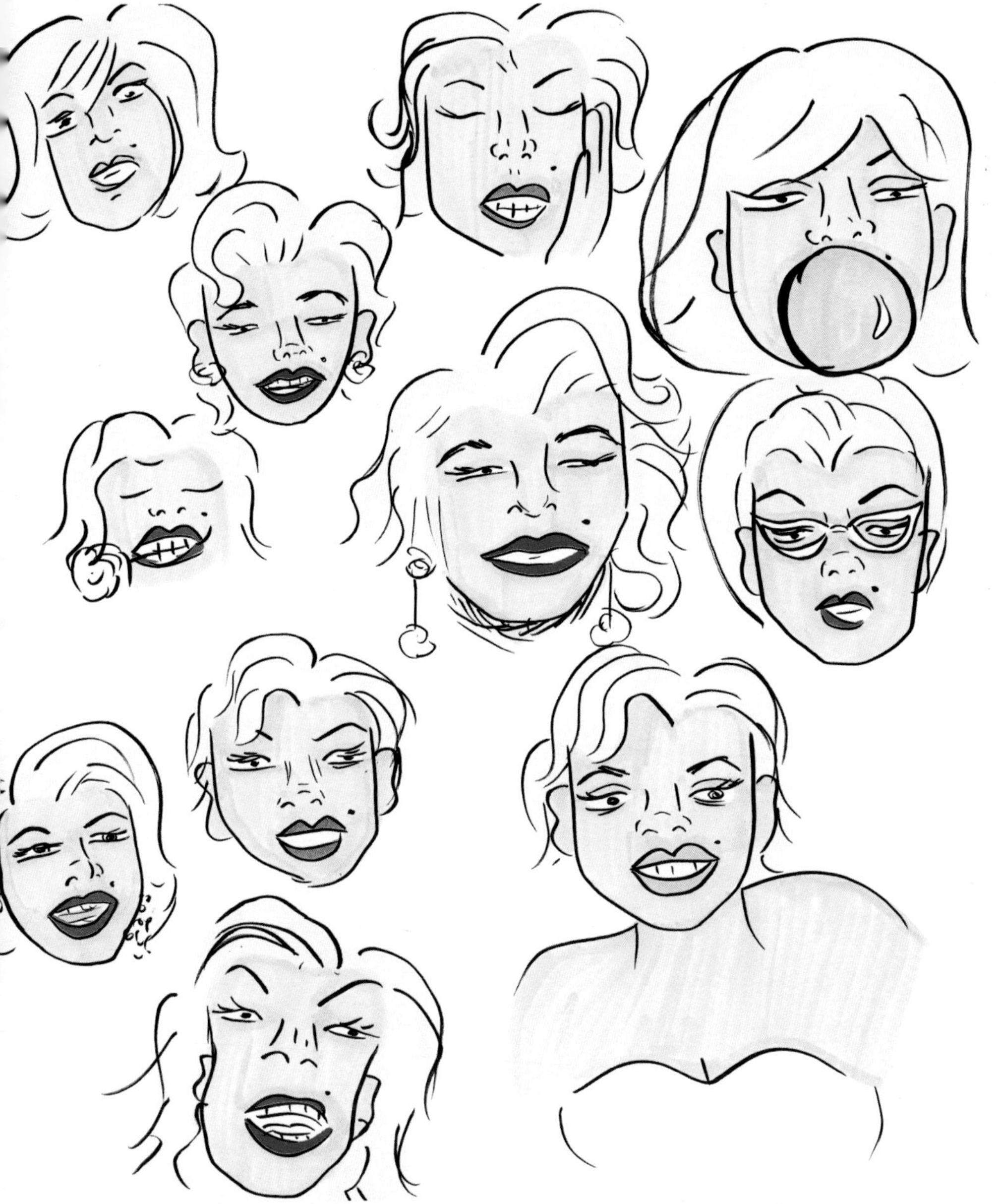

IMPERFECTION IS BEAUTY, MADNESS IS GENIUS, AND IT'S BETTER TO BE ABSOLUTELY RIDICULOUS THAN ABSOLUTELY BORING.

—MARILYN MONROE

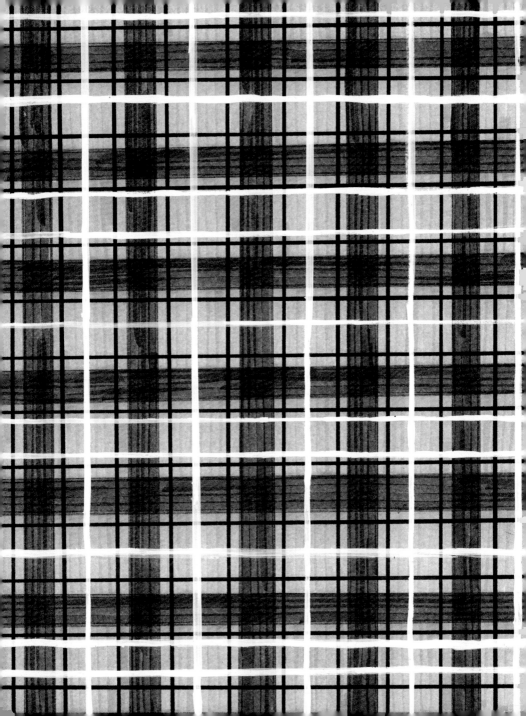

Wallpaper

In that house, there was wallpaper.
Wallpaper like you wouldn't believe!

"We're tearing it down," said Mom, once
the sale went through.

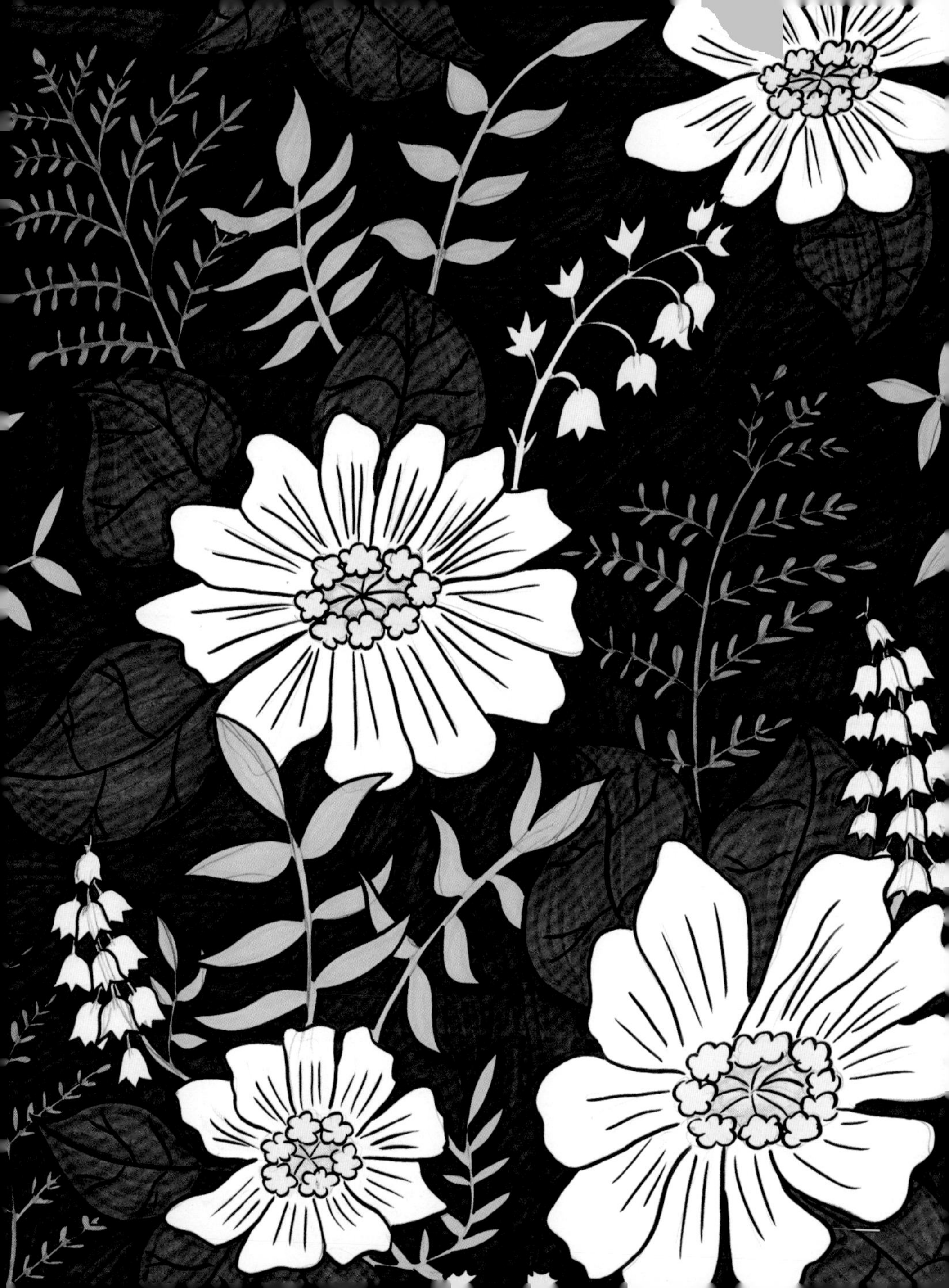

Once we moved in, it all went away,
except for the floral stuff in the
kitchen.

The seafoam bathroom tiles.
The urine-soaked powder blue rug.
Even the dead willow tree.

"I heard that the owners before us
croaked here," I said.

"They were old," Mom mumbled.

That night, I dreamed of eating Willy Wonka's wallpaper. The strawberries, cherries, and grapes.

I ate a Fruit Roll-Up for breakfast.

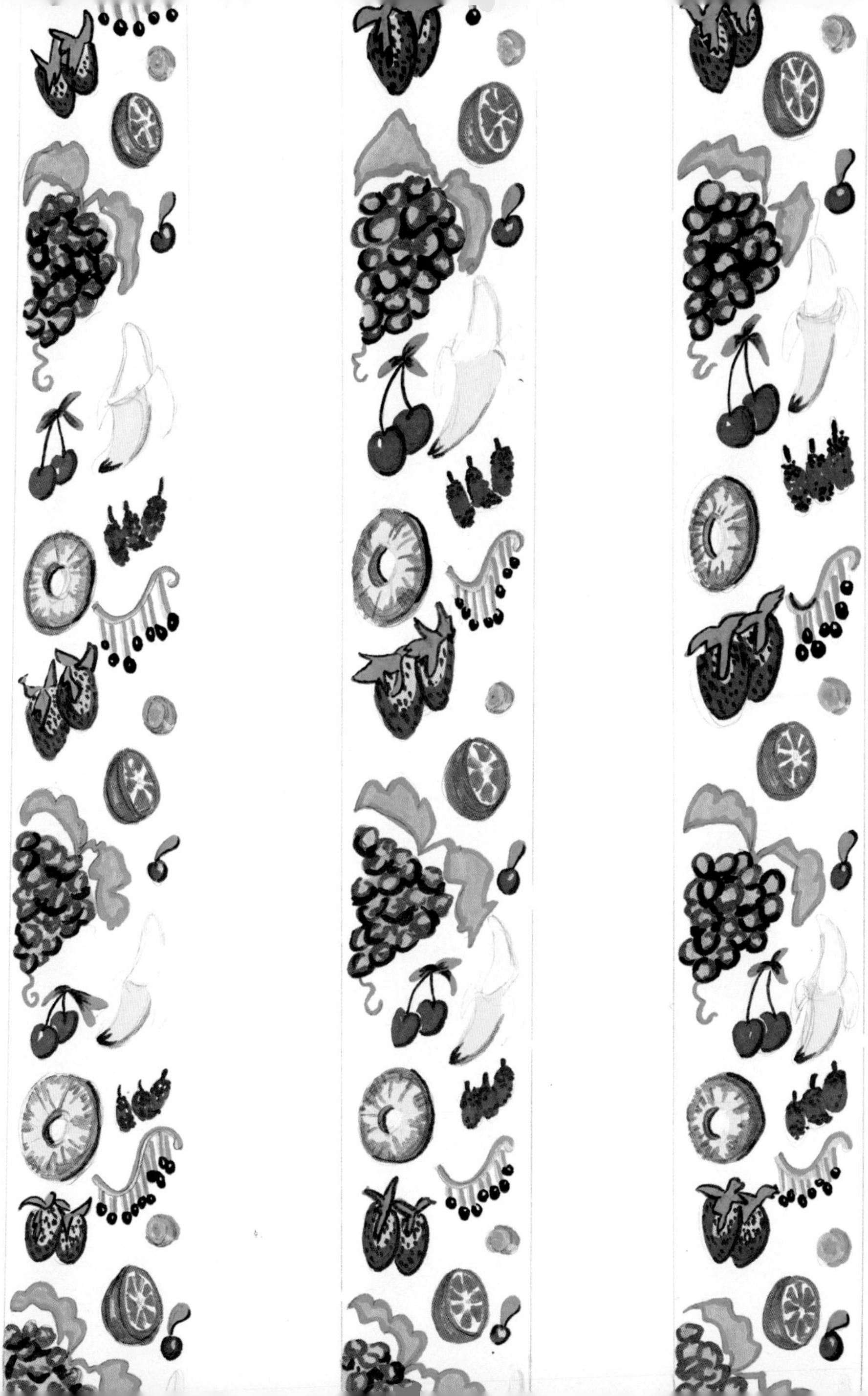

At Grandma's that weekend, my brother Ethan and I went downstairs to play as the adults talked. We wrapped fake Christmas presents, as usual, to occupy ourselves.

"Give Dad that polar bear snow globe," Ethan motioned towards me.

Grandma got the biggest present. She looked shocked. "For me? Why thank you, my Sugahs!"

We chanted "Merry Christmas" as wrapping paper shed like oversized confetti.

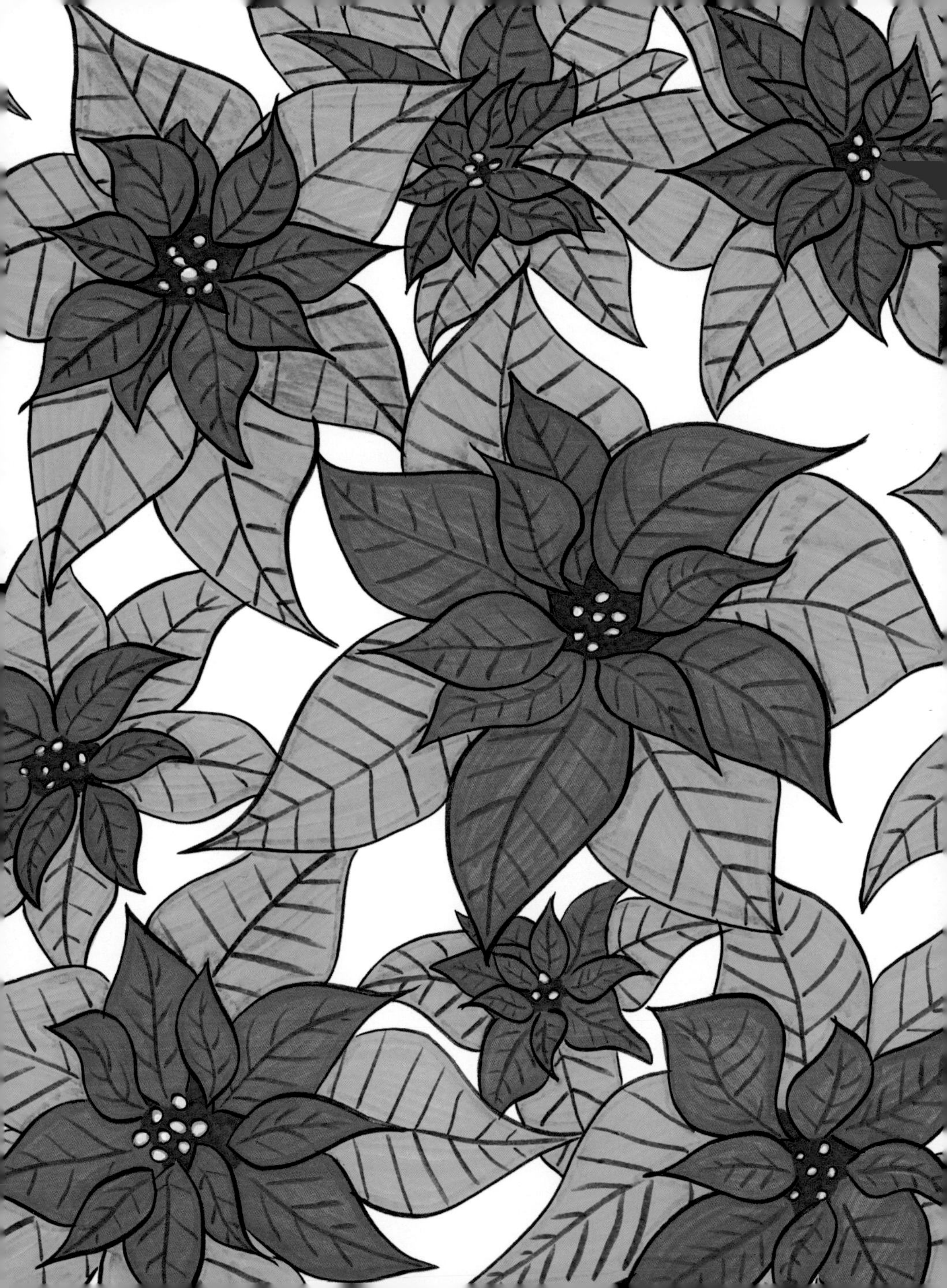

For homework the next week, I read a story about the Egyptian Book of the Dead, where this guy's heart sank. It wasn't supposed to do that if you were good.

I was interrupted by the sound of the linoleum floor being yanked up. The remaining tacky glue looked like clumps of old snot.

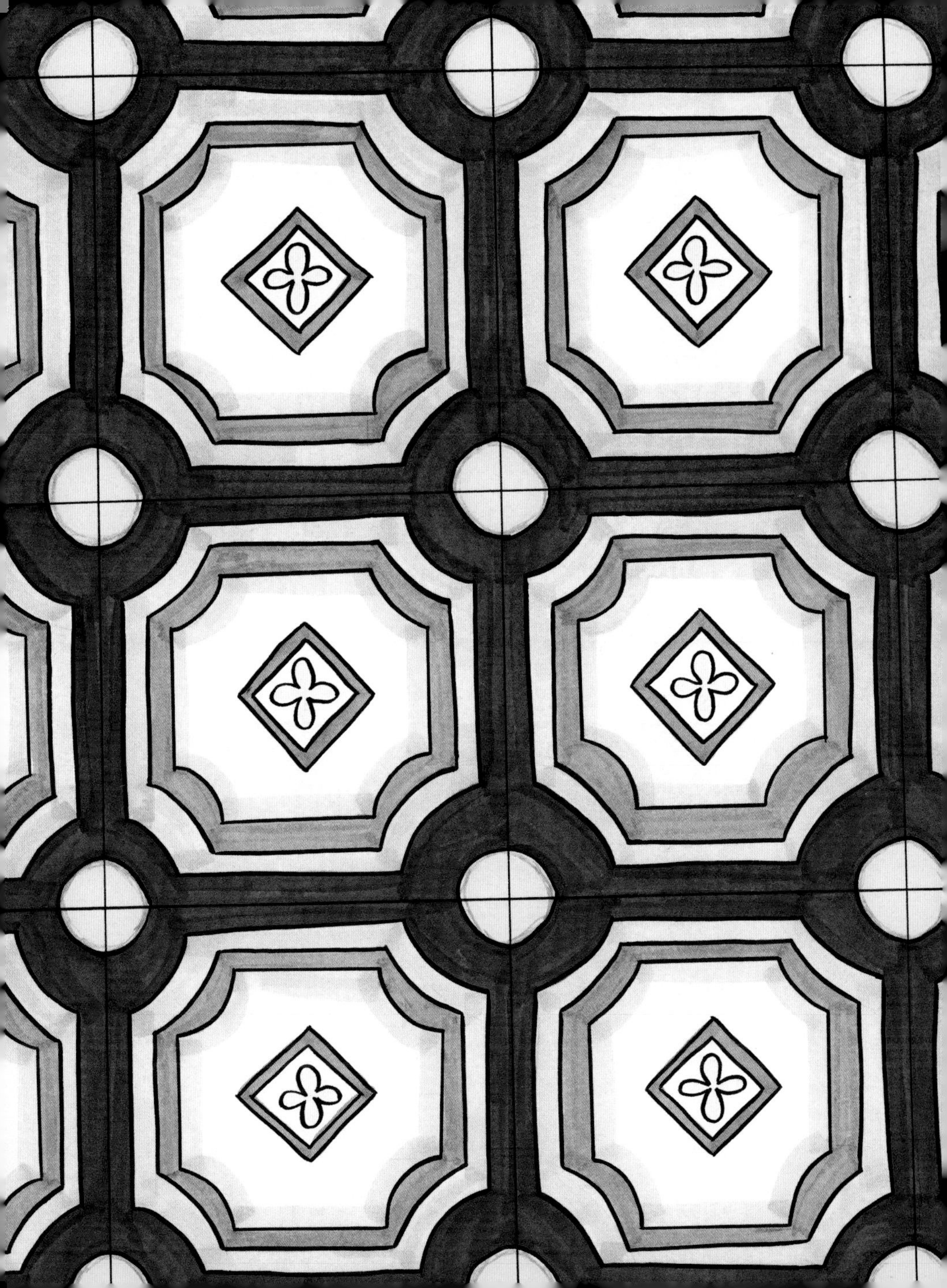

At Lacy's house, the freshly painted walls mimicked a warm southwestern Pueblo.

"It's Santa Fe Red." Lacy's Mom beamed as she showed my Mom. "They used a sponging technique to create the illusion of texture."

"It's wonderful." Mom lightly stroked the wall.

When we got home, Mom sighed as she looked at our kitchen. "I wasn't that impressed, to be honest. I was just trying to be polite."

It took three hours to drive down to Cape May for summer vacation. But I guess it's at the end of the state, so that made sense.

Mom told us about the historic Gingerbread Houses. "They're beautiful Victorian houses with exquisite detail."

"I hope they smell spicy," said Ethan as he fiddled with his broken Scooby Doo Pez dispenser. I tried not to throw up from motion sickness.

"You'll grow out of it," said Dad.

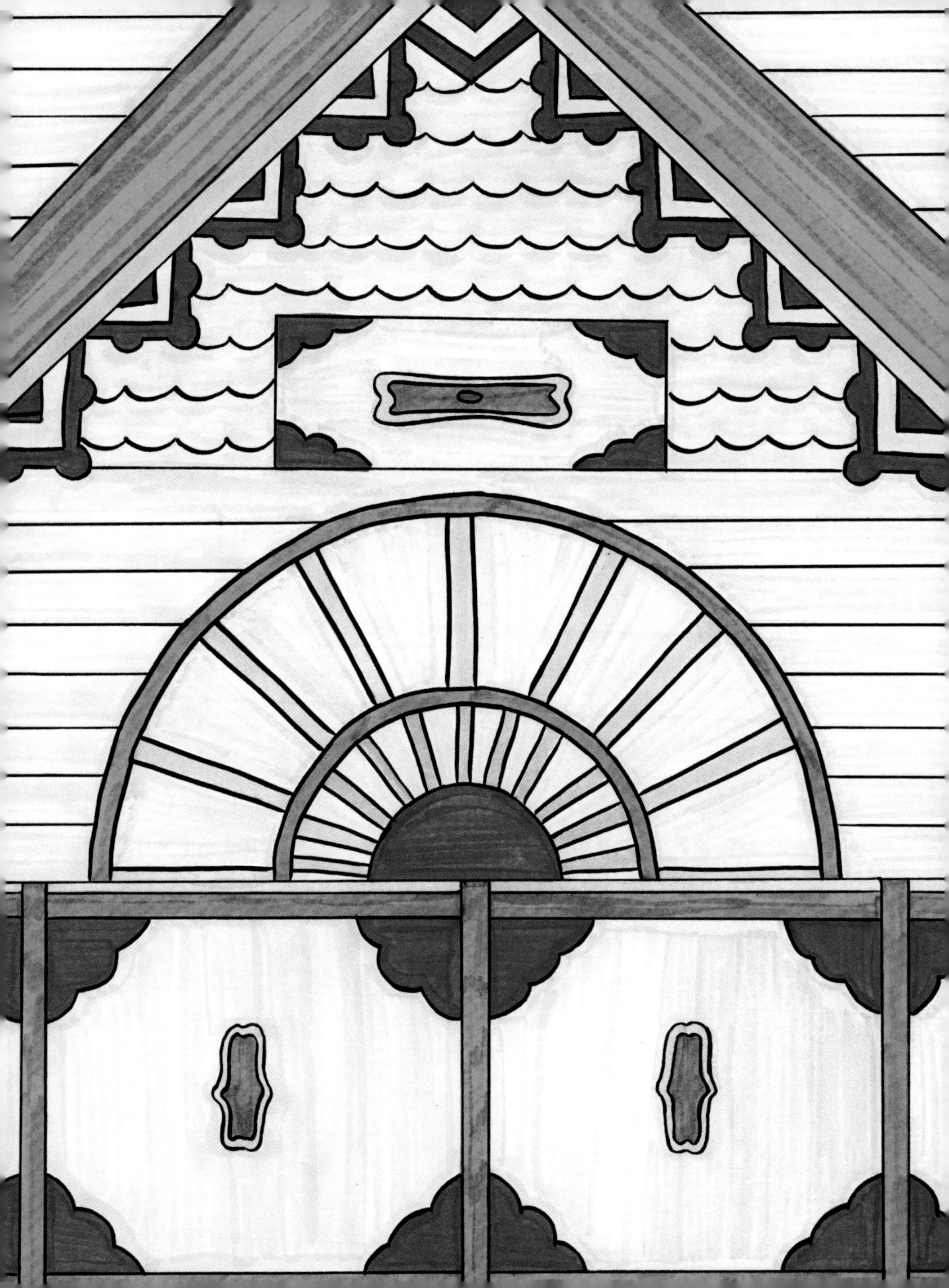

The bed and breakfast was genteel. There was lots of lace and china.

But it was definitely haunted, as confirmed by Ethan, who stopped playing with his action figures to investigate. My breath felt cold with fear, my eyes vigilant.

"This is the best Caesar salad I've EVER had", said Dad at dinner. I didn't know that he had eaten enough Caesar salads to actually prove this.

"What's up with you two?" he asked as he back-forked the remaining dressing, like you see in a froyo commercial. "You hardly ate dinner."

"Nothin'." We both looked down.

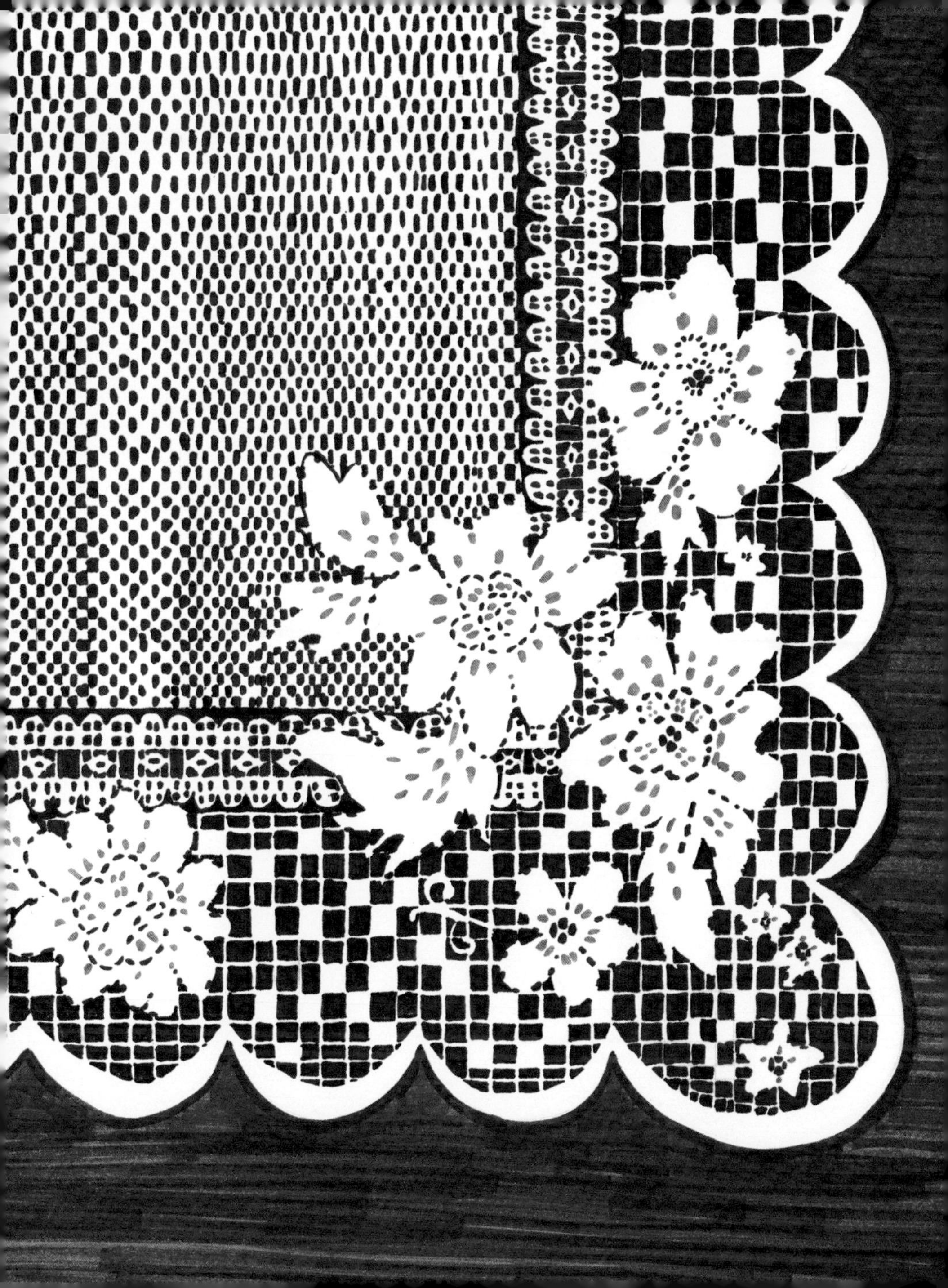

The details of the wallpaper in me and Ethan's room were overwhelming.

"Why did Victorian people like peonies so much? They are so grotesque, like unkempt roses on 'roids," I wondered aloud.

"Ghosts live in between the petals," said Ethan. "They're soft, so they make good mattresses."

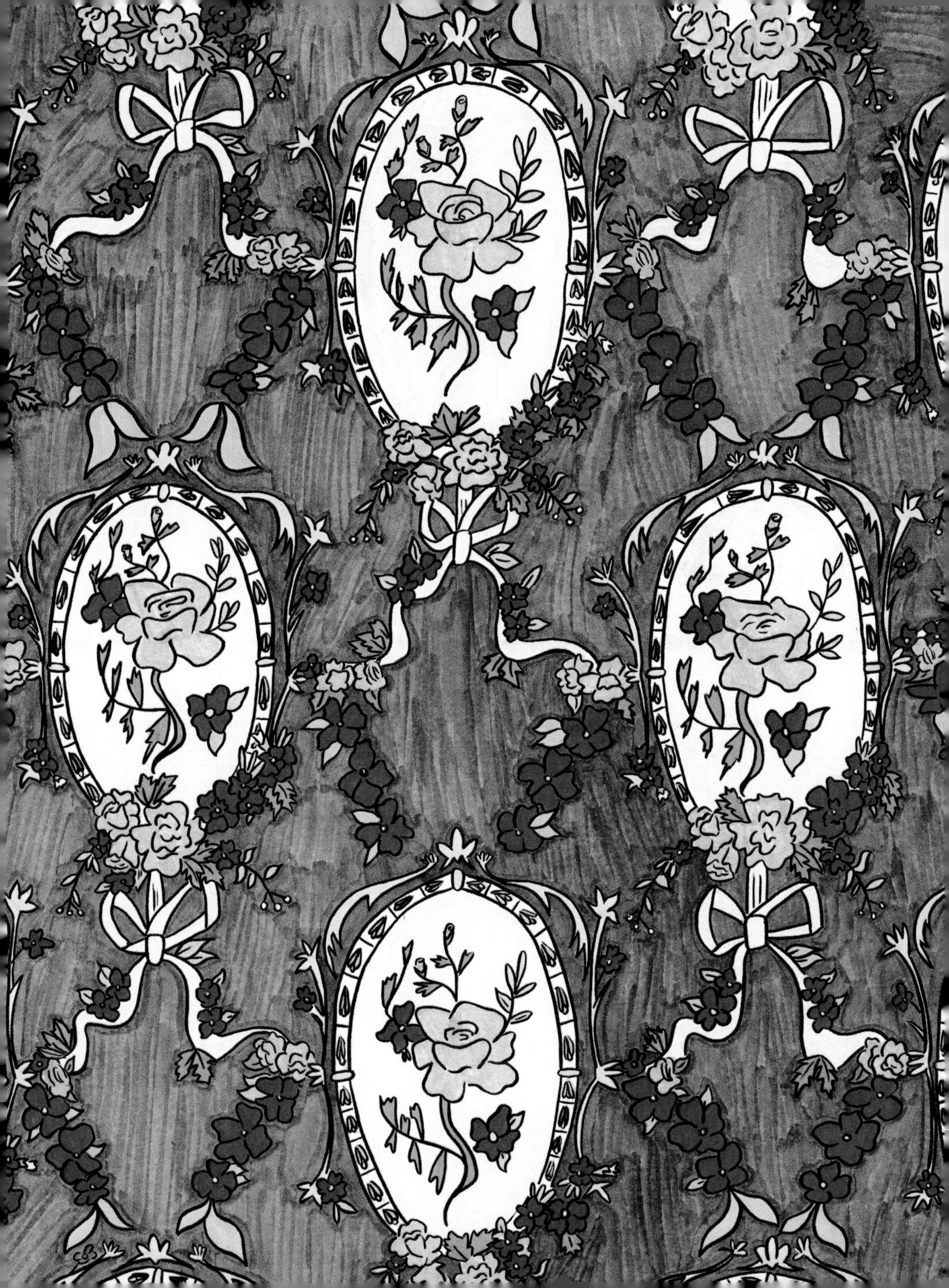

When we got back from vacation, it was time for my room to be fixed up, so I had to sleep in the den. The newly stripped walls were brown, the color of Hershey's chocolate bars.

I kept thinking about chocolate, so I got some after school at the supermarket and ate it later that night while I looked at books in the den.

I accidentally smudged some in a new copy of *Pride and Prejudice* and put the book back quickly.

We got to see Grandma at her new assisted-living apartment for the first time.

Mom said that she was fine but needed some extra support and social opportunities.

We met Grandma for lunch. The vegetables in the cafeteria were very soft, but at least there was Jell-O.

The apartment was all right, but small. It was nice that they gave Grandma a welcome wreath for her door.

I checked in the closet for gift-wrapping supplies, but there were none.

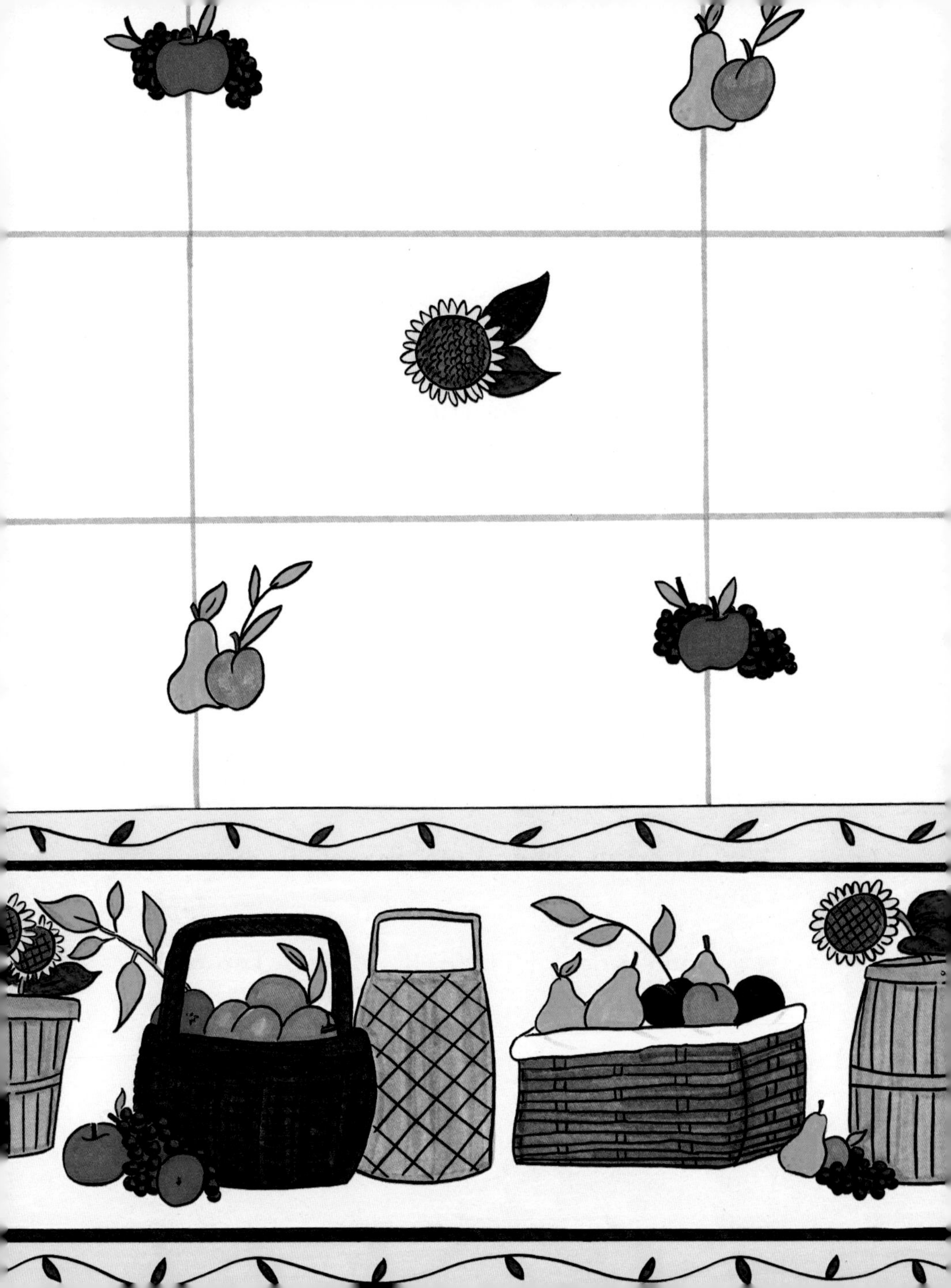

We sat in our half-renovated kitchen after dinner on Monday.

"Someone told me that our house was the site of some gruesome murders back in the day," I mentioned.

"That's ridiculous!" Mom shook her head. "Who told you that?"

"Jon. He's in my class." I didn't tell her that I had a crush on Jon.

"I heard that kid likes smelling other kids' farts," said Ethan.

"YOU smell other kids' farts!" I snapped.

I didn't know, though, if I liked Jon as much anymore.

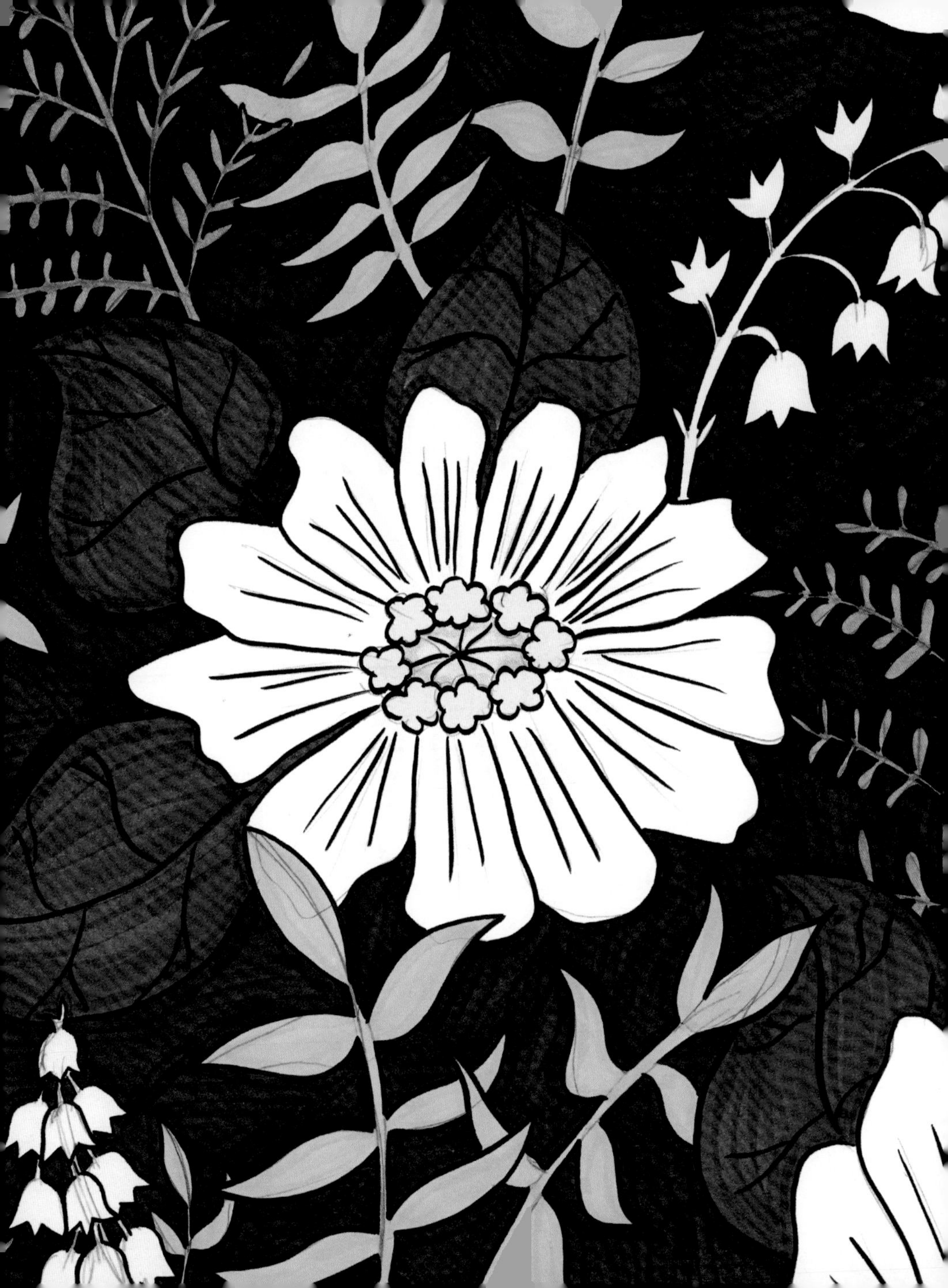

Sometimes, me and Ethan went with Mom to the local jewelry auction.

Mom never bought anything, but she liked to look at the antique stuff. It gave me a chance to eat lots of mini muffins and cheese from the refreshments table.

Each auction piece was introduced by a man that Ethan nicknamed "Mr. Fancy Pants". He always got up to start the auction with much flair. "This 14-karat-gold Edwardian ring with a blah blah blah makes quite the statement, wouldn't you say? The decadence is quite toothsome."

I wondered if people would ever start wearing pocket watches again.

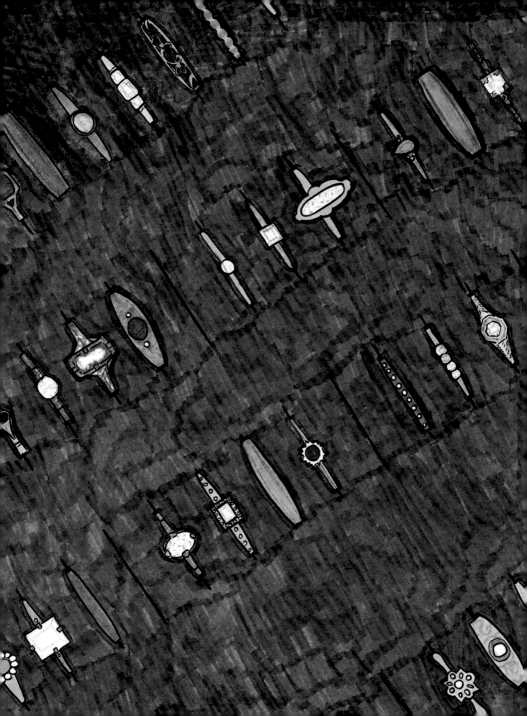

At school the next week, we got to use actual microscopes.

Lacy was my lab partner, but we didn't really talk. Her dad moved out the past weekend and she didn't really want to be bothered.

I looked at her nervously. "I like how the cell slides remind me of kaleidoscopes. You want to take a look? It'll make you happy...maybe."

She considered it, but then just shrugged.

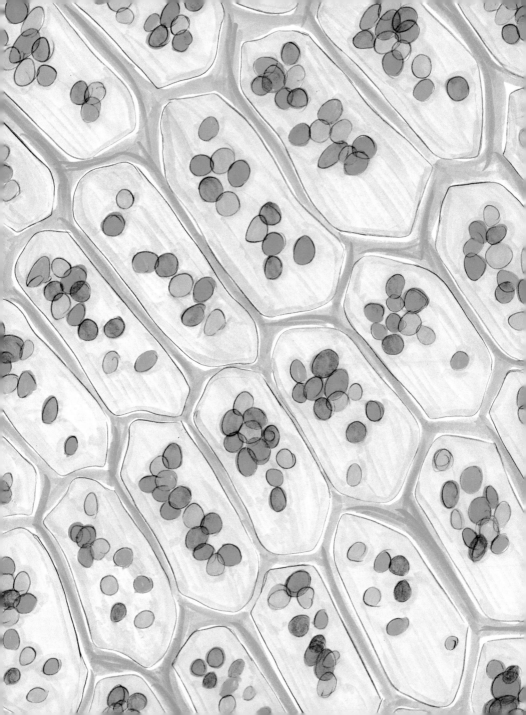

One weekend, Ethan and I clomped around in the leaves, discussing whether it was possible to resell the ketchup packets you get at fast food restaurants for money.

"And Pez candy. I don't like it, but maybe someone else will," he said.

Dad walked up to our pile. "Time to go."

We got in the car to head to Grandma's.

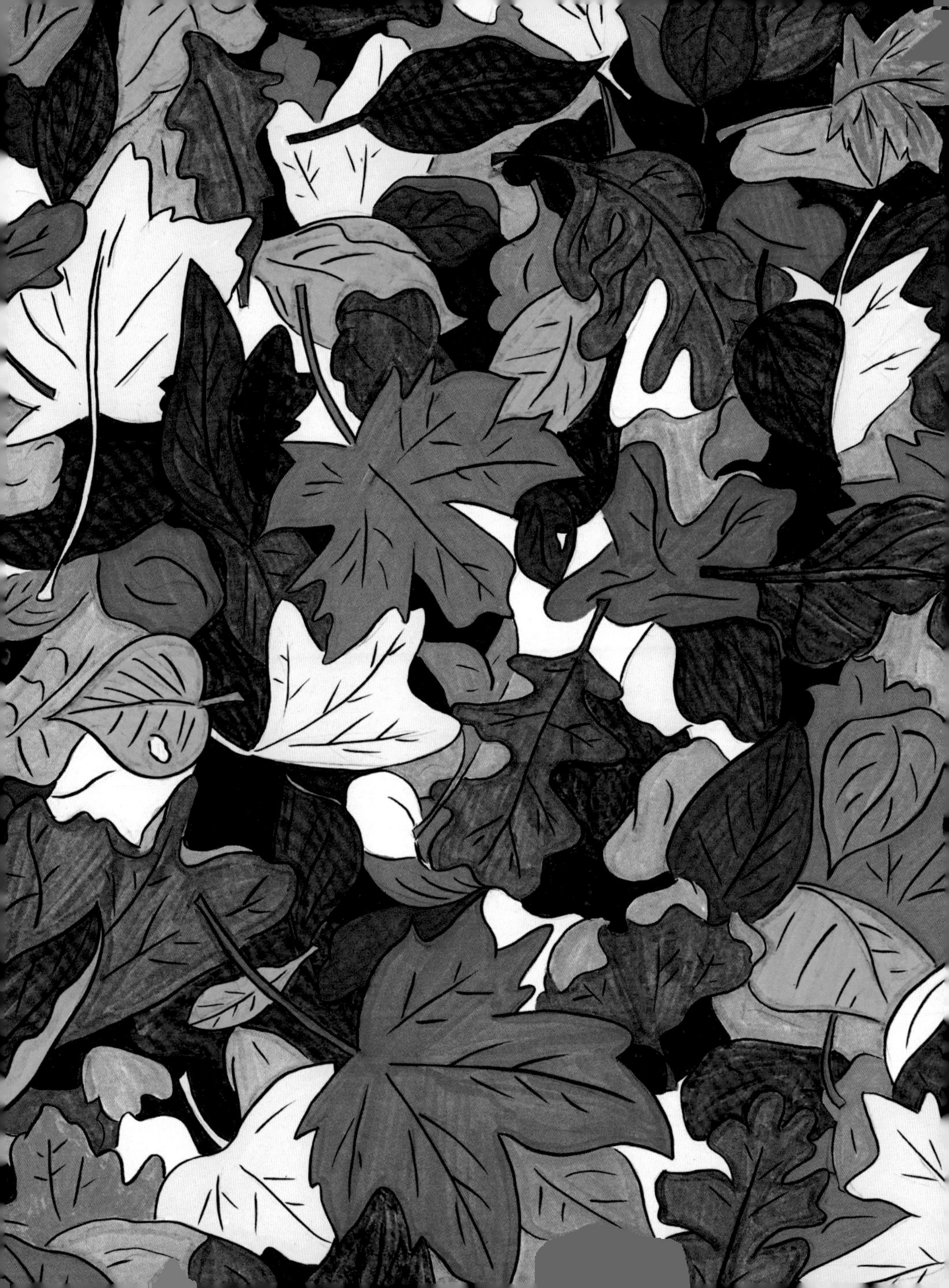

At the hospital, Grandma's breath sounded like a wind tunnel. She moaned, too.

"Not quite yet," Dad mumbled under the bleeps and blips. He looked at Mom, his eyes reddish.

After leaving, we ate at Pizza Hut. No one talked, really.

On the way home, I threw up in the car. Dad pulled over into a strip mall to get me cleaned up. I knew that she was going with the wind.

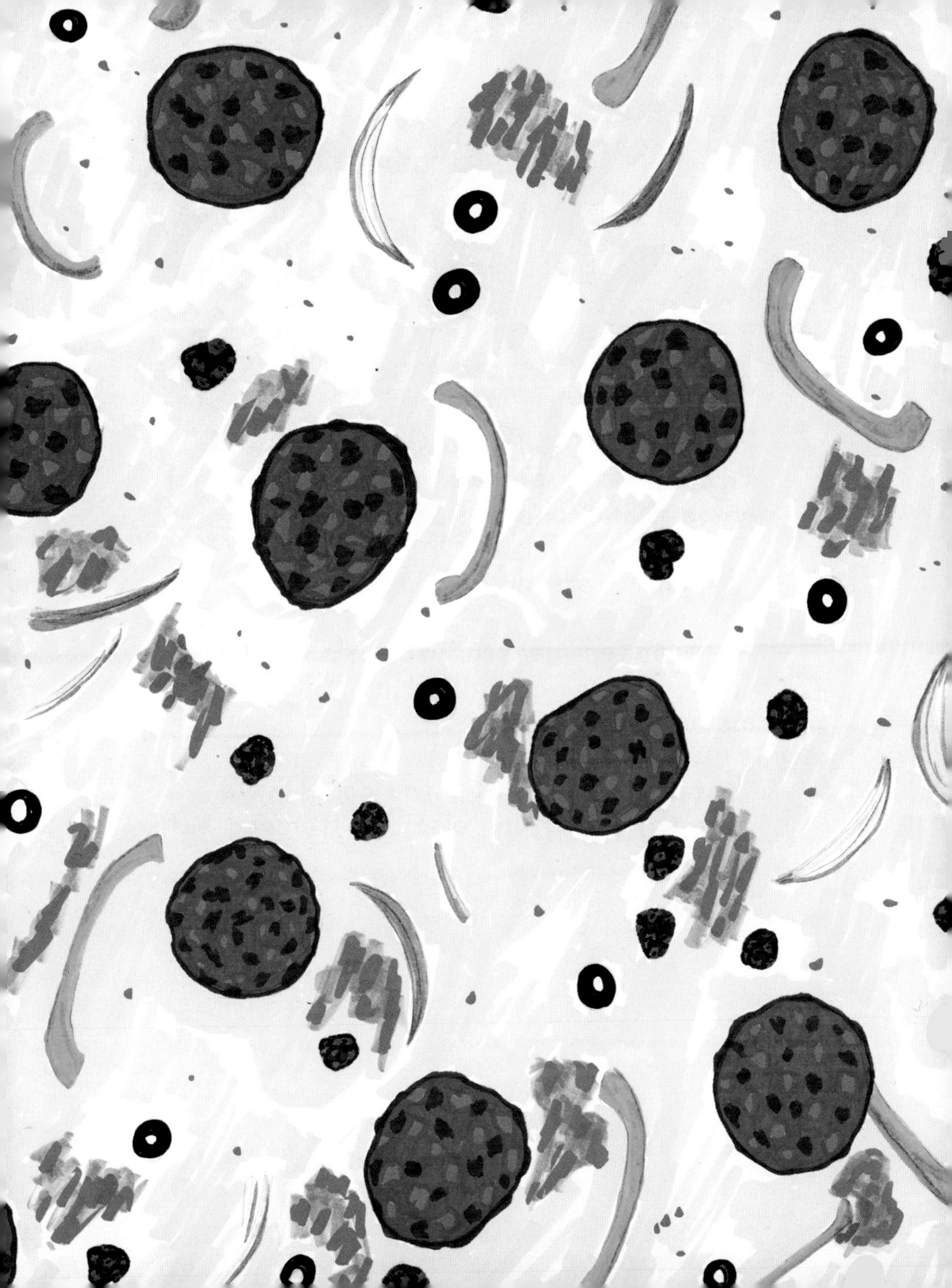

People came today to strip off the kitchen wallpaper and paint. When I got home from school, it was all gone.

"Beige?" I stared in disbelief.

Mom looked pleased. "Yes, it's a neutral color. It'll go well with the other design elements."

"But it's so BORING! You could have gone with anything else!" I stomped out, crying.

The next week, on the way to school, we saw an old dollhouse on the side of the road. Mom picked it up and put it in the car.

She let me fix it up with her help. That was one of the best times I ever had.

Mostly, though, I'm afraid to play with it, because I don't want to screw it up.

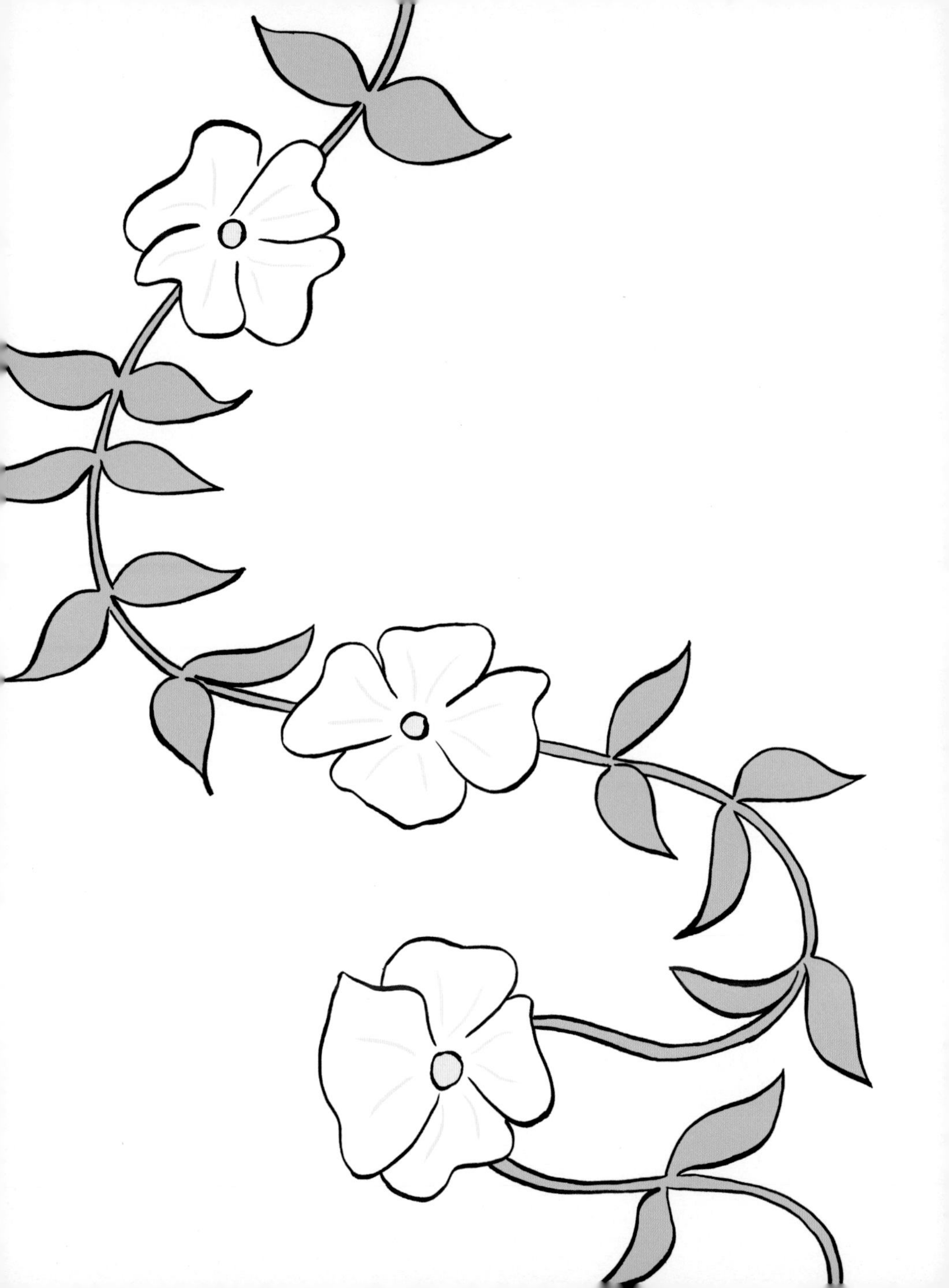

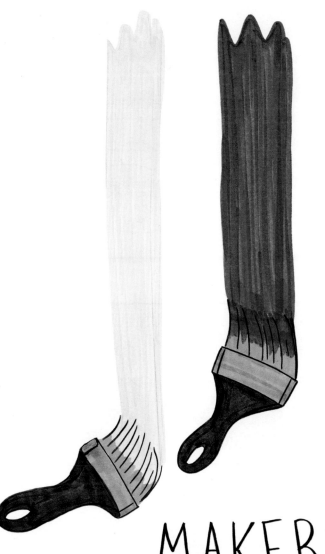

MAKERS

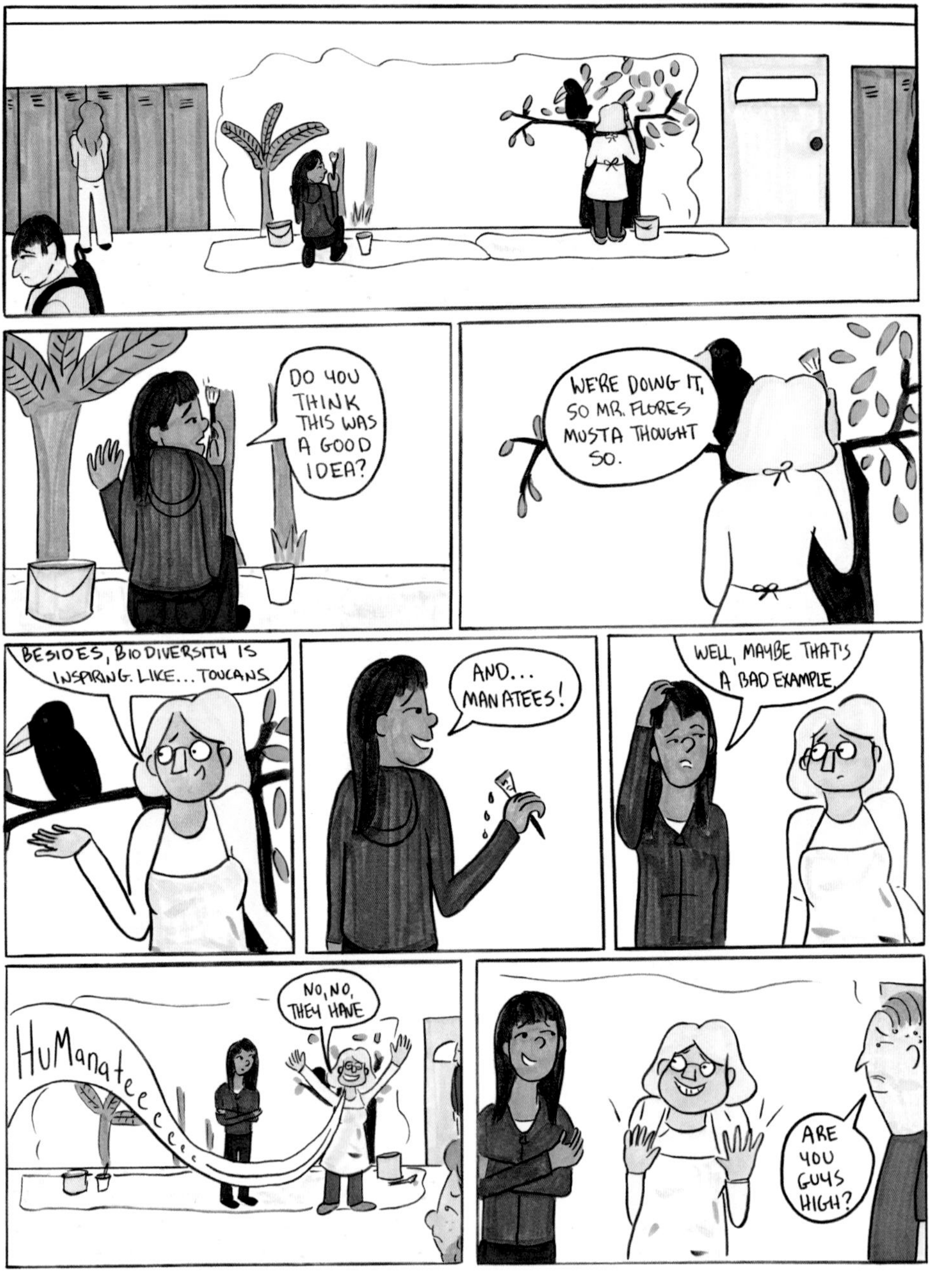

DO YOU THINK THIS WAS A GOOD IDEA?
WE'RE DOING IT, SO MR. FLORES MUSTA THOUGHT SO.
BESIDES, BIODIVERSITY IS INSPIRING. LIKE... TOUCANS.
AND... MANATEES!
WELL, MAYBE THAT'S A BAD EXAMPLE.
NO, NO, THEY HAVE
HuManateeeeeee
ARE YOU GUYS HIGH?

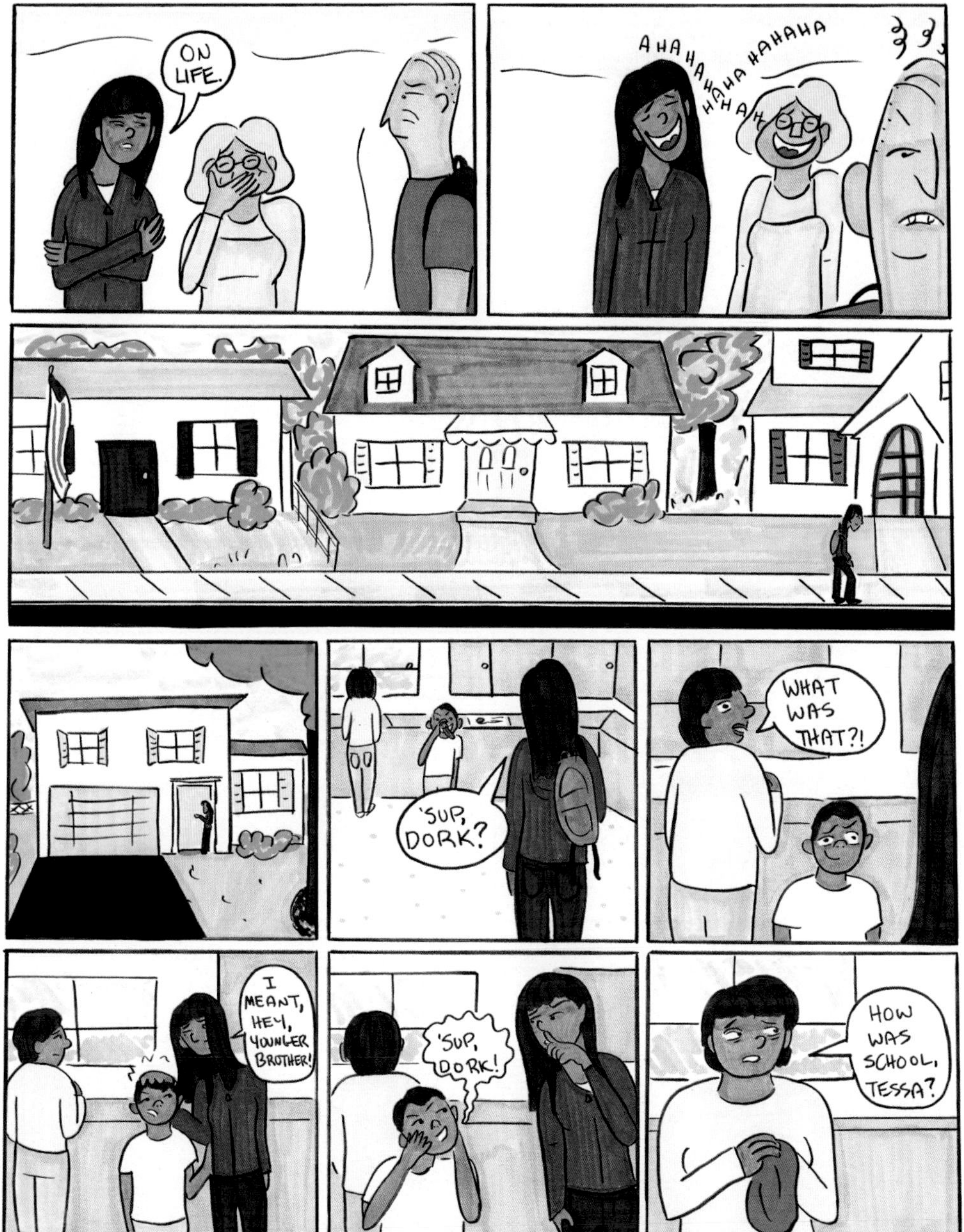
ON LIFE.
AHAHAHAHA HAHAHA HAHAHAHA
'SUP, DORK?
WHAT WAS THAT?!
I MEANT, HEY, YOUNGER BROTHER!
'SUP, DORK!
HOW WAS SCHOOL, TESSA?

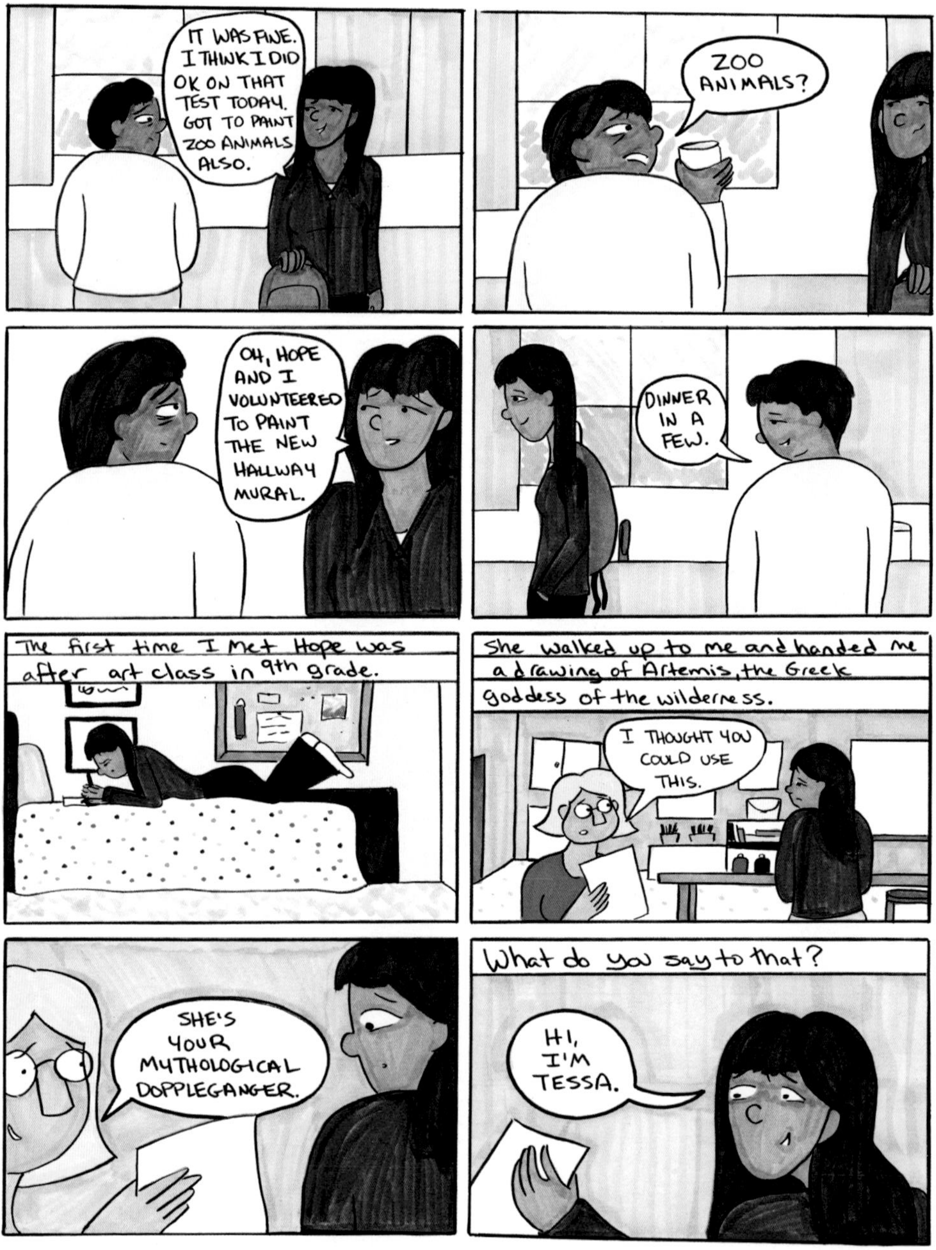
IT WAS FINE. I THINK I DID OK ON THAT TEST TODAY. GOT TO PAINT ZOO ANIMALS ALSO.
ZOO ANIMALS?
OH, HOPE AND I VOLUNTEERED TO PAINT THE NEW HALLWAY MURAL.
DINNER IN A FEW.
The first time I Met Hope was after art class in 9th grade.
She walked up to me and handed me a drawing of Artemis, the Greek goddess of the wilderness.
I THOUGHT YOU COULD USE THIS.
SHE'S YOUR MYTHOLOGICAL DOPPLEGANGER.
What do you say to that?
HI, I'M TESSA.

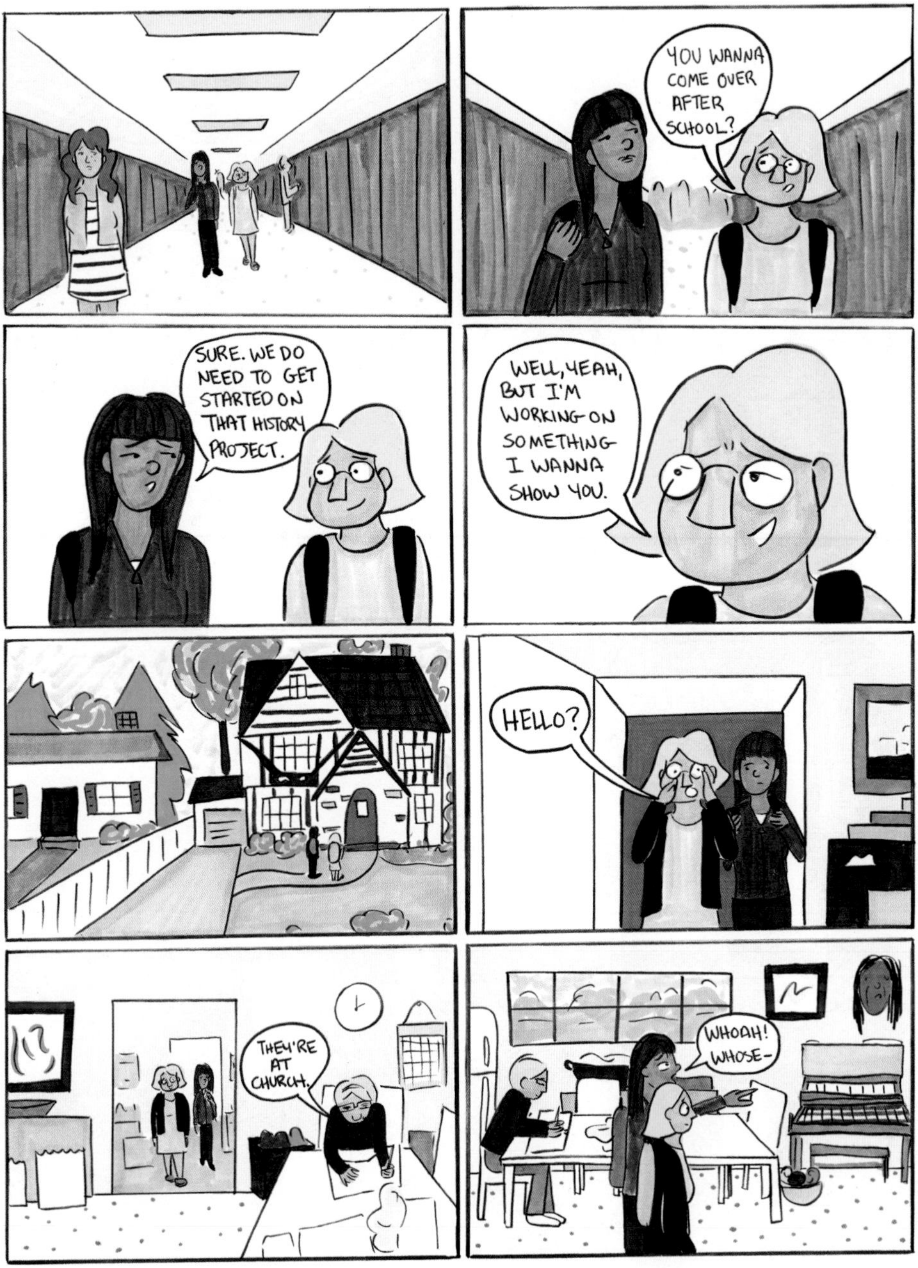
YOU WANNA COME OVER AFTER SCHOOL?
SURE. WE DO NEED TO GET STARTED ON THAT HISTORY PROJECT.
WELL, YEAH, BUT I'M WORKING ON SOMETHING I WANNA SHOW YOU.
HELLO?
THEY'RE AT CHURCH.
WHOAH! WHOSE-

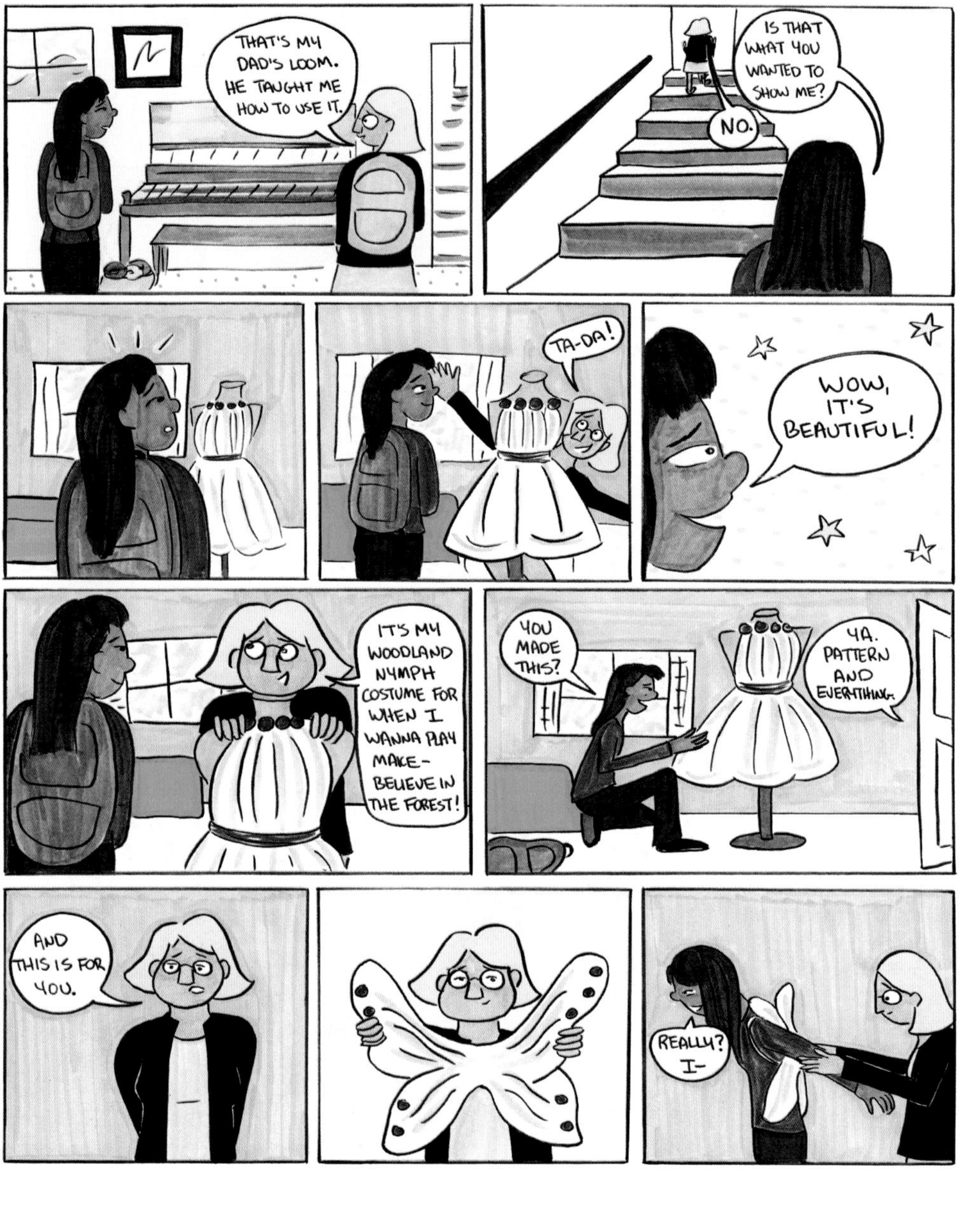
THAT'S MY DAD'S LOOM. HE TAUGHT ME HOW TO USE IT.
IS THAT WHAT YOU WANTED TO SHOW ME?
NO.
TA-DA!
WOW, IT'S BEAUTIFUL!
IT'S MY WOODLAND NYMPH COSTUME FOR WHEN I WANNA PLAY MAKE-BELIEVE IN THE FOREST!
YOU MADE THIS?
YA. PATTERN AND EVERYTHING.
AND THIS IS FOR YOU.
REALLY? I-

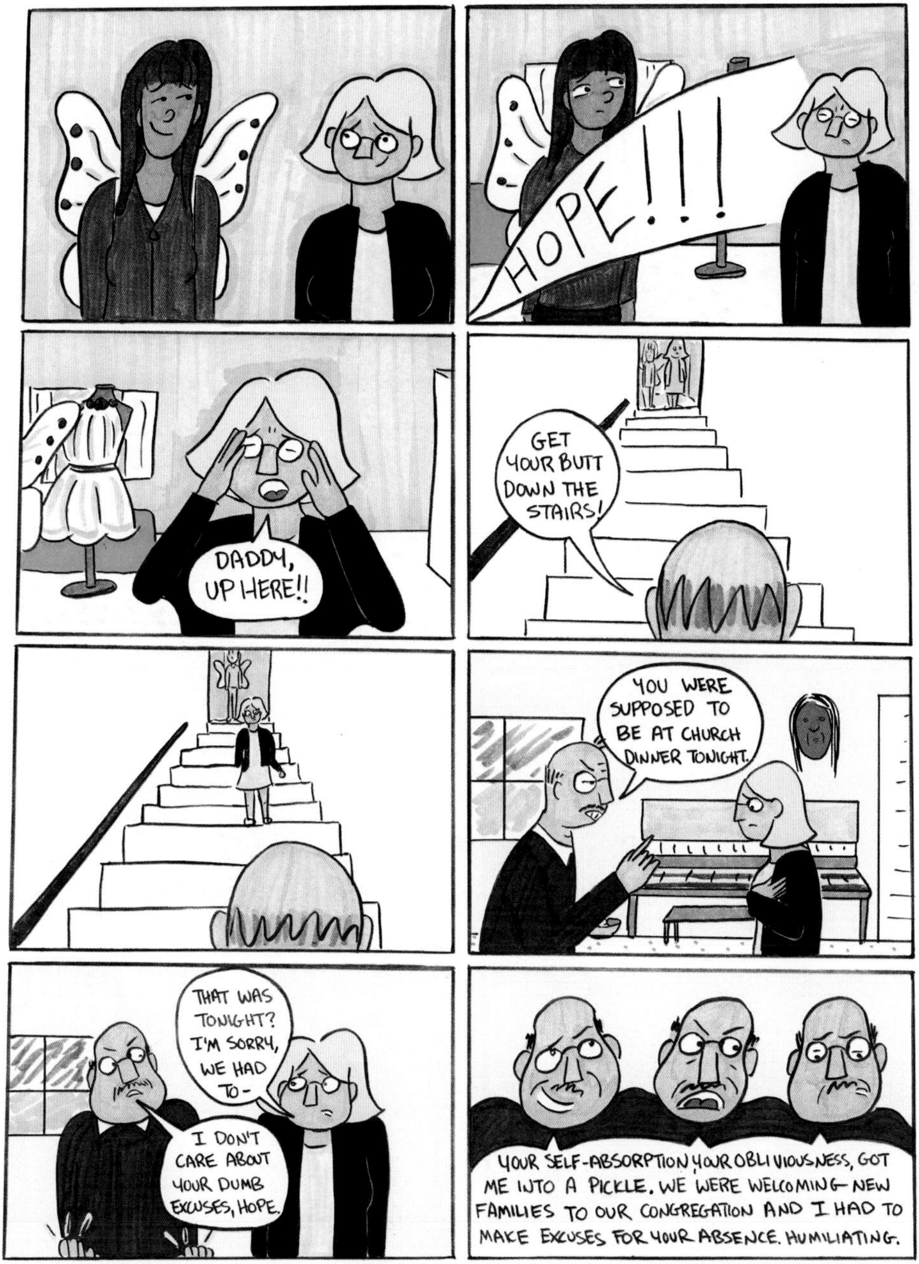
HOPE!!!
DADDY, UP HERE!!
GET YOUR BUTT DOWN THE STAIRS!
YOU WERE SUPPOSED TO BE AT CHURCH DINNER TONIGHT.
THAT WAS TONIGHT? I'M SORRY, WE HAD TO-
I DON'T CARE ABOUT YOUR DUMB EXCUSES, HOPE.
YOUR SELF-ABSORPTION, YOUR OBLIVIOUSNESS, GOT ME INTO A PICKLE. WE WERE WELCOMING NEW FAMILIES TO OUR CONGREGATION AND I HAD TO MAKE EXCUSES FOR YOUR ABSENCE. HUMILIATING.

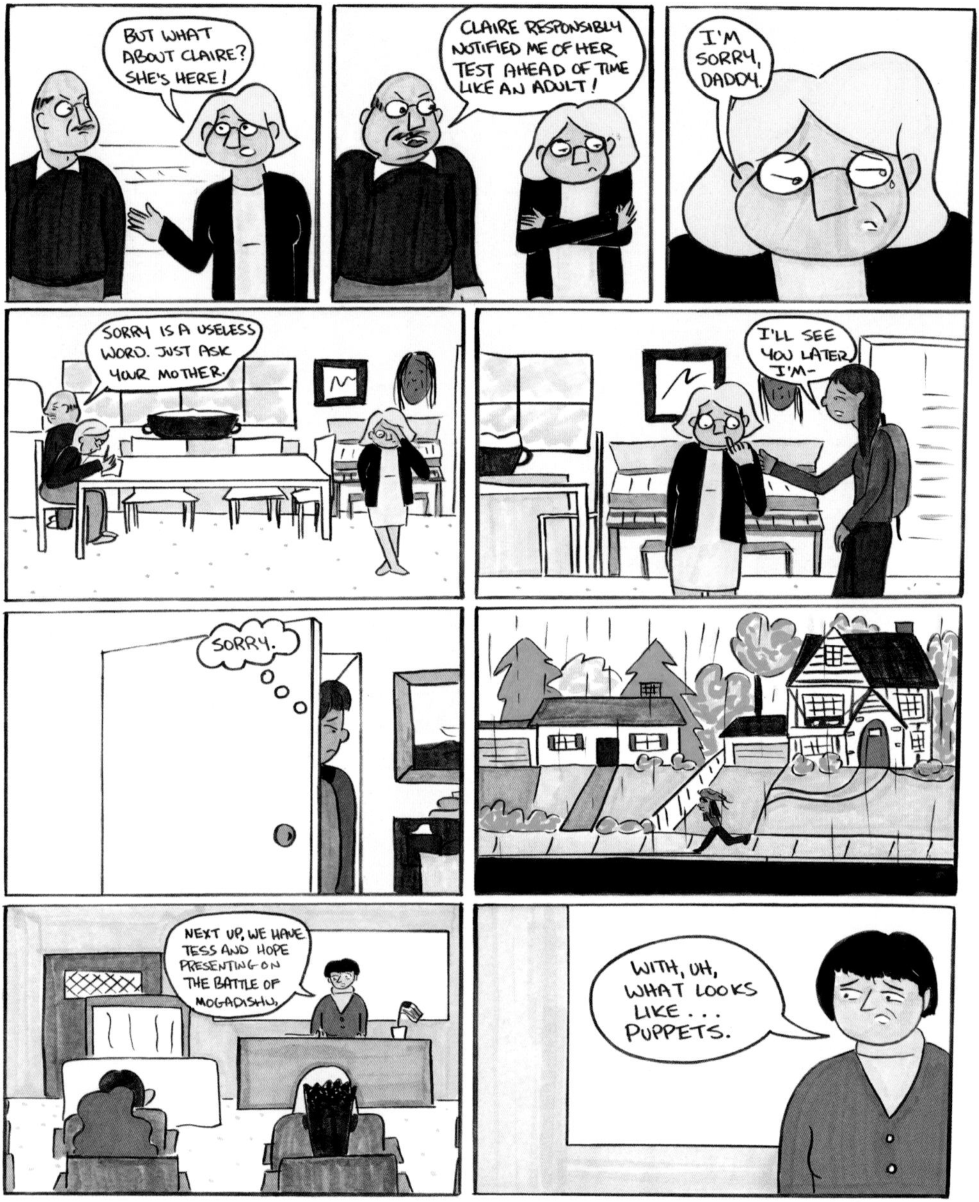
BUT WHAT ABOUT CLAIRE? SHE'S HERE!
CLAIRE RESPONSIBLY NOTIFIED ME OF HER TEST AHEAD OF TIME LIKE AN ADULT!
I'M SORRY, DADDY.
SORRY IS A USELESS WORD. JUST ASK YOUR MOTHER.
I'LL SEE YOU LATER. I'M-
SORRY.
NEXT UP, WE HAVE TESS AND HOPE PRESENTING ON THE BATTLE OF MOGADISHU,
WITH, UH, WHAT LOOKS LIKE . . . PUPPETS.

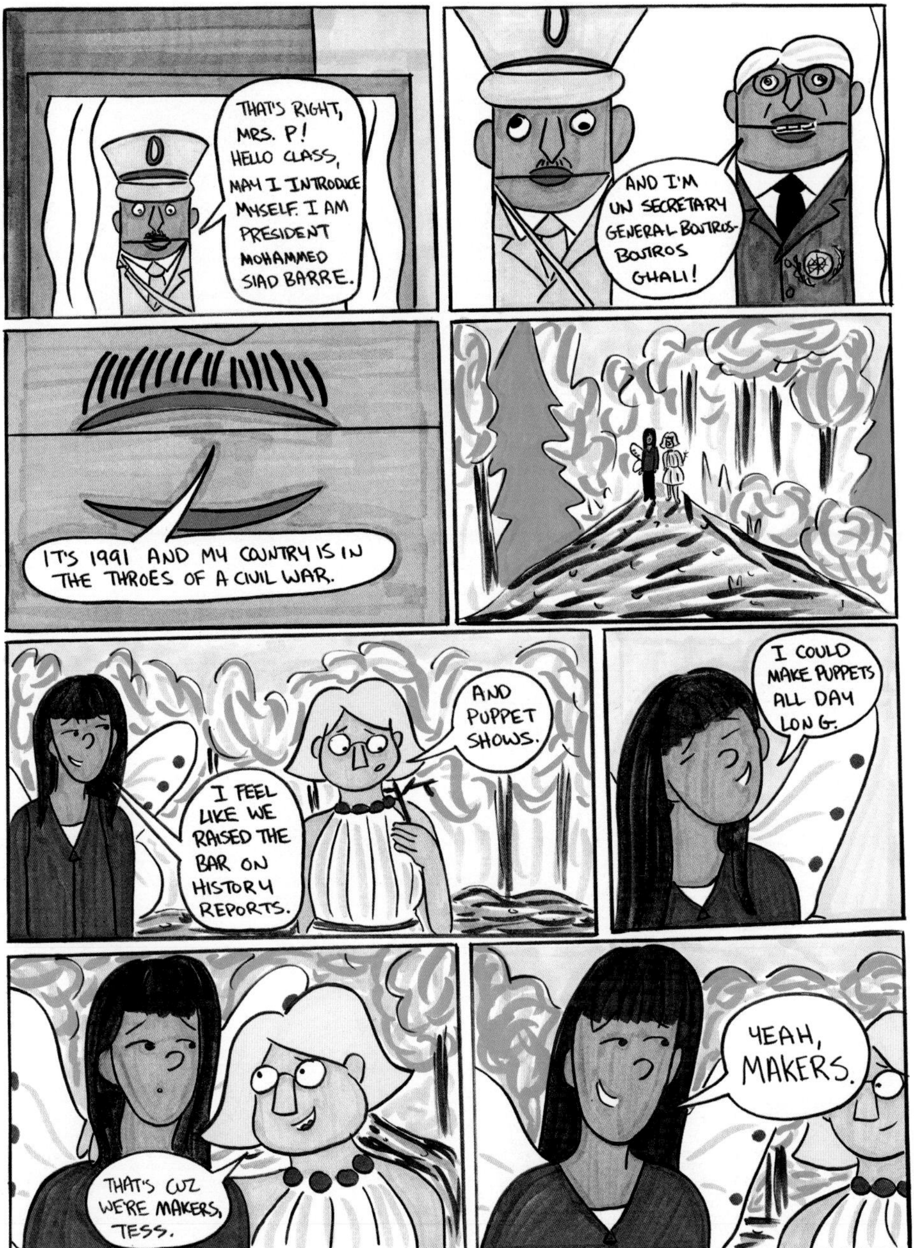
THAT'S RIGHT, MRS. P! HELLO CLASS, MAY I INTRODUCE MYSELF. I AM PRESIDENT MOHAMMED SIAD BARRE.
AND I'M UN SECRETARY GENERAL BOUTROS-BOUTROS GHALI!
IT'S 1991 AND MY COUNTRY IS IN THE THROES OF A CIVIL WAR.
I FEEL LIKE WE RAISED THE BAR ON HISTORY REPORTS.
AND PUPPET SHOWS.
I COULD MAKE PUPPETS ALL DAY LONG.
THAT'S CUZ WE'RE MAKERS, TESS.
YEAH, MAKERS.

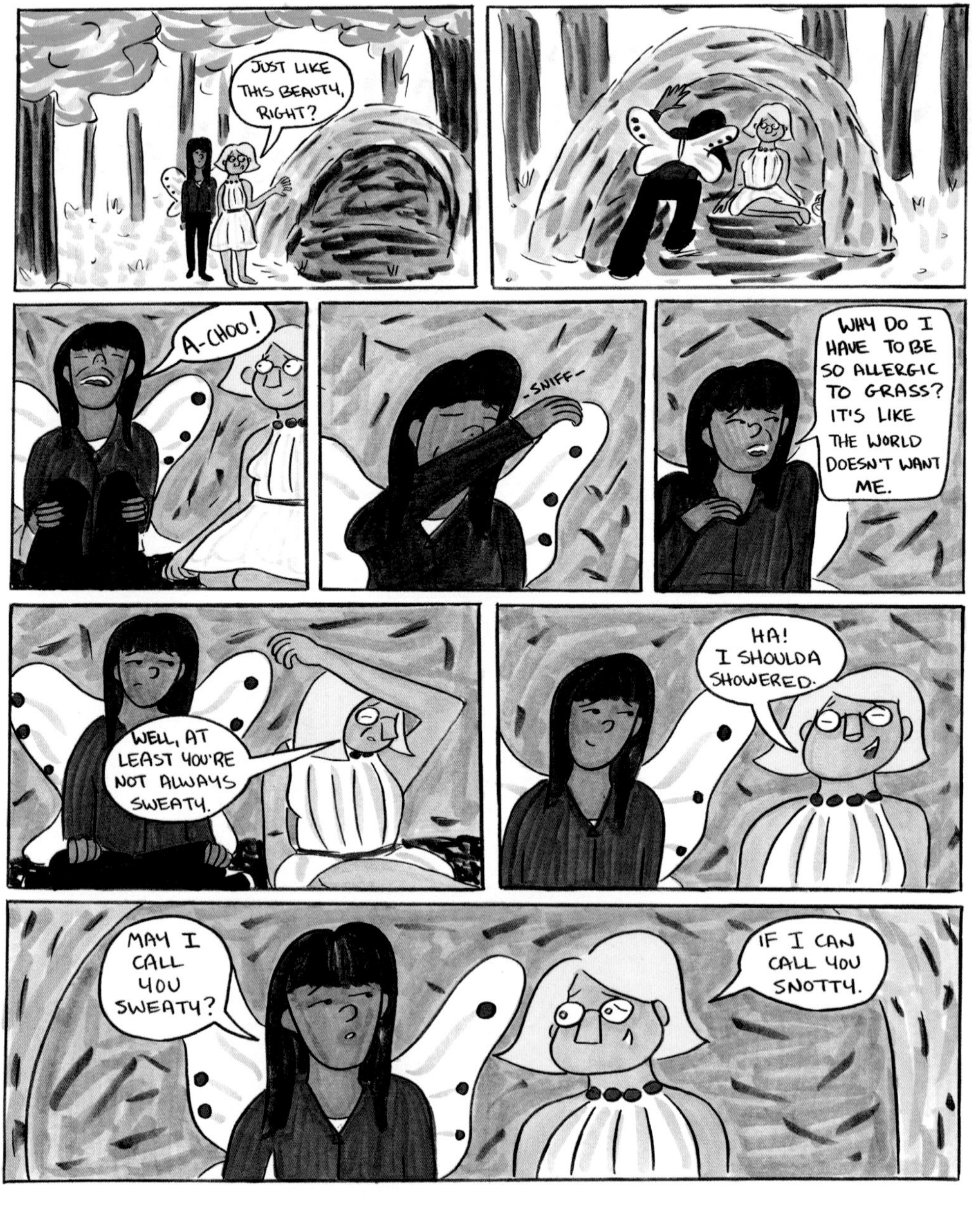
JUST LIKE THIS BEAUTY, RIGHT?
A-CHOO!
-SNIFF-
WHY DO I HAVE TO BE SO ALLERGIC TO GRASS? IT'S LIKE THE WORLD DOESN'T WANT ME.
WELL, AT LEAST YOU'RE NOT ALWAYS SWEATY.
HA! I SHOULDA SHOWERED.
MAY I CALL YOU SWEATY?
IF I CAN CALL YOU SNOTTY.

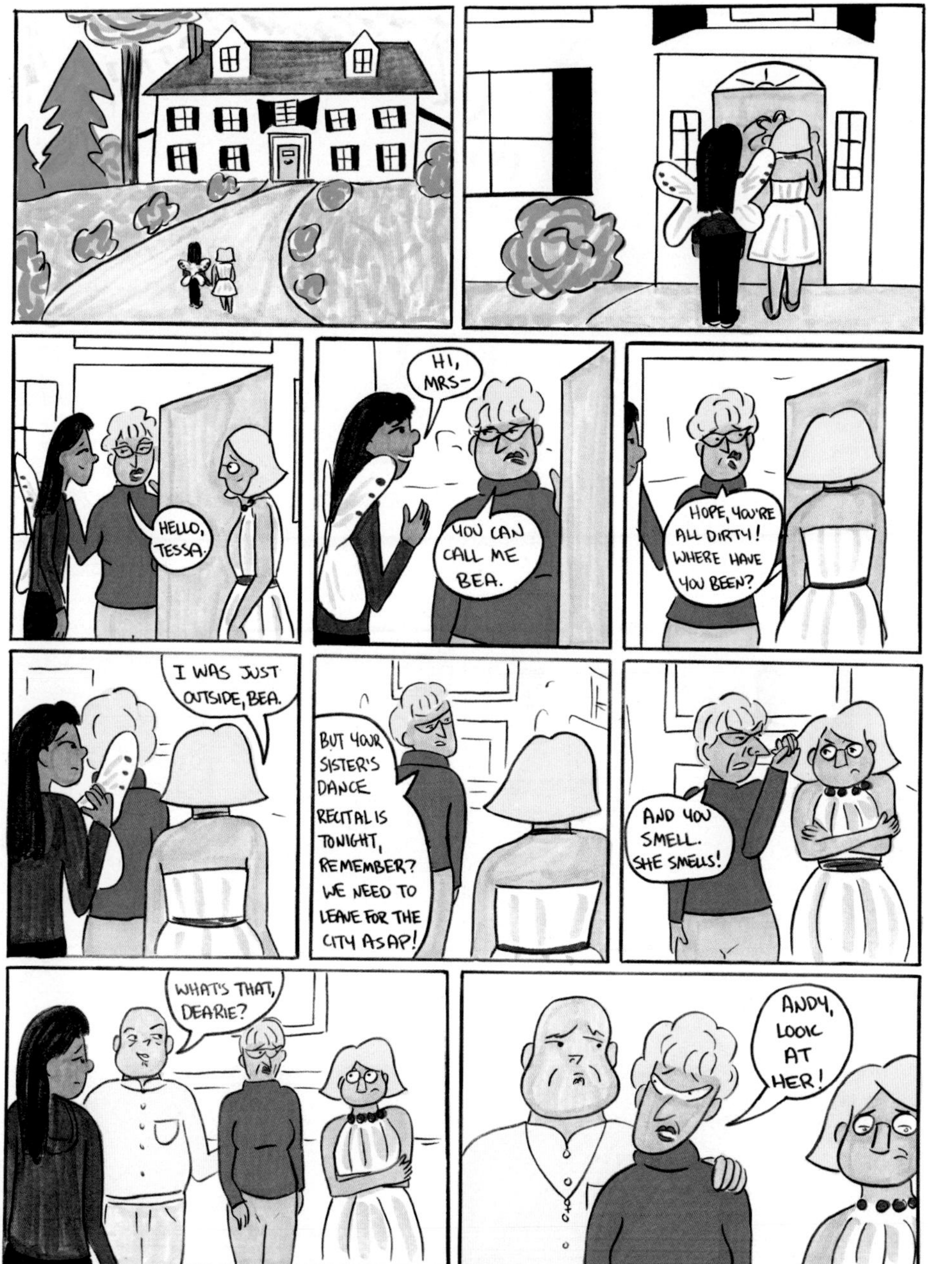

HELLO, TESSA.
HI, MRS-
YOU CAN CALL ME BEA.
HOPE, YOU'RE ALL DIRTY! WHERE HAVE YOU BEEN?
I WAS JUST OUTSIDE, BEA.
BUT YOUR SISTER'S DANCE RECITAL IS TONIGHT, REMEMBER? WE NEED TO LEAVE FOR THE CITY ASAP!
AND YOU SMELL. SHE SMELLS!
WHAT'S THAT, DEARIE?
ANDY, LOOK AT HER!

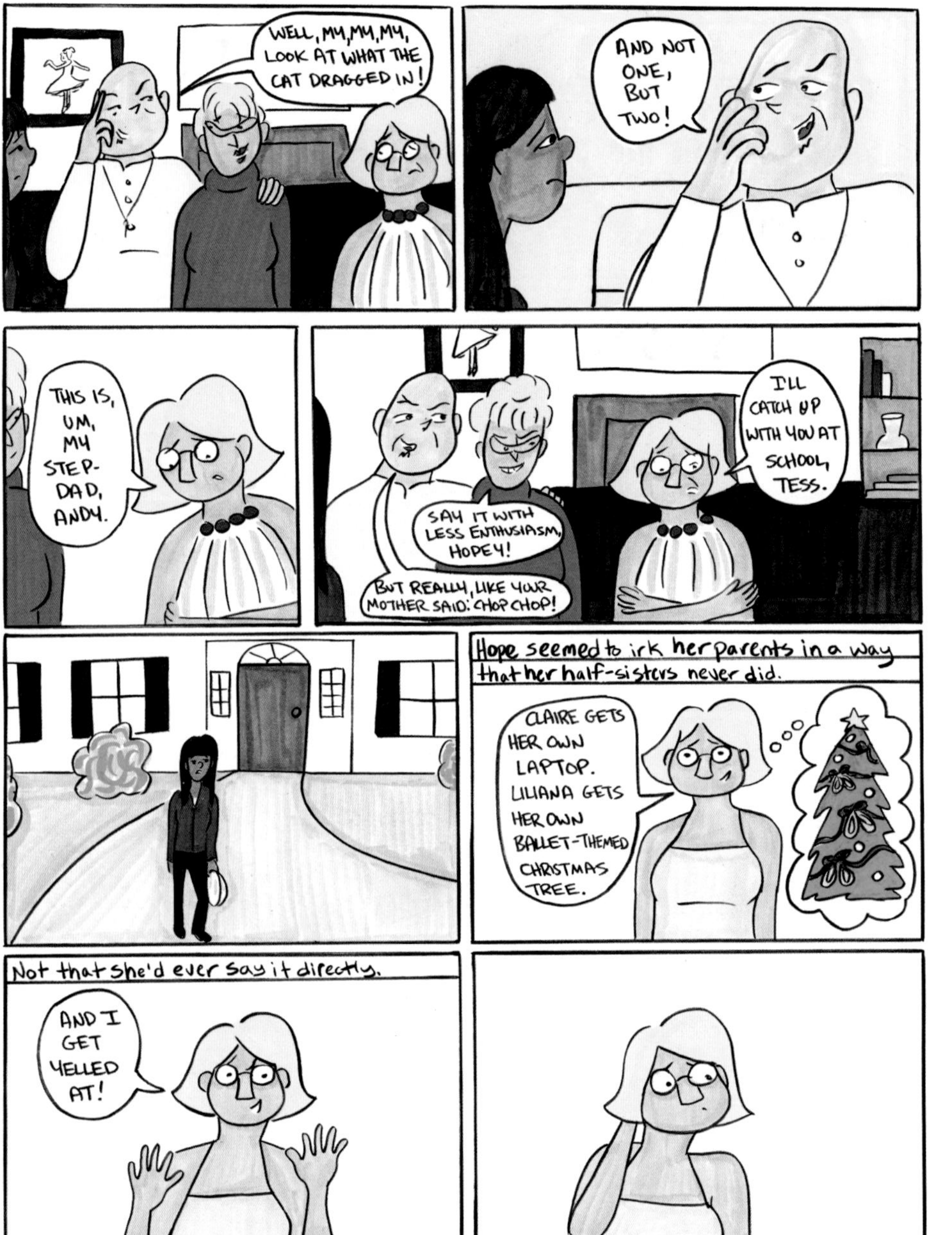

WELL, MY, MY, MY, LOOK AT WHAT THE CAT DRAGGED IN!
AND NOT ONE, BUT TWO!
THIS IS, UM, MY STEP-DAD, ANDY.
I'LL CATCH UP WITH YOU AT SCHOOL, TESS.
SAY IT WITH LESS ENTHUSIASM, HOPEY!
BUT REALLY, LIKE YOUR MOTHER SAID: CHOP CHOP!
Hope seemed to irk her parents in a way that her half-sisters never did.
CLAIRE GETS HER OWN LAPTOP. LILIANA GETS HER OWN BALLET-THEMED CHRISTMAS TREE.
Not that she'd ever say it directly.
AND I GET YELLED AT!

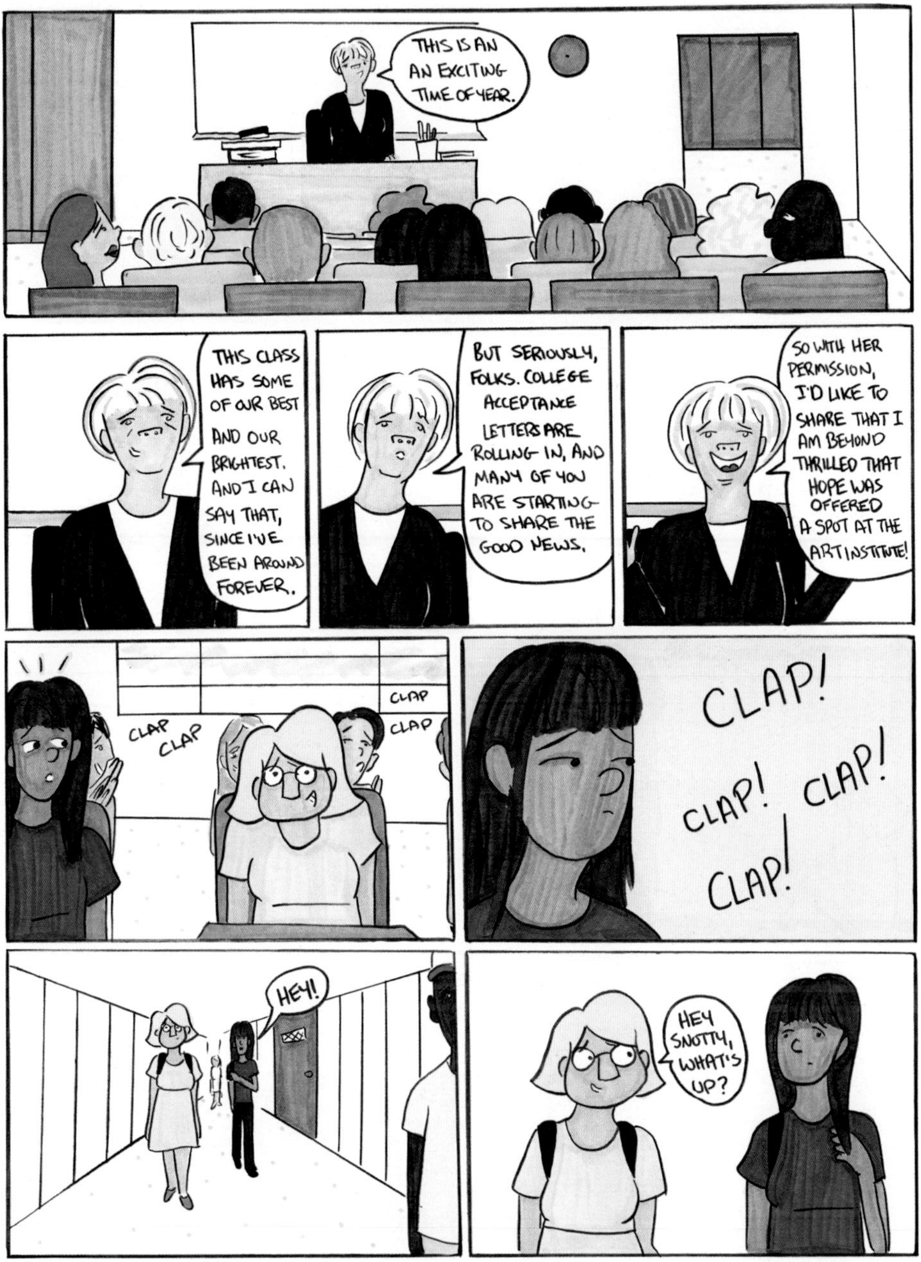
THIS IS AN AN EXCITING TIME OF YEAR.
THIS CLASS HAS SOME OF OUR BEST AND OUR BRIGHTEST. AND I CAN SAY THAT, SINCE I'VE BEEN AROUND FOREVER.
BUT SERIOUSLY, FOLKS. COLLEGE ACCEPTANCE LETTERS ARE ROLLING IN, AND MANY OF YOU ARE STARTING TO SHARE THE GOOD NEWS.
SO WITH HER PERMISSION, I'D LIKE TO SHARE THAT I AM BEYOND THRILLED THAT HOPE WAS OFFERED A SPOT AT THE ART INSTITUTE!
CLAP CLAP
CLAP
CLAP
CLAP!
CLAP!
CLAP!
CLAP!
HEY!
HEY SNOTTY, WHAT'S UP?

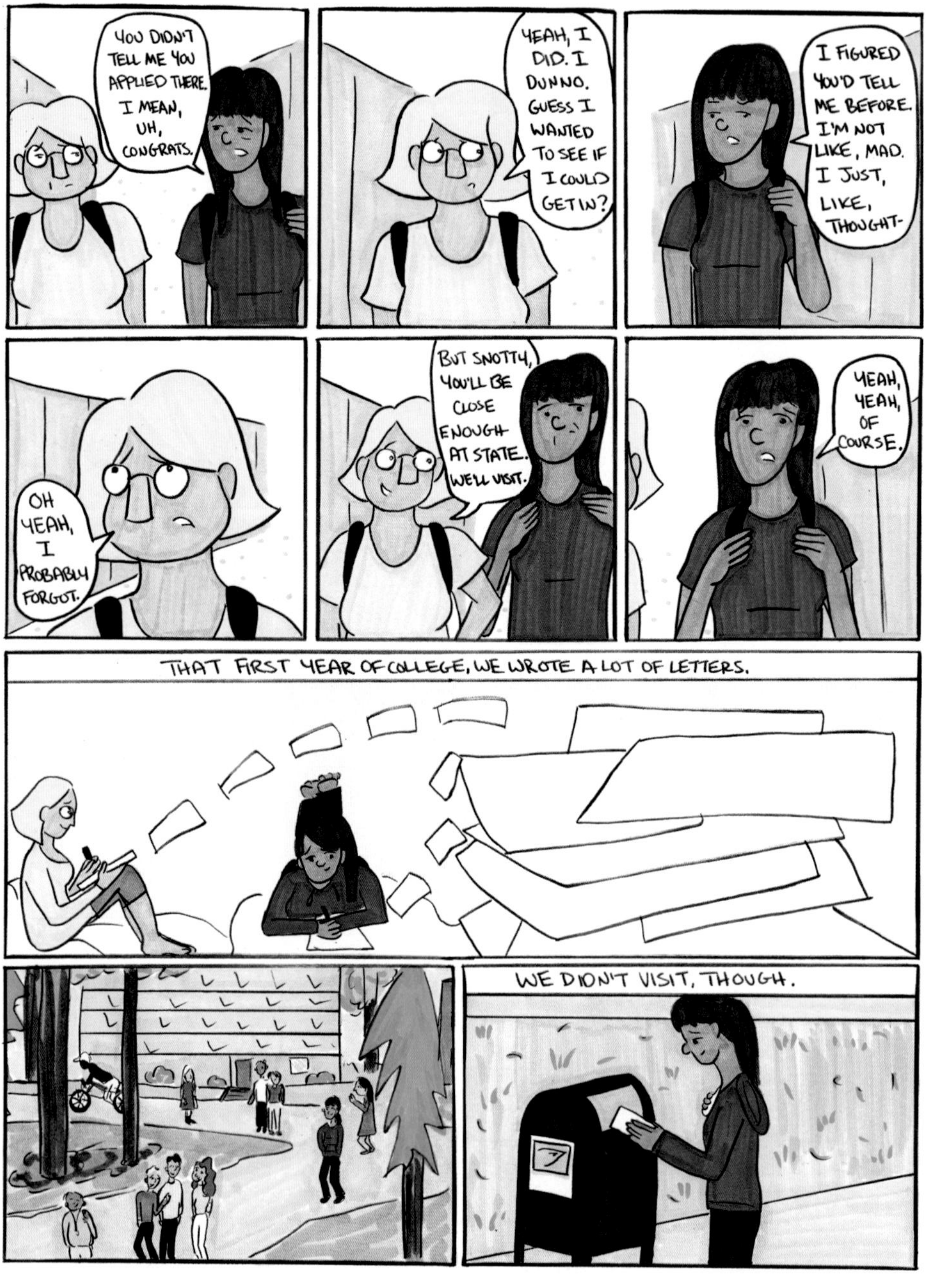
YOU DIDN'T TELL ME YOU APPLIED THERE. I MEAN, UH, CONGRATS.
YEAH, I DID. I DUNNO. GUESS I WANTED TO SEE IF I COULD GET IN?
I FIGURED YOU'D TELL ME BEFORE. I'M NOT LIKE, MAD. I JUST, LIKE, THOUGHT-
OH YEAH, I PROBABLY FORGOT.
BUT SNOTTY, YOU'LL BE CLOSE ENOUGH AT STATE. WE'LL VISIT.
YEAH, YEAH, OF COURSE.
THAT FIRST YEAR OF COLLEGE, WE WROTE A LOT OF LETTERS.
WE DIDN'T VISIT, THOUGH.

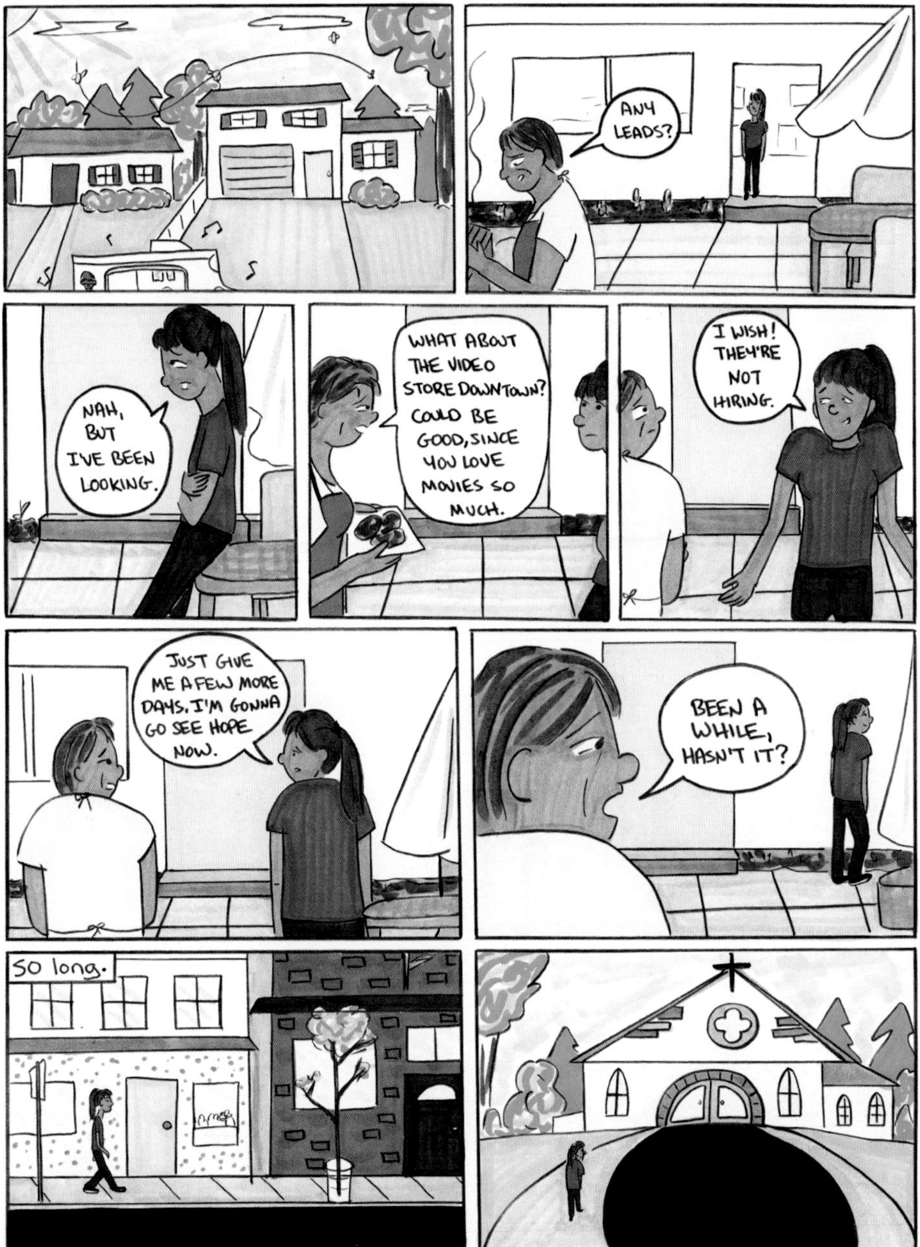
ANY LEADS?
NAH, BUT I'VE BEEN LOOKING.
WHAT ABOUT THE VIDEO STORE DOWNTOWN? COULD BE GOOD, SINCE YOU LOVE MOVIES SO MUCH.
I WISH! THEY'RE NOT HIRING.
JUST GIVE ME A FEW MORE DAYS. I'M GONNA GO SEE HOPE NOW.
BEEN A WHILE, HASN'T IT?
SO long.

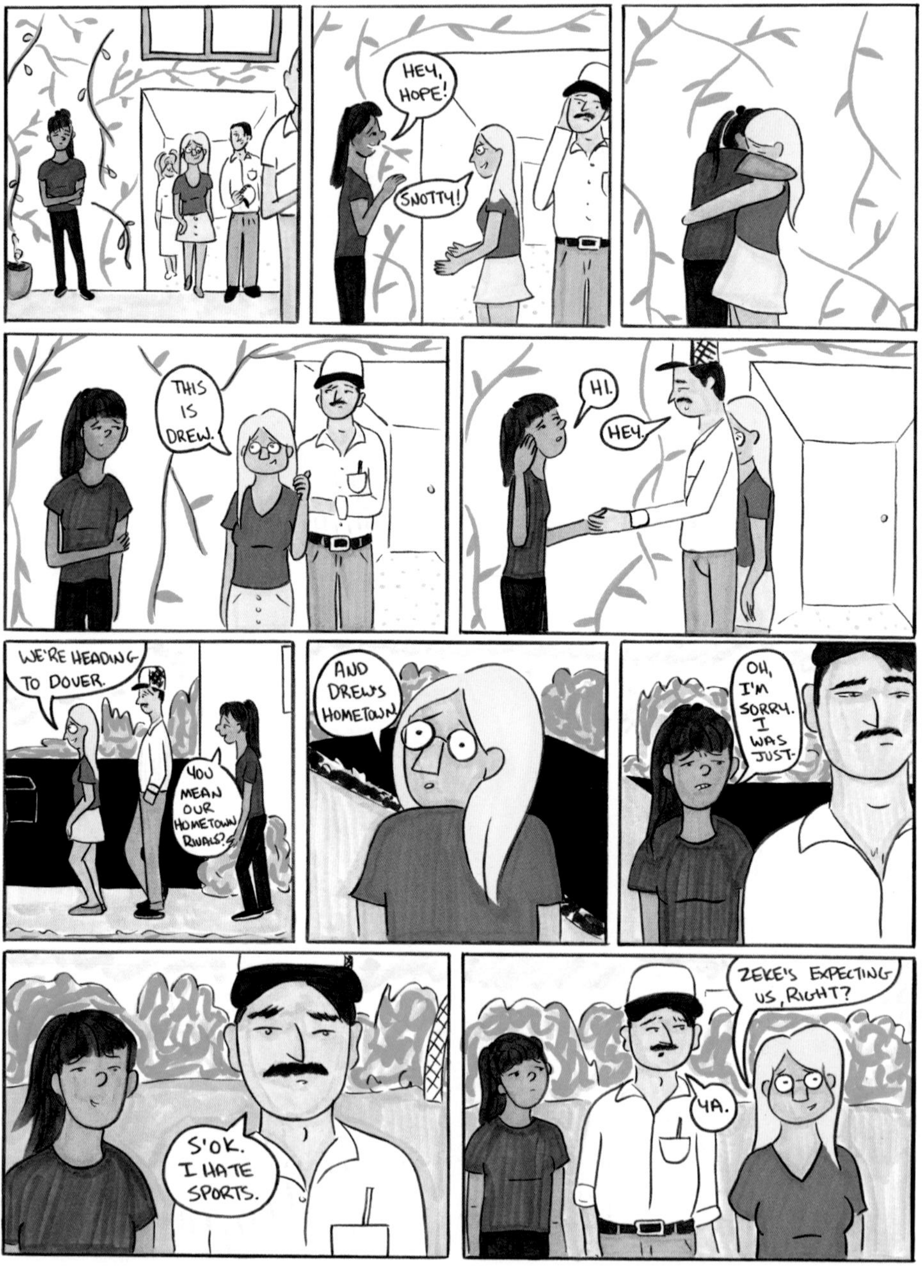
HEY, HOPE!
SNOTTY!
THIS IS DREW.
HI.
HEY.
WE'RE HEADING TO DOVER.
YOU MEAN OUR HOMETOWN RIVALS?
AND DREW'S HOMETOWN.
OH, I'M SORRY. I WAS JUST-
S'OK. I HATE SPORTS.
ZEKE'S EXPECTING US, RIGHT?
YA.

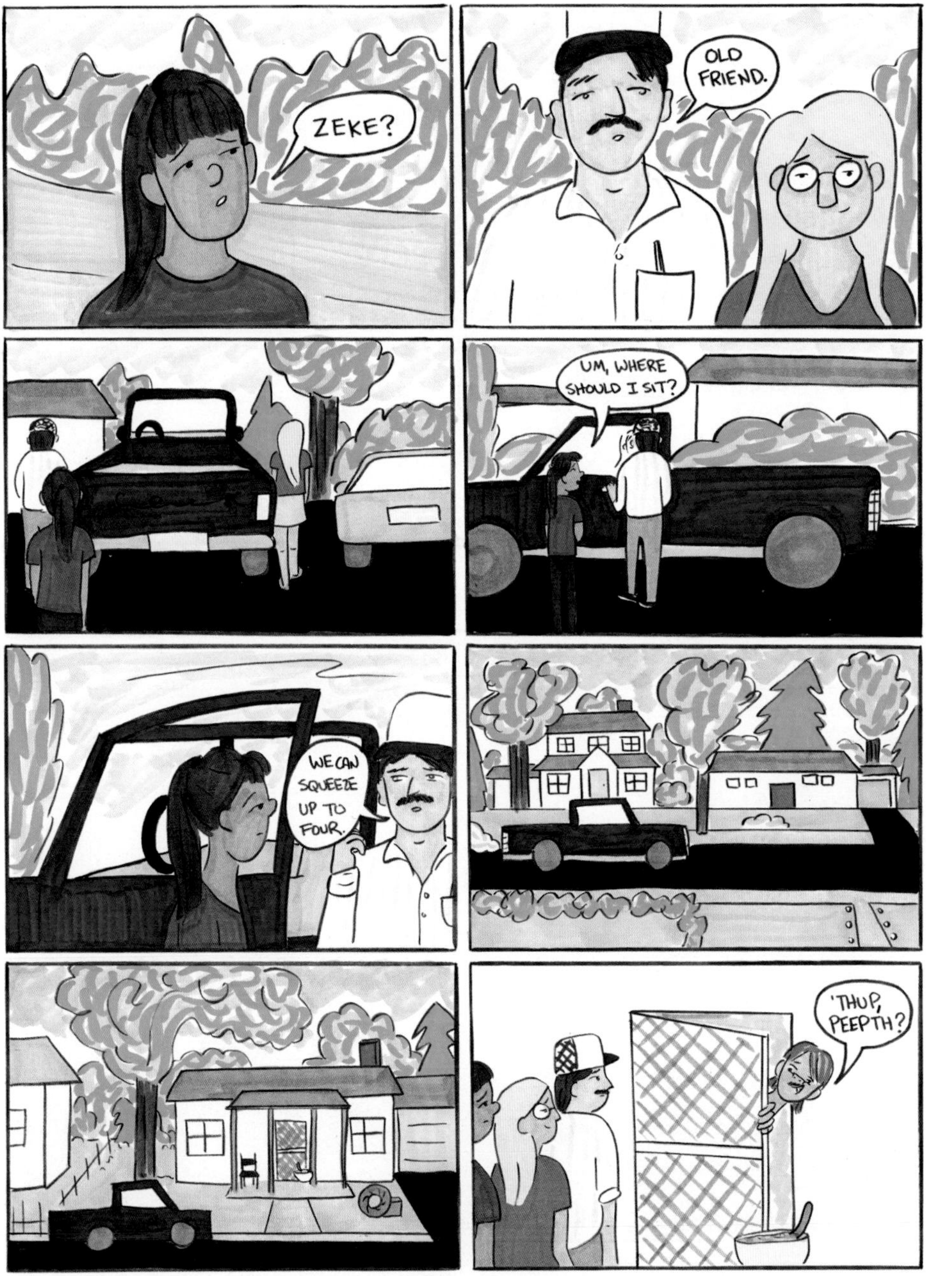
ZEKE?
OLD FRIEND.
UM, WHERE SHOULD I SIT?
WE CAN SQUEEZE UP TO FOUR.
'THUP, PEEPTH?

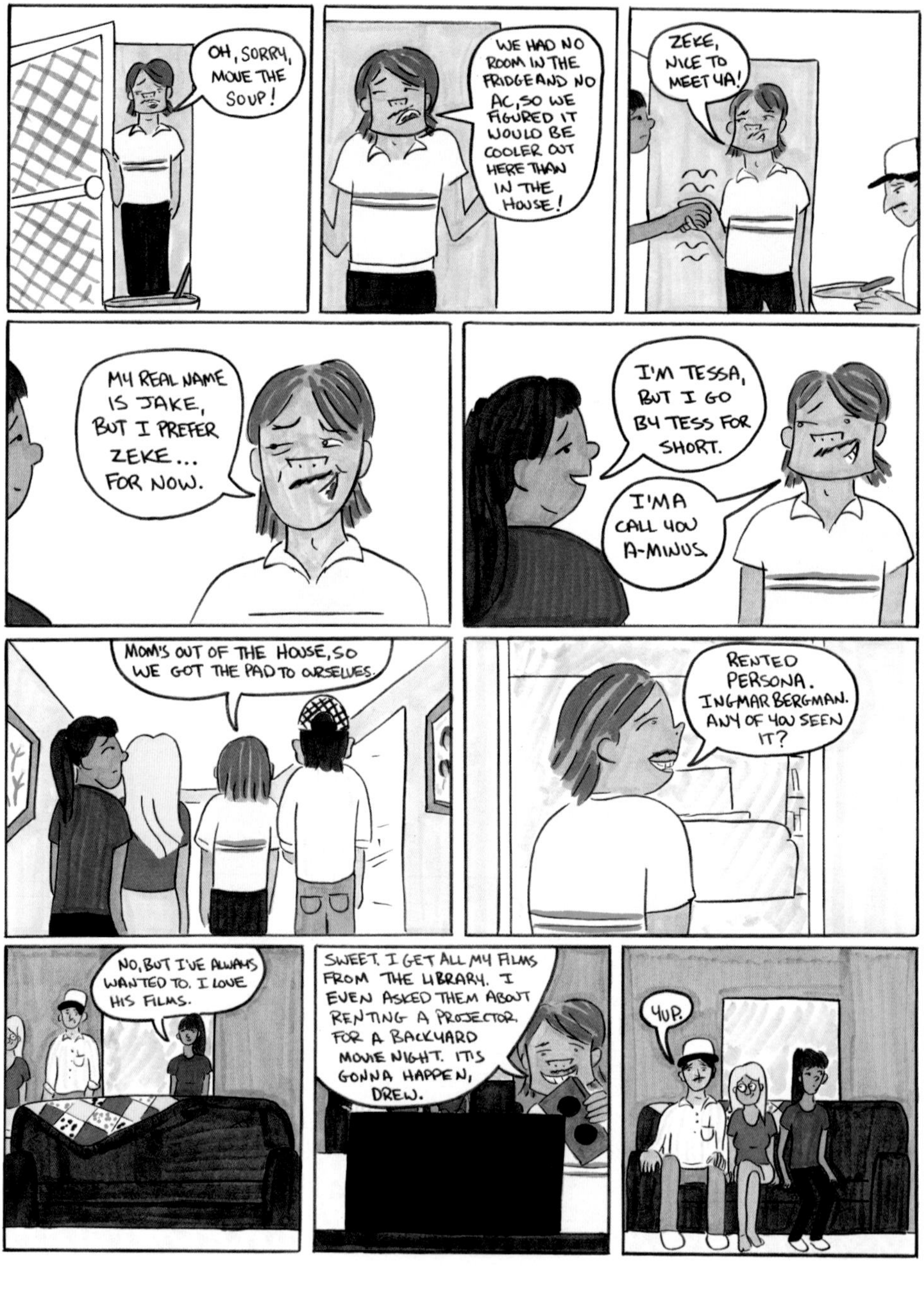
OH, SORRY, MOVE THE SOUP!
WE HAD NO ROOM IN THE FRIDGE AND NO AC, SO WE FIGURED IT WOULD BE COOLER OUT HERE THAN IN THE HOUSE!
ZEKE, NICE TO MEET YA!
MY REAL NAME IS JAKE, BUT I PREFER ZEKE... FOR NOW.
I'M TESSA, BUT I GO BY TESS FOR SHORT.
I'MA CALL YOU A-MINUS.
MOM'S OUT OF THE HOUSE, SO WE GOT THE PAD TO OURSELVES.
RENTED PERSONA. INGMAR BERGMAN. ANY OF YOU SEEN IT?
NO, BUT I'VE ALWAYS WANTED TO. I LOVE HIS FILMS.
SWEET. I GET ALL MY FILMS FROM THE LIBRARY. I EVEN ASKED THEM ABOUT RENTING A PROJECTOR FOR A BACKYARD MOVIE NIGHT. IT'S GONNA HAPPEN, DREW.
YUP.

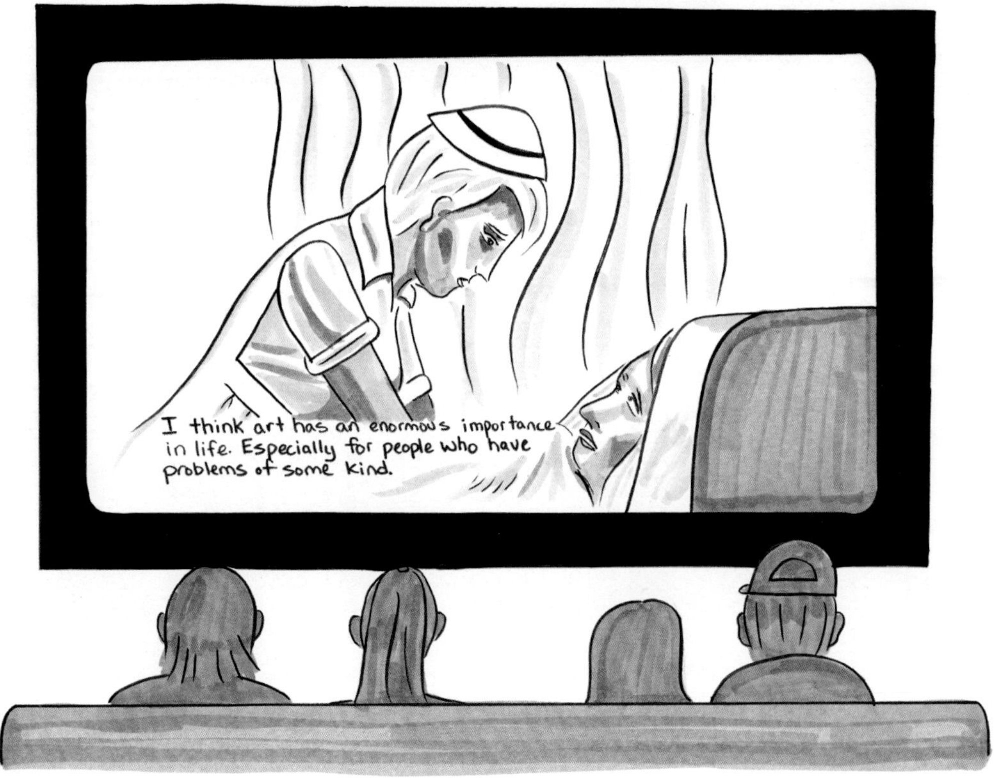
I think art has an enormous importance in life. Especially for people who have problems of some kind.

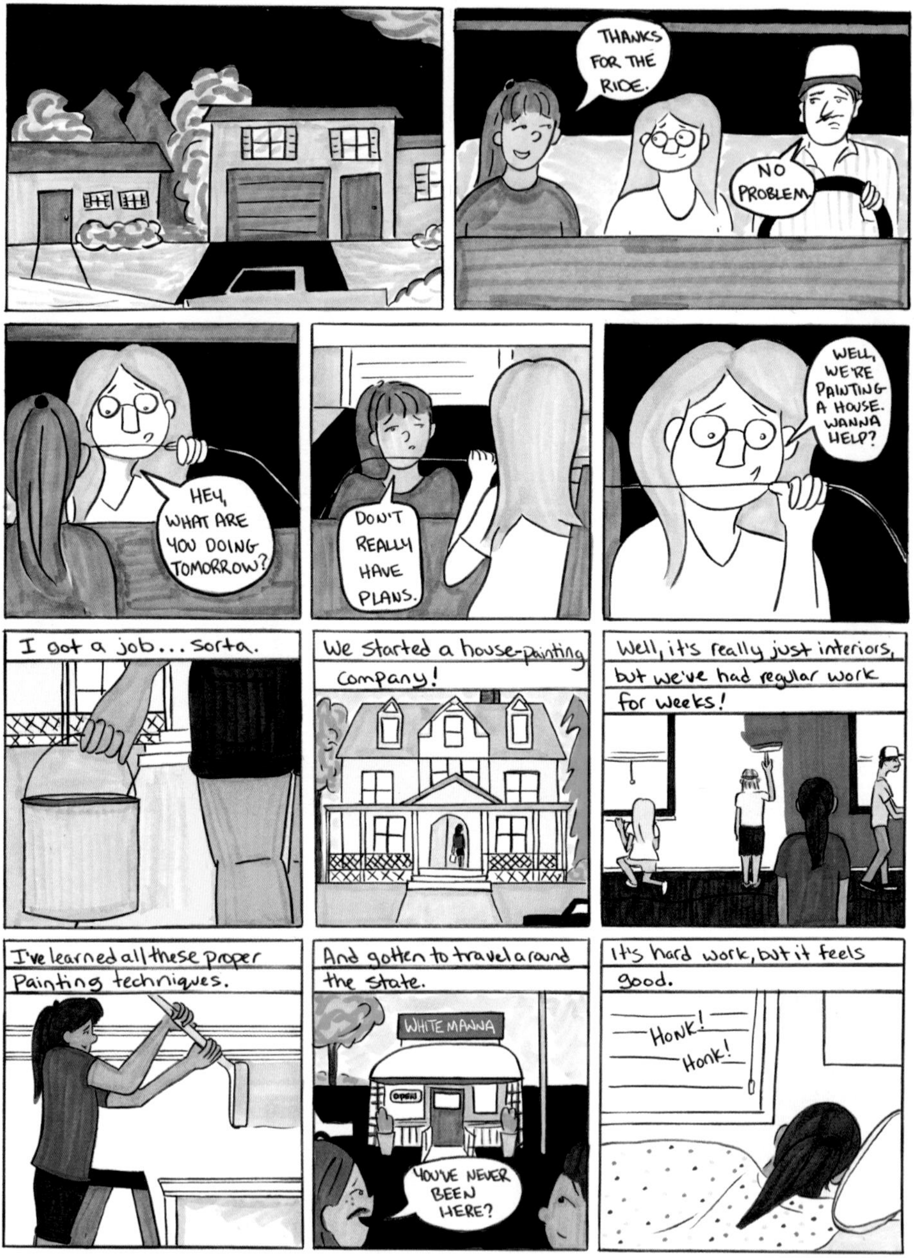
THANKS FOR THE RIDE.
NO PROBLEM.
HEY, WHAT ARE YOU DOING TOMORROW?
DON'T REALLY HAVE PLANS.
WELL, WE'RE PAINTING A HOUSE. WANNA HELP?
I got a job... sorta.
We started a house-painting company!
Well, it's really just interiors, but we've had regular work for weeks!
I've learned all these proper Painting techniques.
And gotten to travel around the state.
WHITE MANNA
OPEN
YOU'VE NEVER BEEN HERE?
It's hard work, but it feels good.
Honk!
Honk!

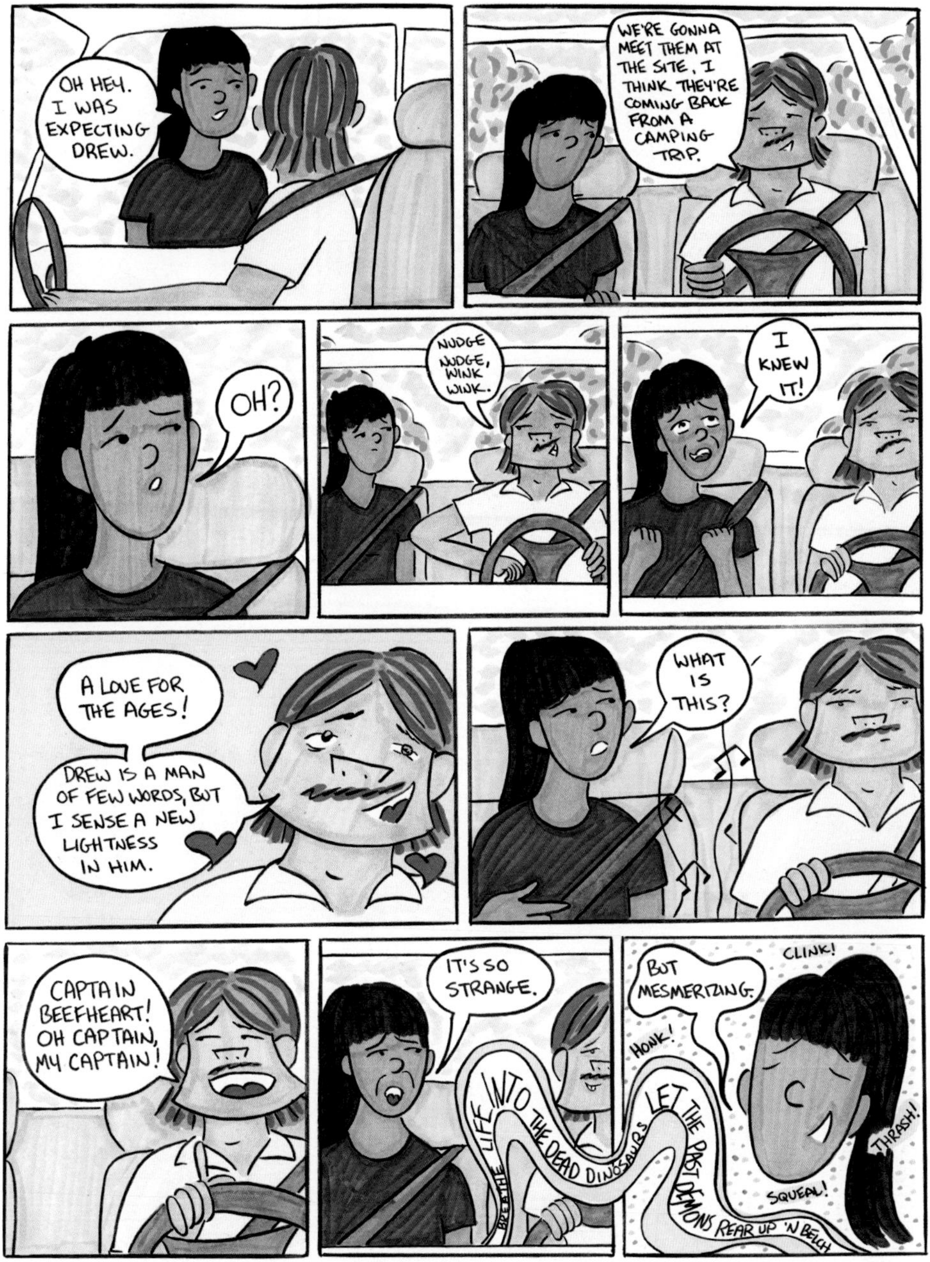
OH HEY. I WAS EXPECTING DREW.
WE'RE GONNA MEET THEM AT THE SITE, I THINK THEY'RE COMING BACK FROM A CAMPING TRIP.
OH?
NUDGE NUDGE, WINK WINK.
I KNEW IT!
A LOVE FOR THE AGES!
DREW IS A MAN OF FEW WORDS, BUT I SENSE A NEW LIGHTNESS IN HIM.
WHAT IS THIS?
CAPTAIN BEEFHEART! OH CAPTAIN, MY CAPTAIN!
IT'S SO STRANGE.
BREATHE LIFE INTO THE DEAD DINOSAURS LET THE PAST DEMONS REAR UP 'N BELCH
BUT MESMERIZING.
CLINK!
HONK!
THRASH!
SQUEAL!

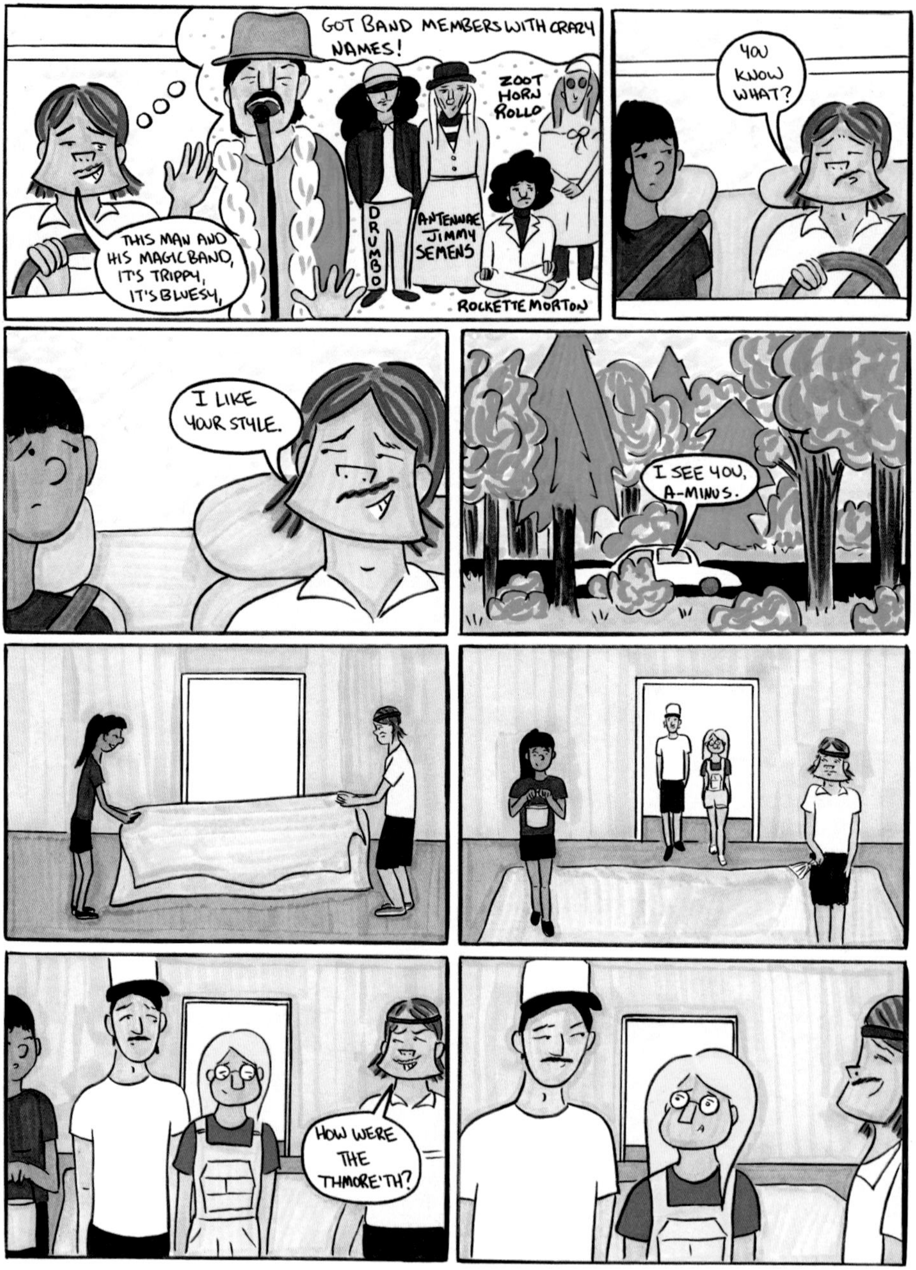
GOT BAND MEMBERS WITH CRAZY NAMES!
THIS MAN AND HIS MAGIC BAND, IT'S TRIPPY, IT'S BLUESY,
DRUMBO
ANTENNAE JIMMY SEMENS
ZOOT HORN ROLLO
ROCKETTE MORTON
YOU KNOW WHAT?
I LIKE YOUR STYLE.
I SEE YOU, A-MINUS.
HOW WERE THE THMORE'TH?

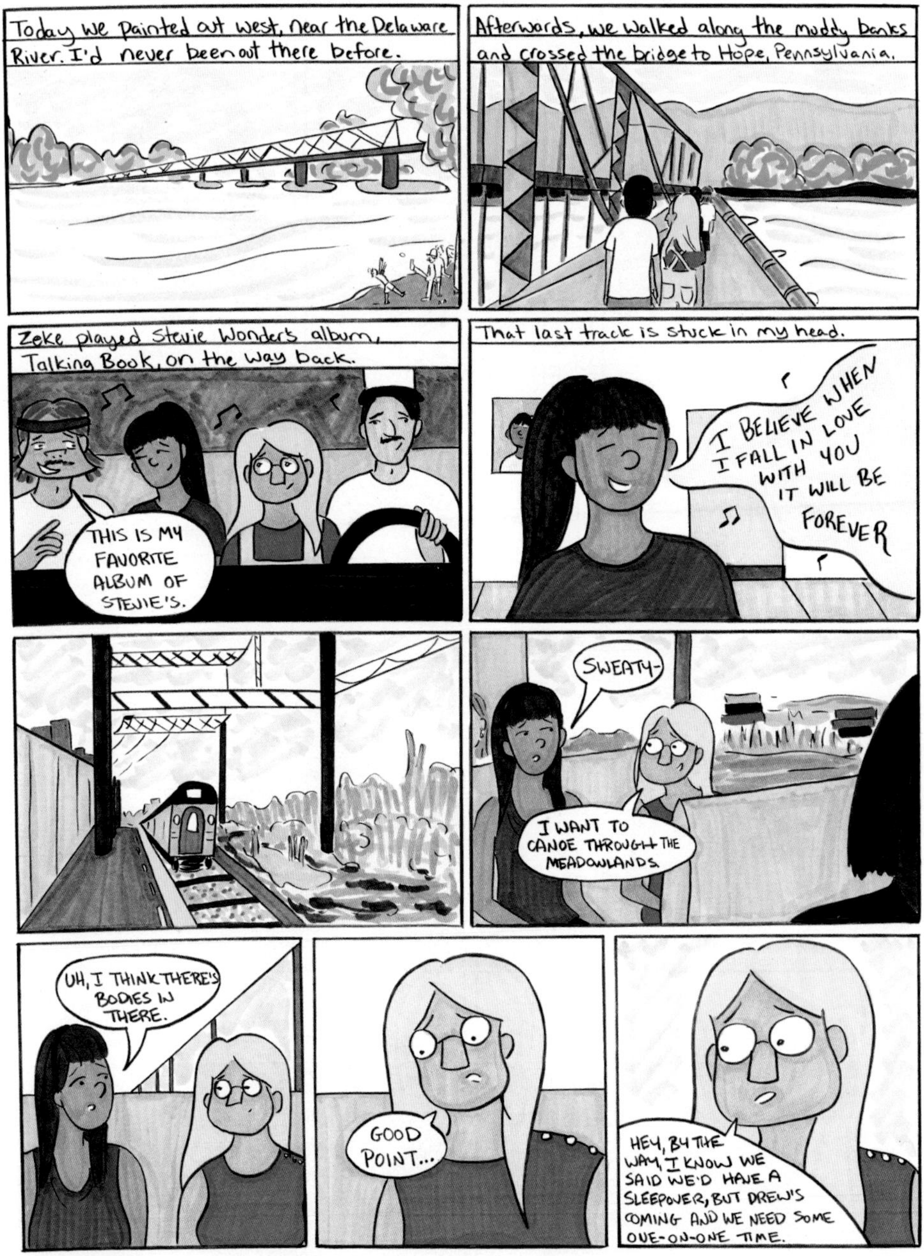
Today we painted out west, near the Delaware River. I'd never been out there before.
Afterwards, we walked along the muddy banks and crossed the bridge to Hope, Pennsylvania.
Zeke played Stevie Wonder's album, Talking Book, on the way back.
THIS IS MY FAVORITE ALBUM OF STEVIE'S.
That last track is stuck in my head.
I BELIEVE WHEN I FALL IN LOVE WITH YOU IT WILL BE FOREVER
SWEATY-
I WANT TO CANOE THROUGH THE MEADOWLANDS.
UH, I THINK THERE'S BODIES IN THERE.
GOOD POINT...
HEY, BY THE WAY, I KNOW WE SAID WE'D HAVE A SLEEPOVER, BUT DREW'S COMING AND WE NEED SOME ONE-ON-ONE TIME.

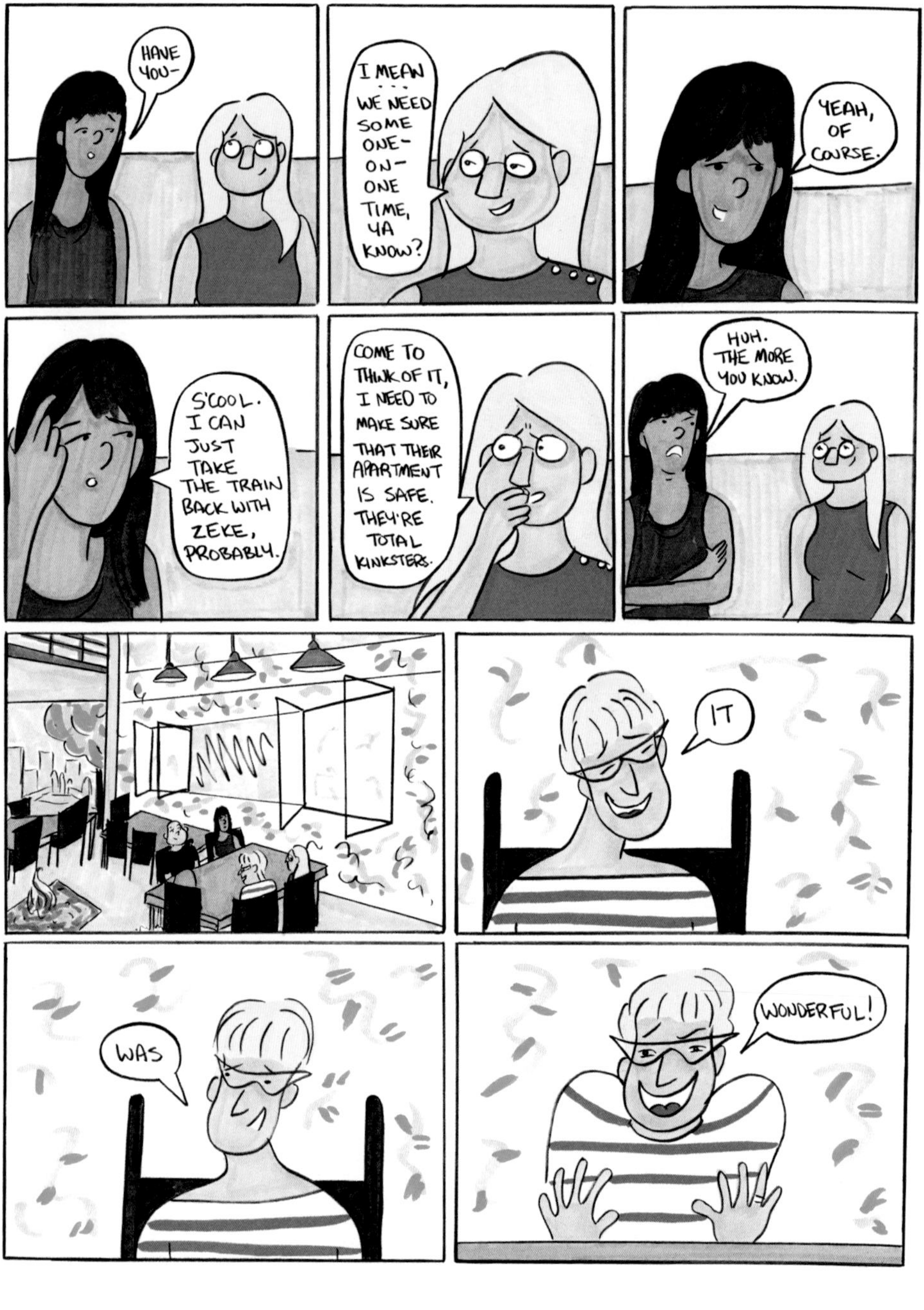
HAVE YOU-
I MEAN ... WE NEED SOME ONE-ON-ONE TIME, YA KNOW?
YEAH, OF COURSE.
S'COOL. I CAN JUST TAKE THE TRAIN BACK WITH ZEKE, PROBABLY.
COME TO THINK OF IT, I NEED TO MAKE SURE THAT THEIR APARTMENT IS SAFE. THEY'RE TOTAL KINKSTERS.
HUH. THE MORE YOU KNOW.
IT
WAS
WONDERFUL!

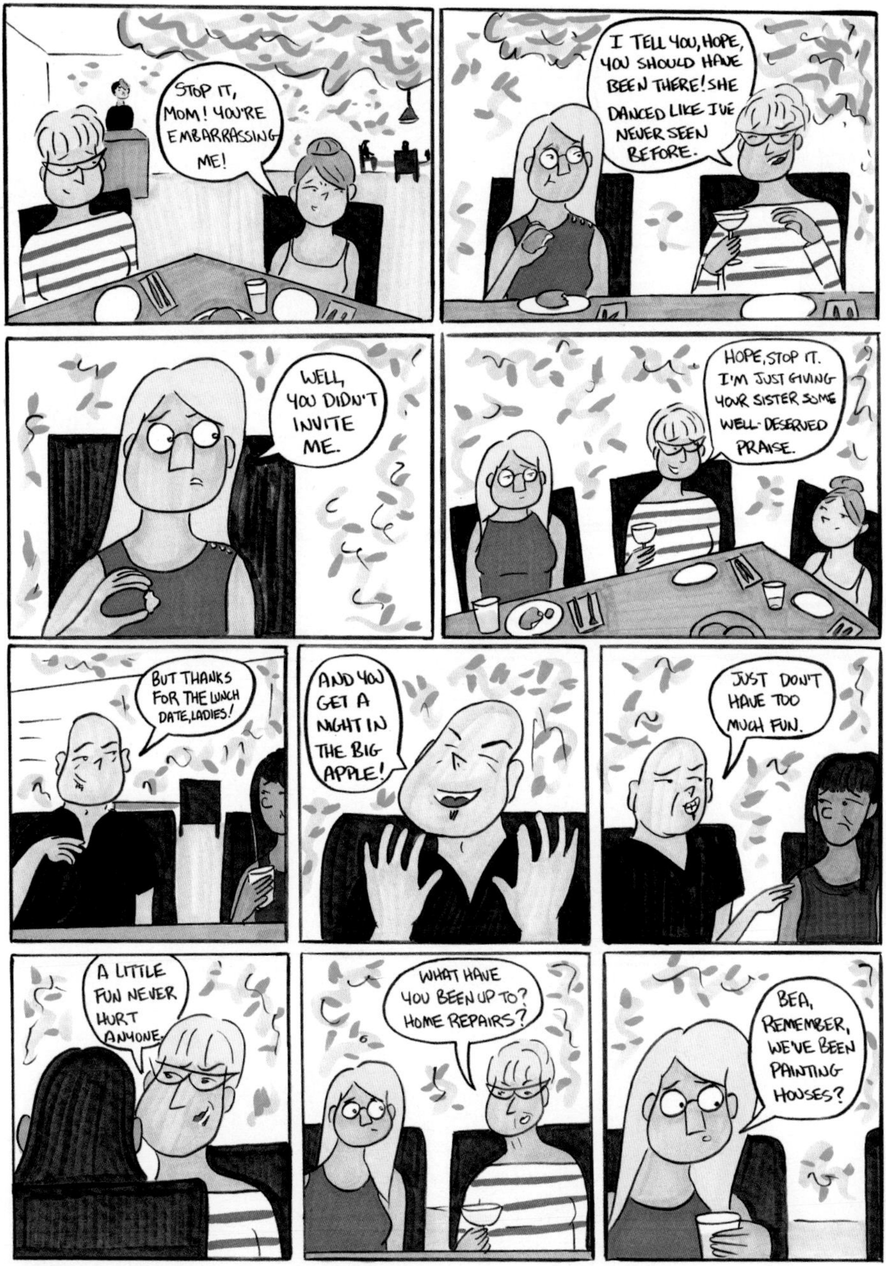
STOP IT, MOM! YOU'RE EMBARRASSING ME!
I TELL YOU, HOPE, YOU SHOULD HAVE BEEN THERE! SHE DANCED LIKE I'VE NEVER SEEN BEFORE.
WELL, YOU DIDN'T INVITE ME.
HOPE, STOP IT. I'M JUST GIVING YOUR SISTER SOME WELL-DESERVED PRAISE.
BUT THANKS FOR THE LUNCH DATE, LADIES!
AND YOU GET A NIGHT IN THE BIG APPLE!
JUST DON'T HAVE TOO MUCH FUN.
A LITTLE FUN NEVER HURT ANYONE.
WHAT HAVE YOU BEEN UP TO? HOME REPAIRS?
BEA, REMEMBER, WE'VE BEEN PAINTING HOUSES?

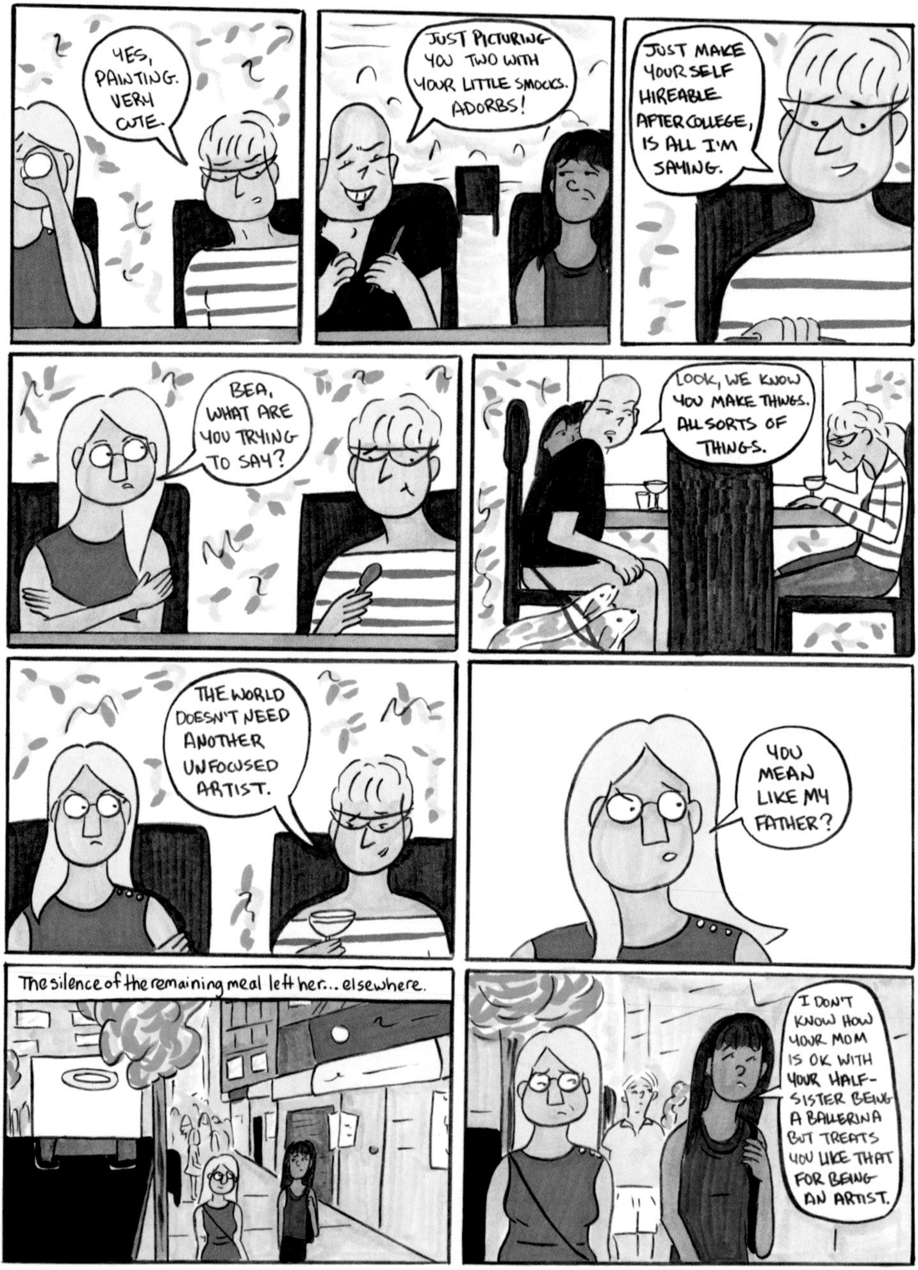
YES, PAINTING. VERY CUTE.
JUST PICTURING YOU TWO WITH YOUR LITTLE SMOCKS. ADORBS!
JUST MAKE YOURSELF HIREABLE AFTER COLLEGE, IS ALL I'M SAYING.
BEA, WHAT ARE YOU TRYING TO SAY?
LOOK, WE KNOW YOU MAKE THINGS. ALL SORTS OF THINGS.
THE WORLD DOESN'T NEED ANOTHER UNFOCUSED ARTIST.
YOU MEAN LIKE MY FATHER?
The silence of the remaining meal left her... elsewhere.
I DON'T KNOW HOW YOUR MOM IS OK WITH YOUR HALF-SISTER BEING A BALLERINA BUT TREATS YOU LIKE THAT FOR BEING AN ARTIST.

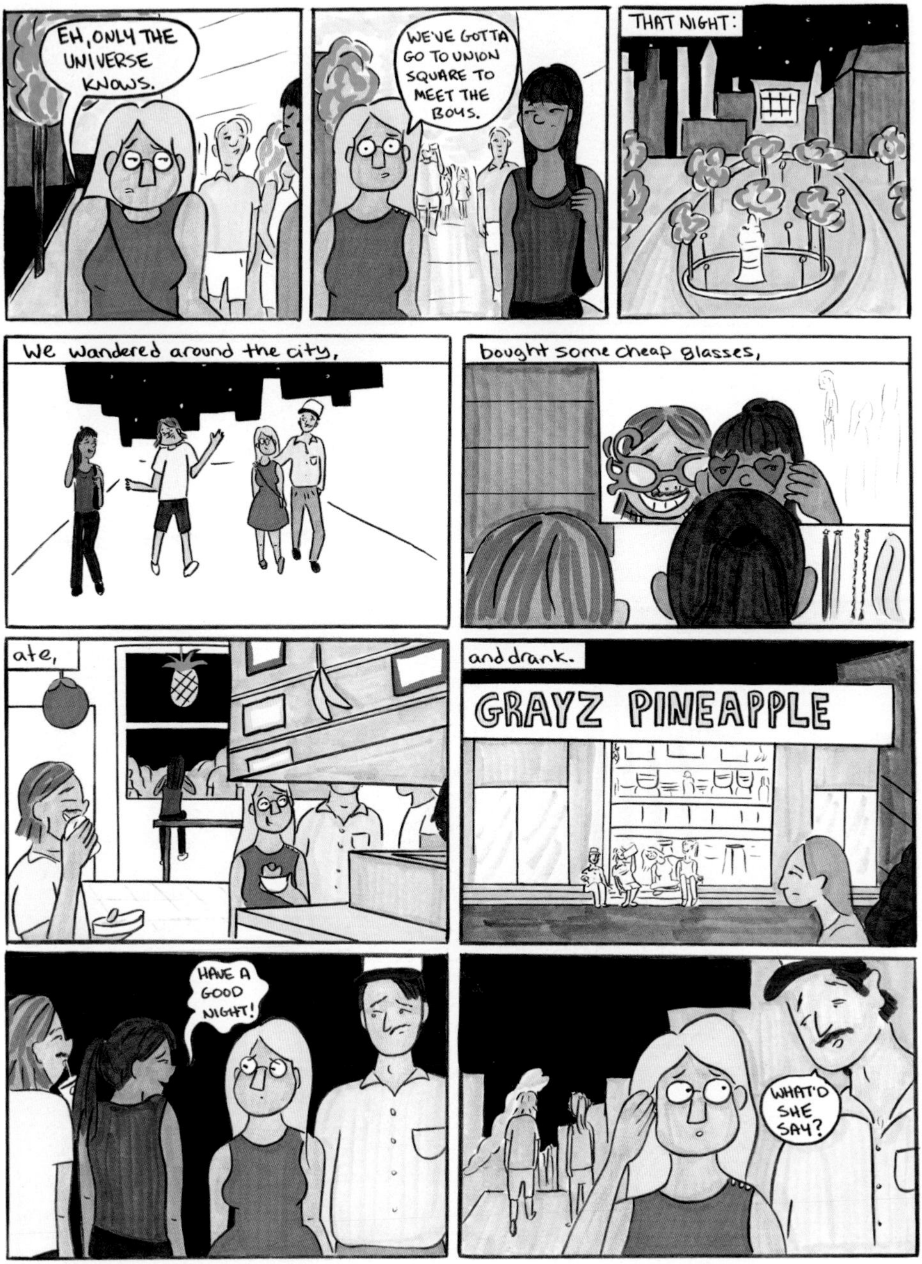
EH, ONLY THE UNIVERSE KNOWS.
WE'VE GOTTA GO TO UNION SQUARE TO MEET THE BOYS.
THAT NIGHT:
We wandered around the city,
bought some cheap glasses,
ate,
and drank.
GRAYZ PINEAPPLE
HAVE A GOOD NIGHT!
WHAT'D SHE SAY?

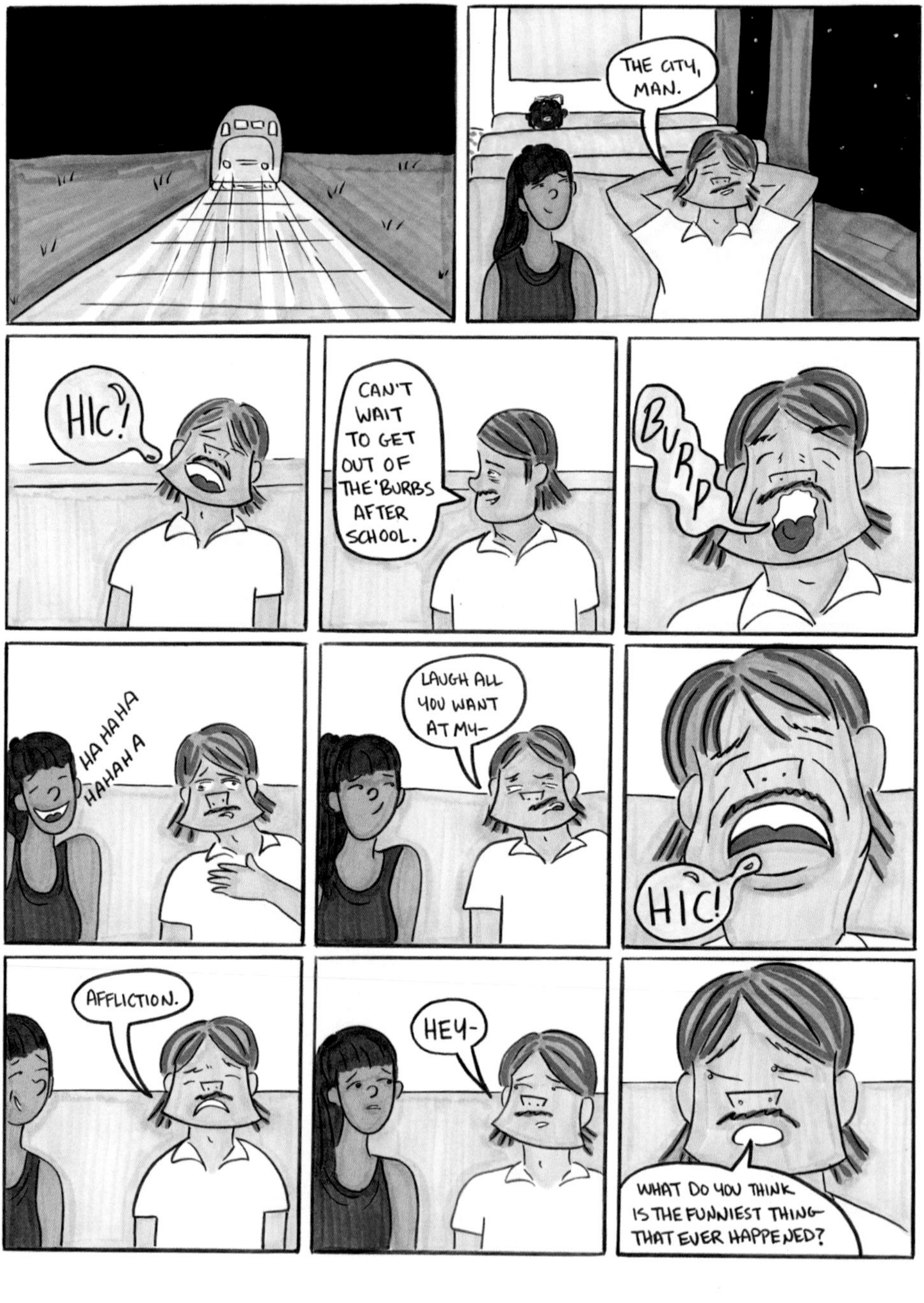
THE CITY, MAN.
HIC!
CAN'T WAIT TO GET OUT OF THE 'BURBS AFTER SCHOOL.
BURP
HA HA HA HA HA HA
LAUGH ALL YOU WANT AT MY-
HIC!
AFFLICTION.
HEY-
WHAT DO YOU THINK IS THE FUNNIEST THING THAT EVER HAPPENED?

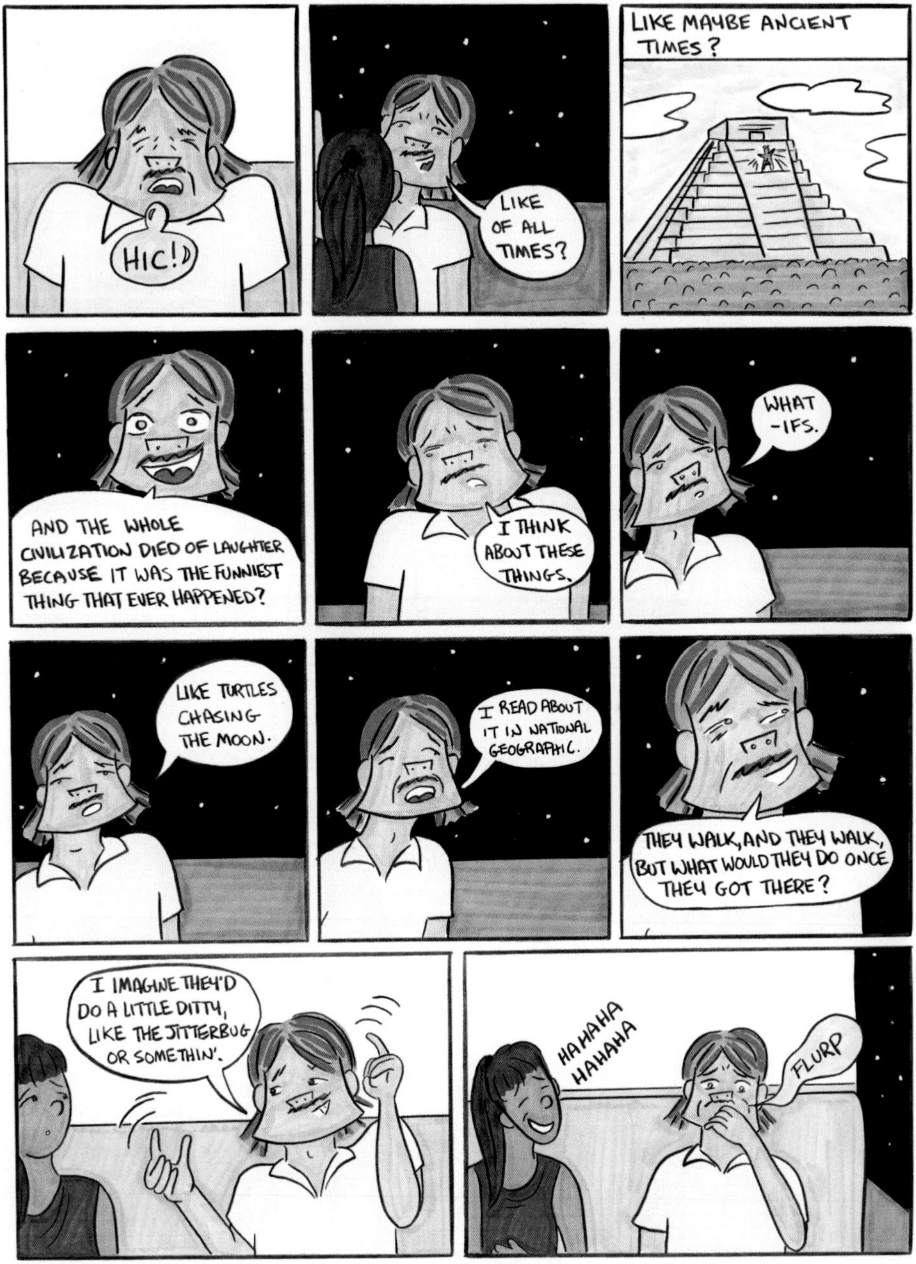
HIC!
LIKE OF ALL TIMES?
LIKE MAYBE ANCIENT TIMES?
AND THE WHOLE CIVILIZATION DIED OF LAUGHTER BECAUSE IT WAS THE FUNNIEST THING THAT EVER HAPPENED?
I THINK ABOUT THESE THINGS.
WHAT -IFS.
LIKE TURTLES CHASING THE MOON.
I READ ABOUT IT IN NATIONAL GEOGRAPHIC.
THEY WALK, AND THEY WALK, BUT WHAT WOULD THEY DO ONCE THEY GOT THERE?
I IMAGINE THEY'D DO A LITTLE DITTY, LIKE THE JITTERBUG OR SOMETHIN'.
HAHAHA HAHAHA
FLURP

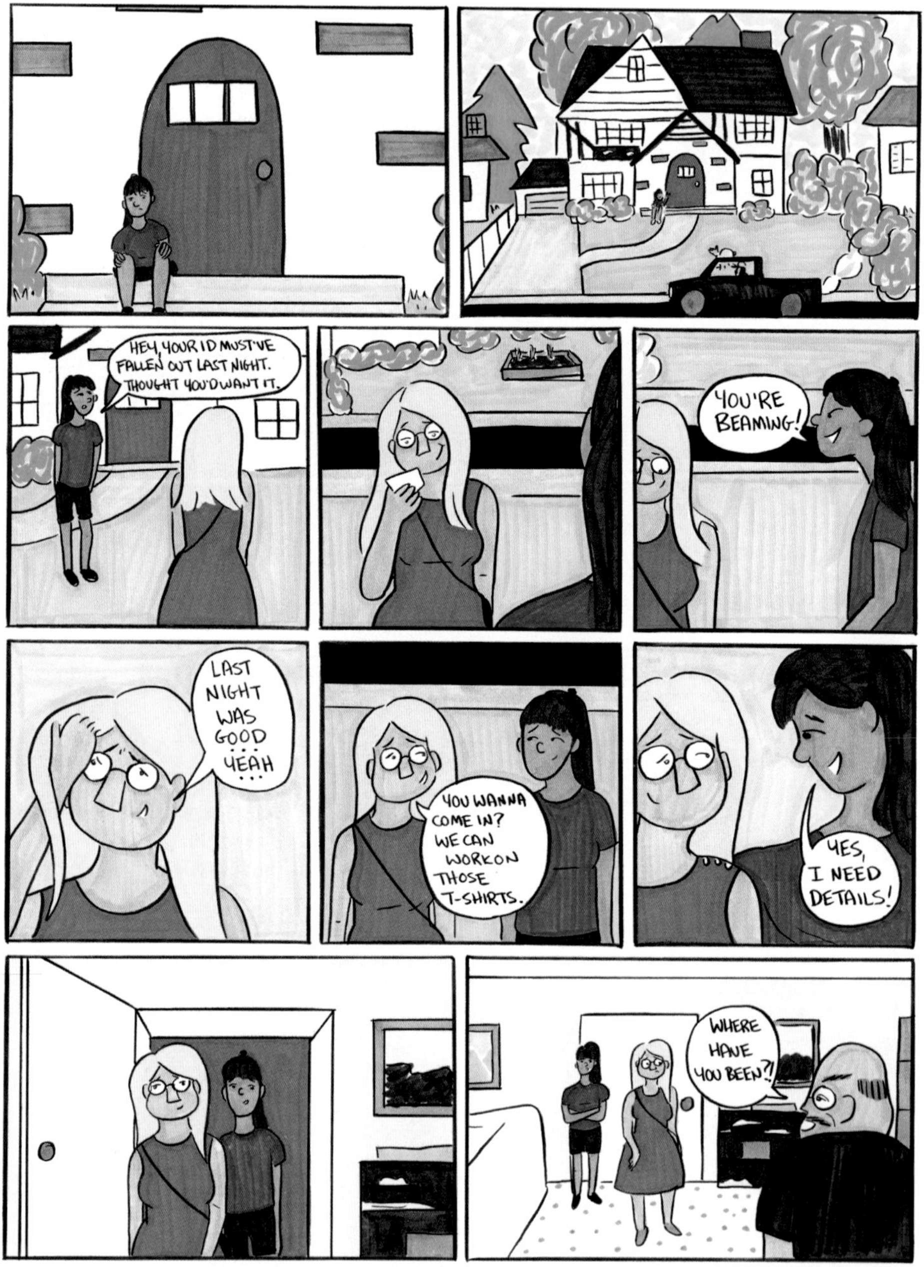
HEY, YOUR ID MUST'VE FALLEN OUT LAST NIGHT. THOUGHT YOU'D WANT IT.
YOU'RE BEAMING!
LAST NIGHT WAS GOOD . . . YEAH . . .
YOU WANNA COME IN? WE CAN WORK ON THOSE T-SHIRTS.
YES, I NEED DETAILS!
WHERE HAVE YOU BEEN?!

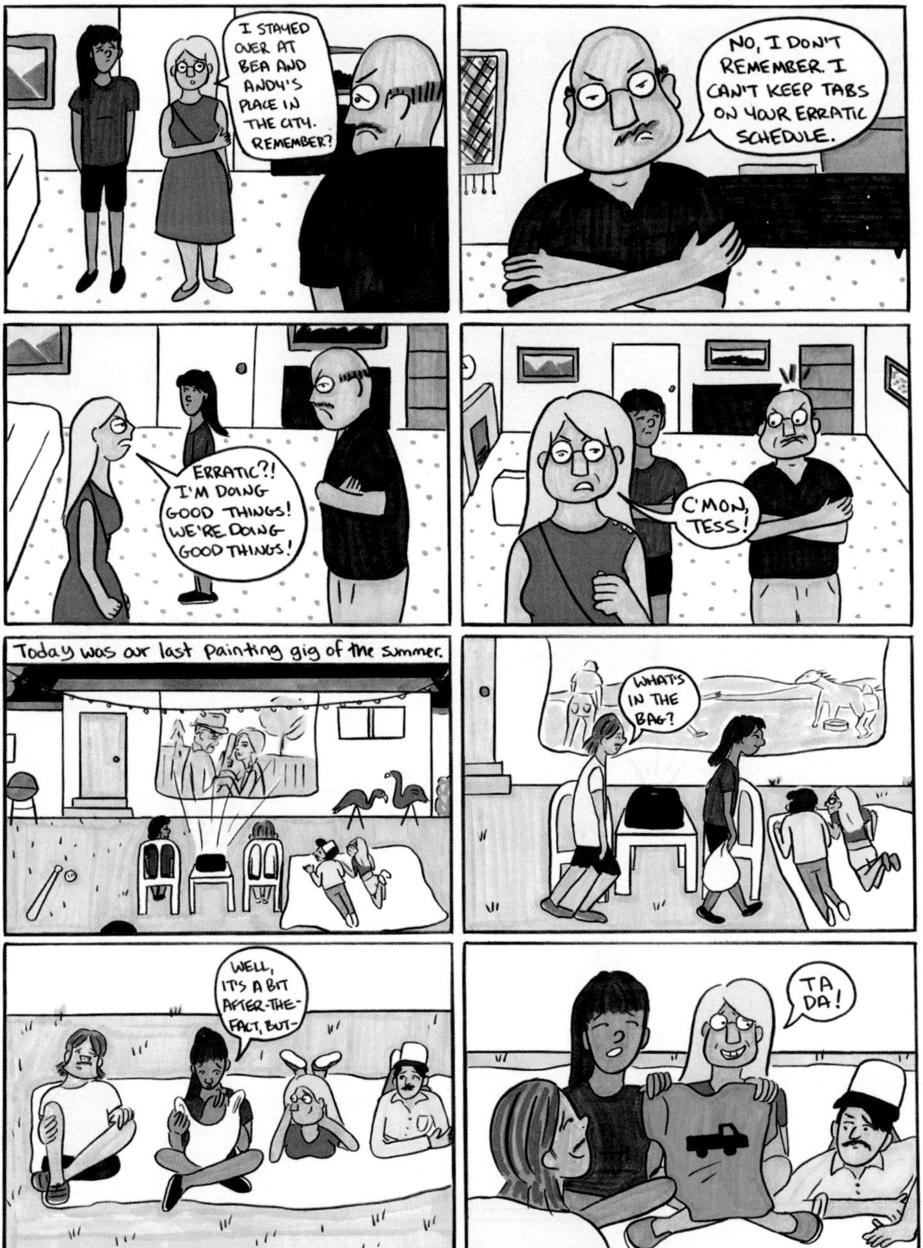

I STAYED OVER AT BEA AND ANDY'S PLACE IN THE CITY. REMEMBER?
NO, I DON'T REMEMBER. I CAN'T KEEP TABS ON YOUR ERRATIC SCHEDULE.
ERRATIC?! I'M DOING GOOD THINGS! WE'RE DOING GOOD THINGS!
C'MON, TESS!
Today was our last painting gig of the summer.
WHAT'S IN THE BAG?
WELL, IT'S A BIT AFTER-THE-FACT, BUT-
TA DA!

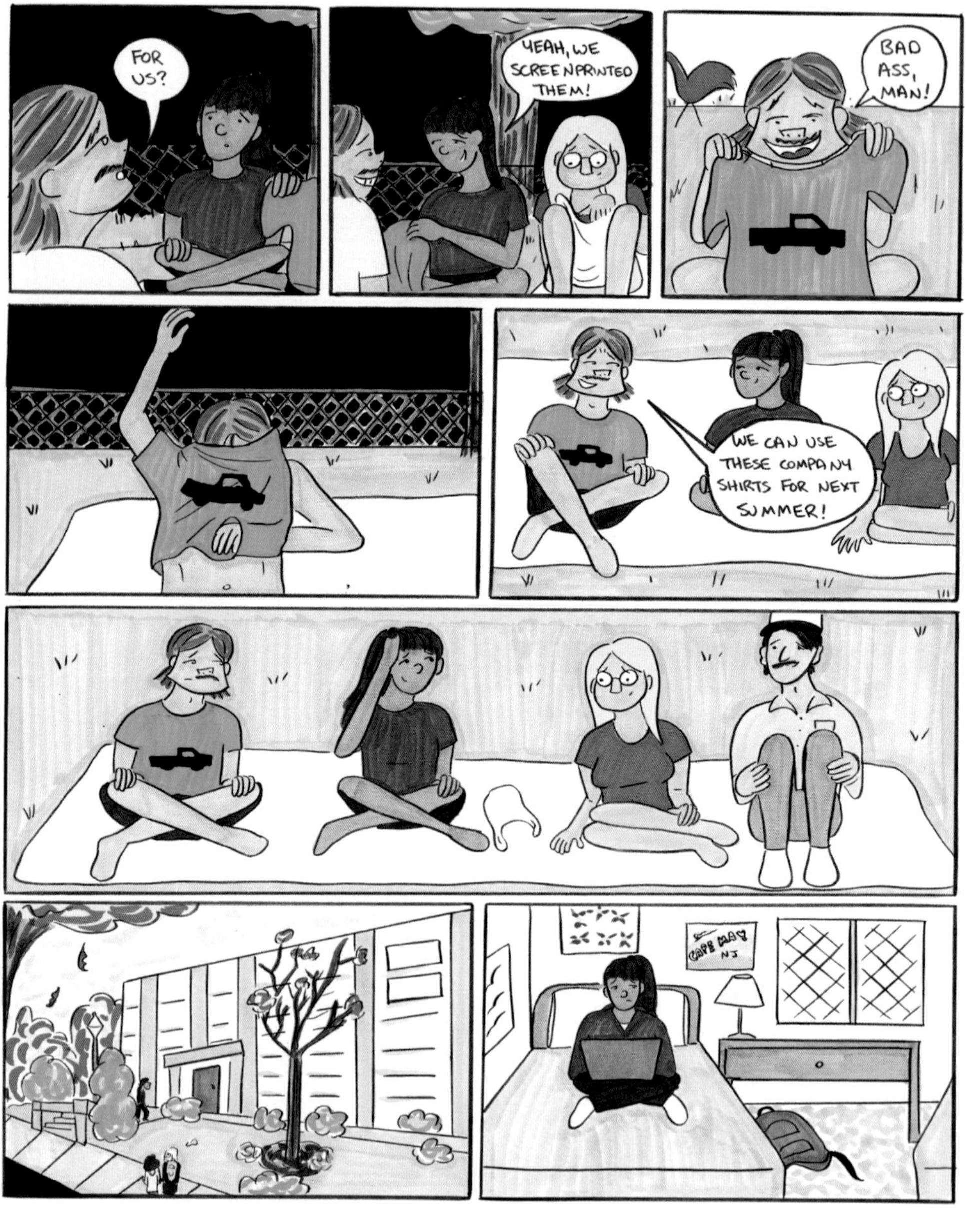
FOR US?
YEAH, WE SCREENPRINTED THEM!
BAD ASS, MAN!
WE CAN USE THESE COMPANY SHIRTS FOR NEXT SUMMER!
CAPE MAY NJ

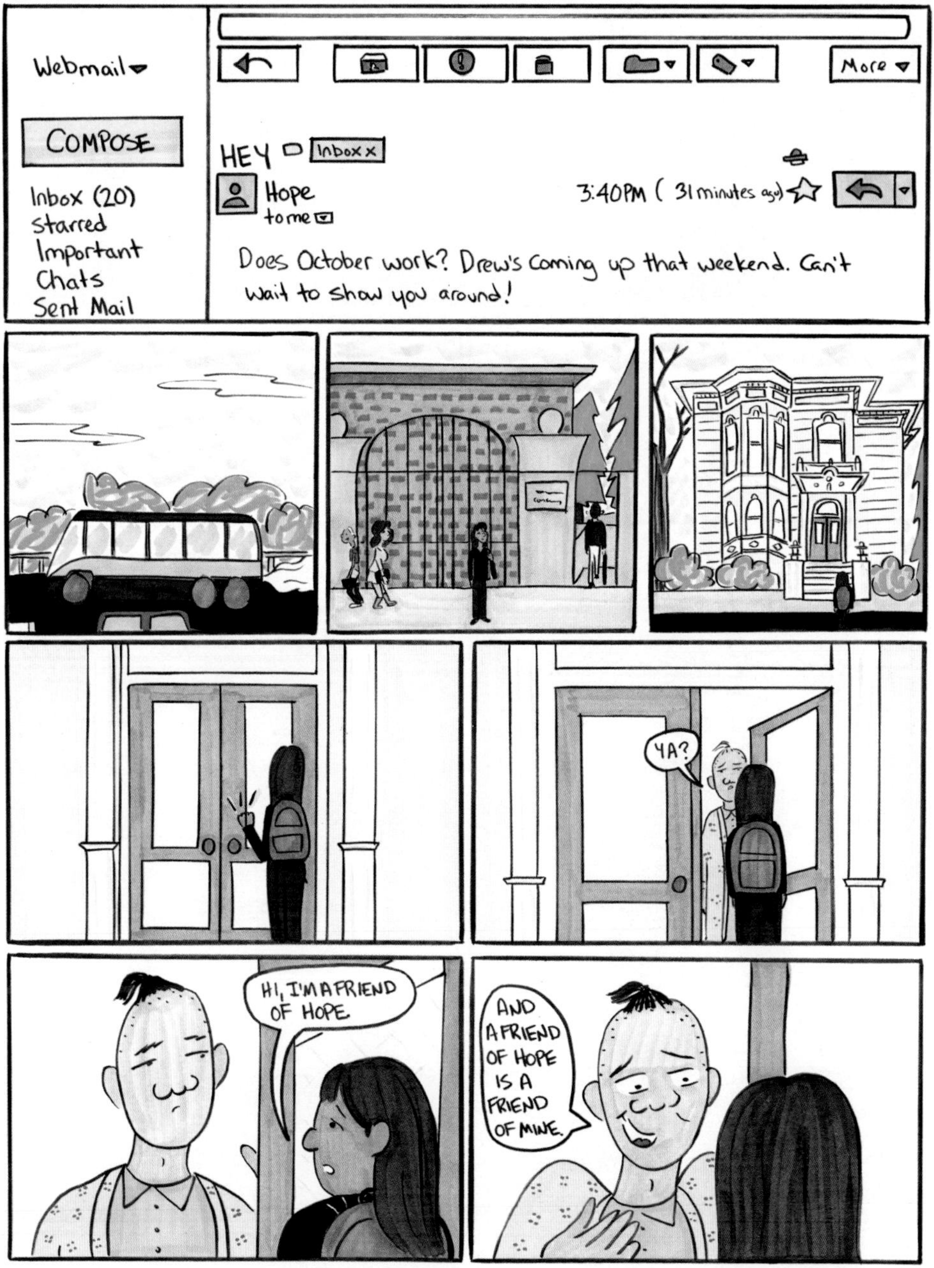
Webmail
COMPOSE
Inbox (20)
Starred
Important
Chats
Sent Mail
More
HEY
Inbox x
Hope
to me
3:40PM (31 minutes ago)
Does October work? Drew's coming up that weekend. Can't wait to show you around!
YA?
HI, I'M A FRIEND OF HOPE.
AND A FRIEND OF HOPE IS A FRIEND OF MINE.

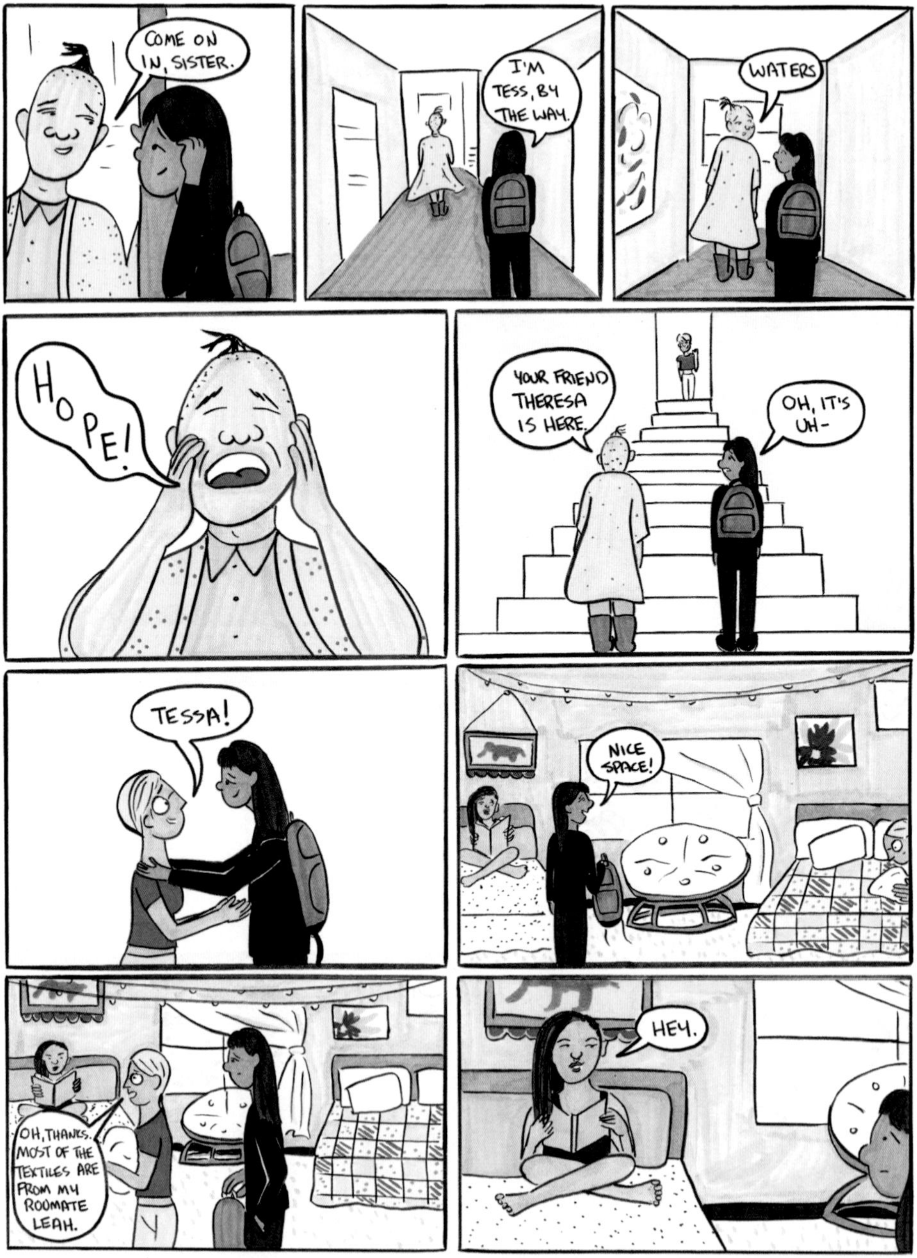
COME ON IN, SISTER.
I'M TESS, BY THE WAY.
WATERS
HOPE!
YOUR FRIEND THERESA IS HERE.
OH, IT'S UH-
TESSA!
NICE SPACE!
OH, THANKS. MOST OF THE TEXTILES ARE FROM MY ROOMATE LEAH.
HEY.

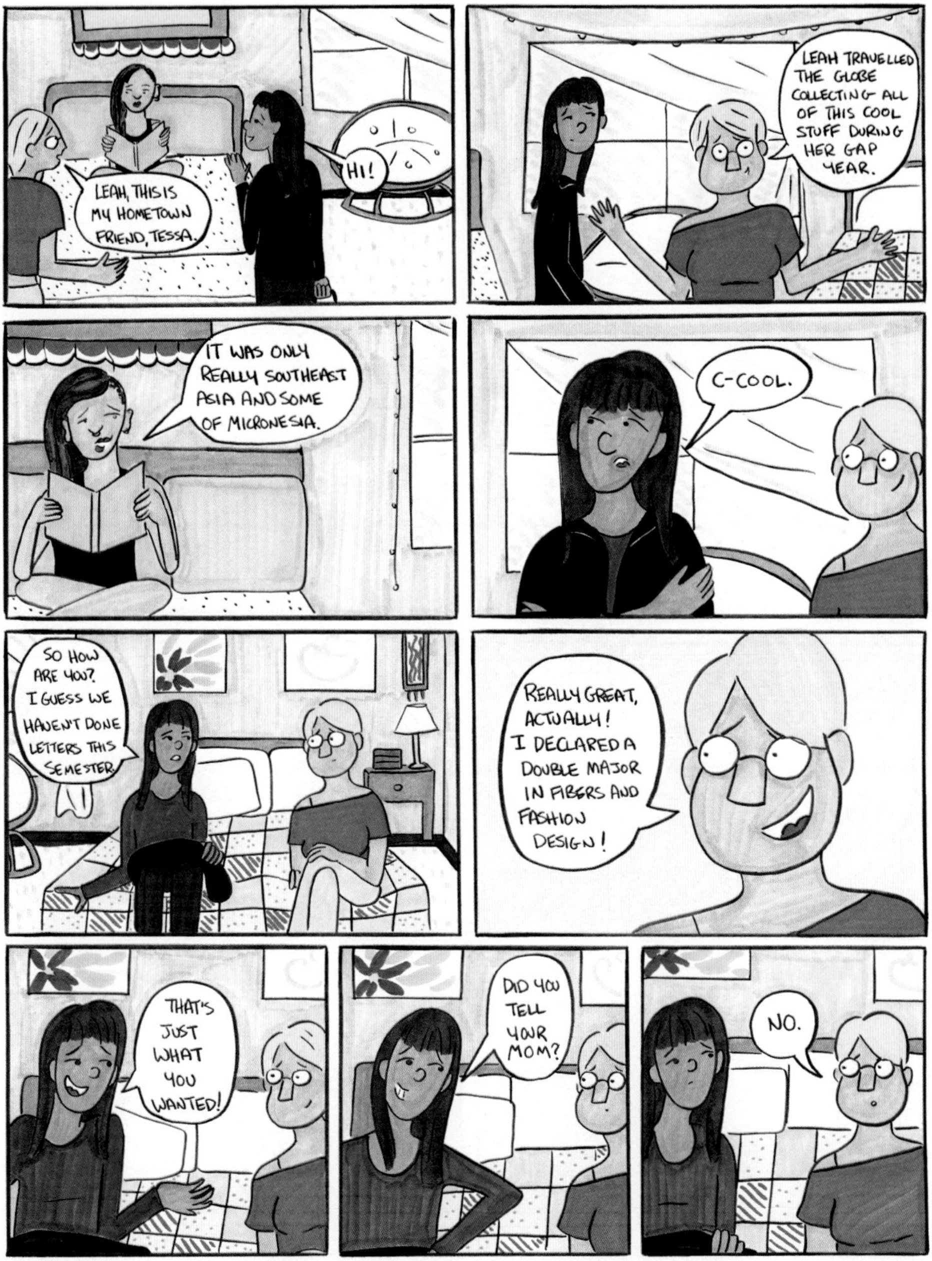
LEAH, THIS IS MY HOMETOWN FRIEND, TESSA.
HI!
LEAH TRAVELLED THE GLOBE COLLECTING ALL OF THIS COOL STUFF DURING HER GAP YEAR.
IT WAS ONLY REALLY SOUTHEAST ASIA AND SOME OF MICRONESIA.
C-COOL.
SO HOW ARE YOU? I GUESS WE HAVEN'T DONE LETTERS THIS SEMESTER.
REALLY GREAT, ACTUALLY! I DECLARED A DOUBLE MAJOR IN FIBERS AND FASHION DESIGN!
THAT'S JUST WHAT YOU WANTED!
DID YOU TELL YOUR MOM?
NO.

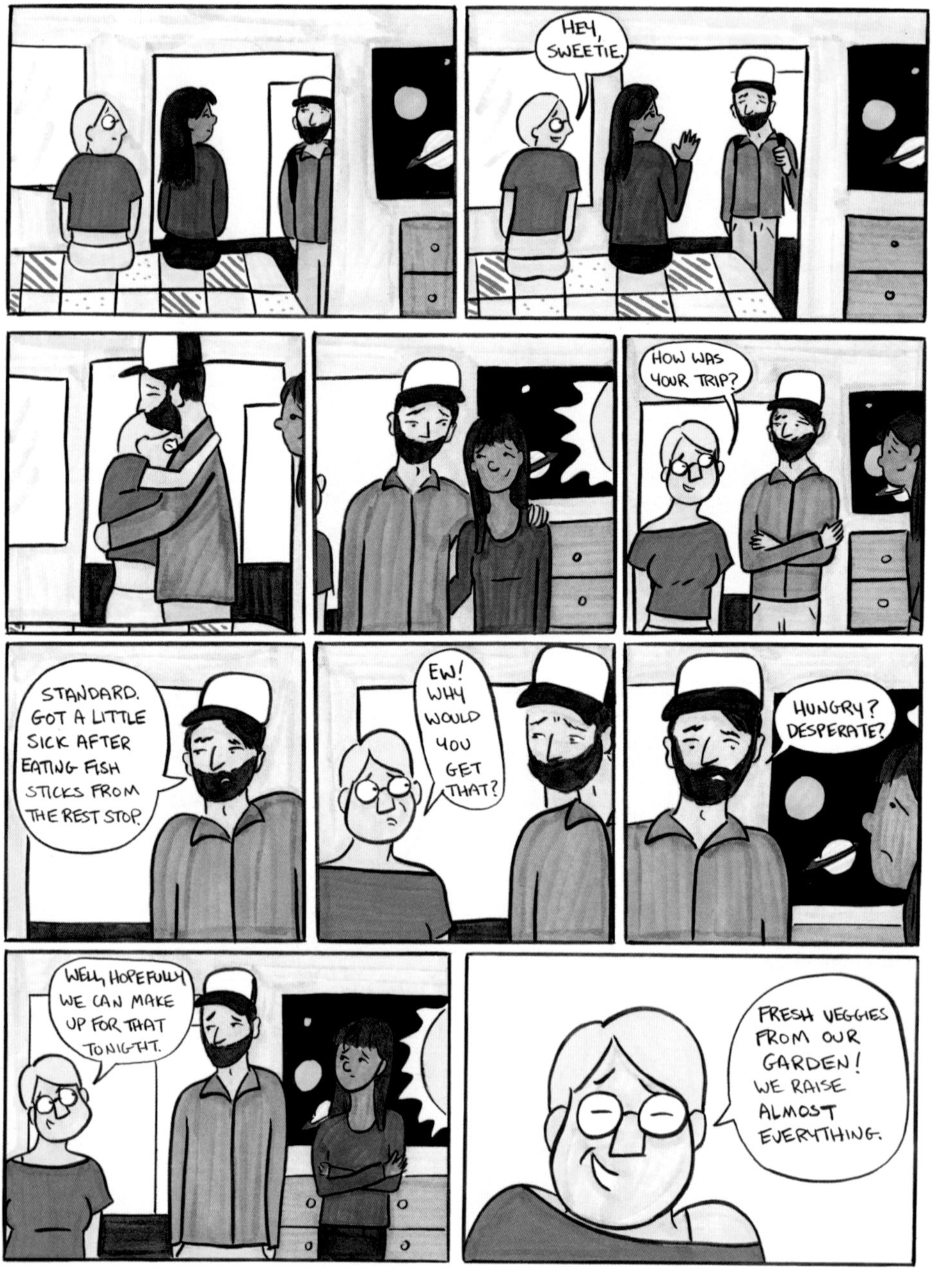
HEY, SWEETIE.
HOW WAS YOUR TRIP?
STANDARD. GOT A LITTLE SICK AFTER EATING FISH STICKS FROM THE REST STOP.
EW! WHY WOULD YOU GET THAT?
HUNGRY? DESPERATE?
WELL, HOPEFULLY WE CAN MAKE UP FOR THAT TONIGHT.
FRESH VEGGIES FROM OUR GARDEN! WE RAISE ALMOST EVERYTHING.

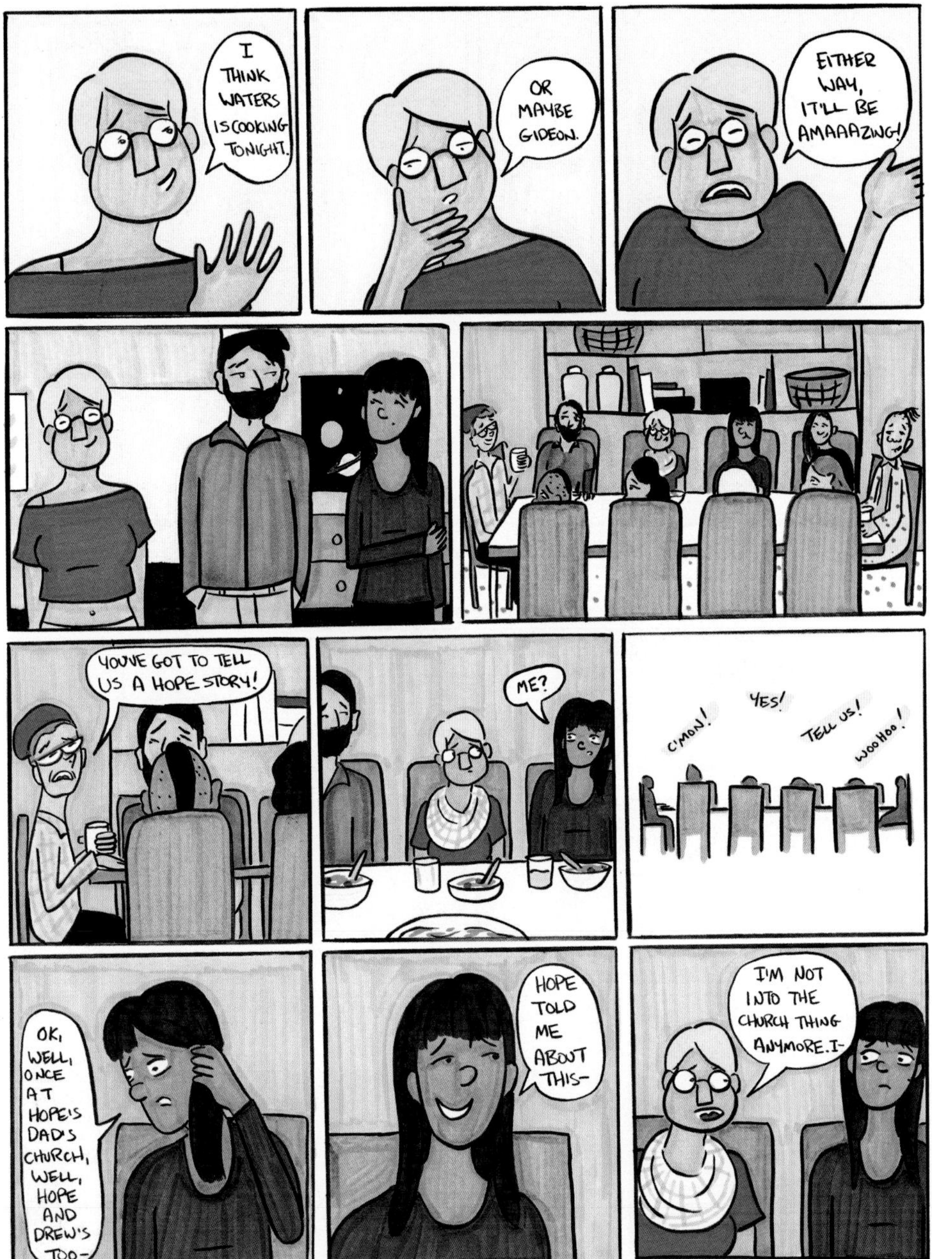
I THINK WATERS IS COOKING TONIGHT.
OR MAYBE GIDEON.
EITHER WAY, IT'LL BE AMAAAZING!
YOU'VE GOT TO TELL US A HOPE STORY!
ME?
C'MON!
YES!
TELL US!
WOOHOO!
OK, WELL, ONCE AT HOPE'S DAD'S CHURCH, WELL, HOPE AND DREW'S TOO-
HOPE TOLD ME ABOUT THIS-
I'M NOT INTO THE CHURCH THING ANYMORE. I-

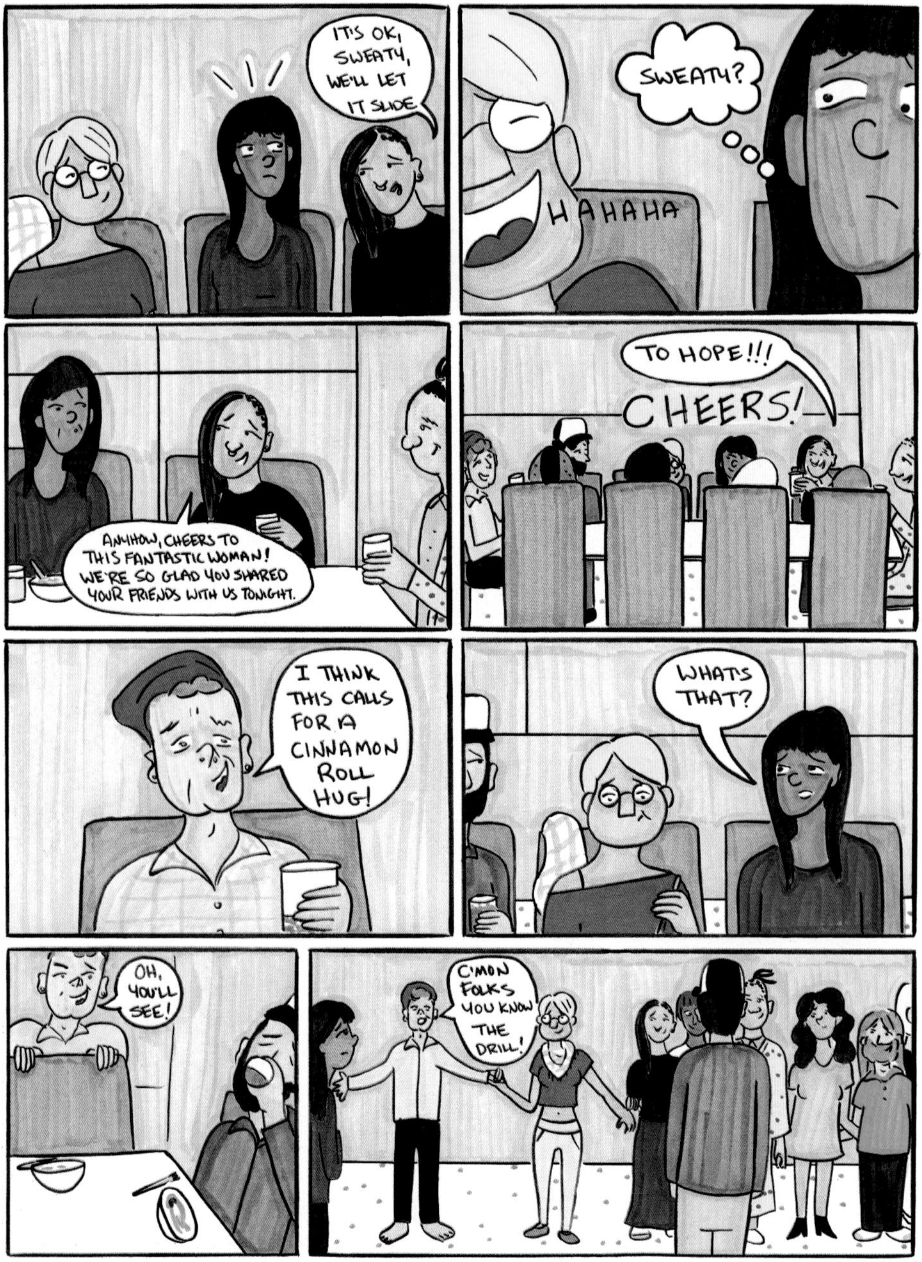
IT'S OK, SWEATY, WE'LL LET IT SLIDE
SWEATY?
HAHAHA
ANYHOW, CHEERS TO THIS FANTASTIC WOMAN! WE'RE SO GLAD YOU SHARED YOUR FRIENDS WITH US TONIGHT.
TO HOPE!!!
CHEERS!
I THINK THIS CALLS FOR A CINNAMON ROLL HUG!
WHAT'S THAT?
OH, YOU'LL SEE!
C'MON FOLKS YOU KNOW THE DRILL!

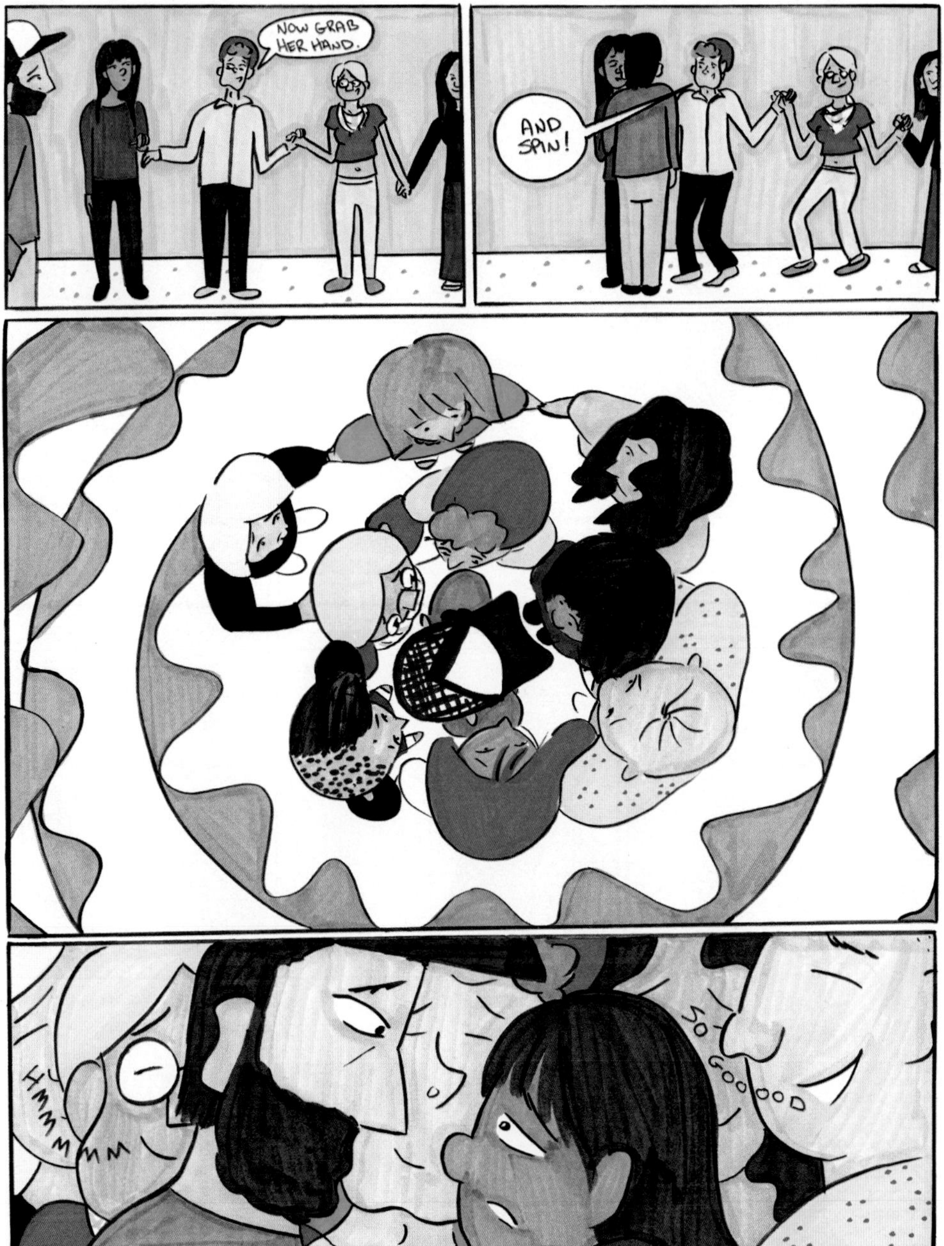
NOW GRAB HER HAND.
AND SPIN!
HMMMMMM
SO GOOOOD

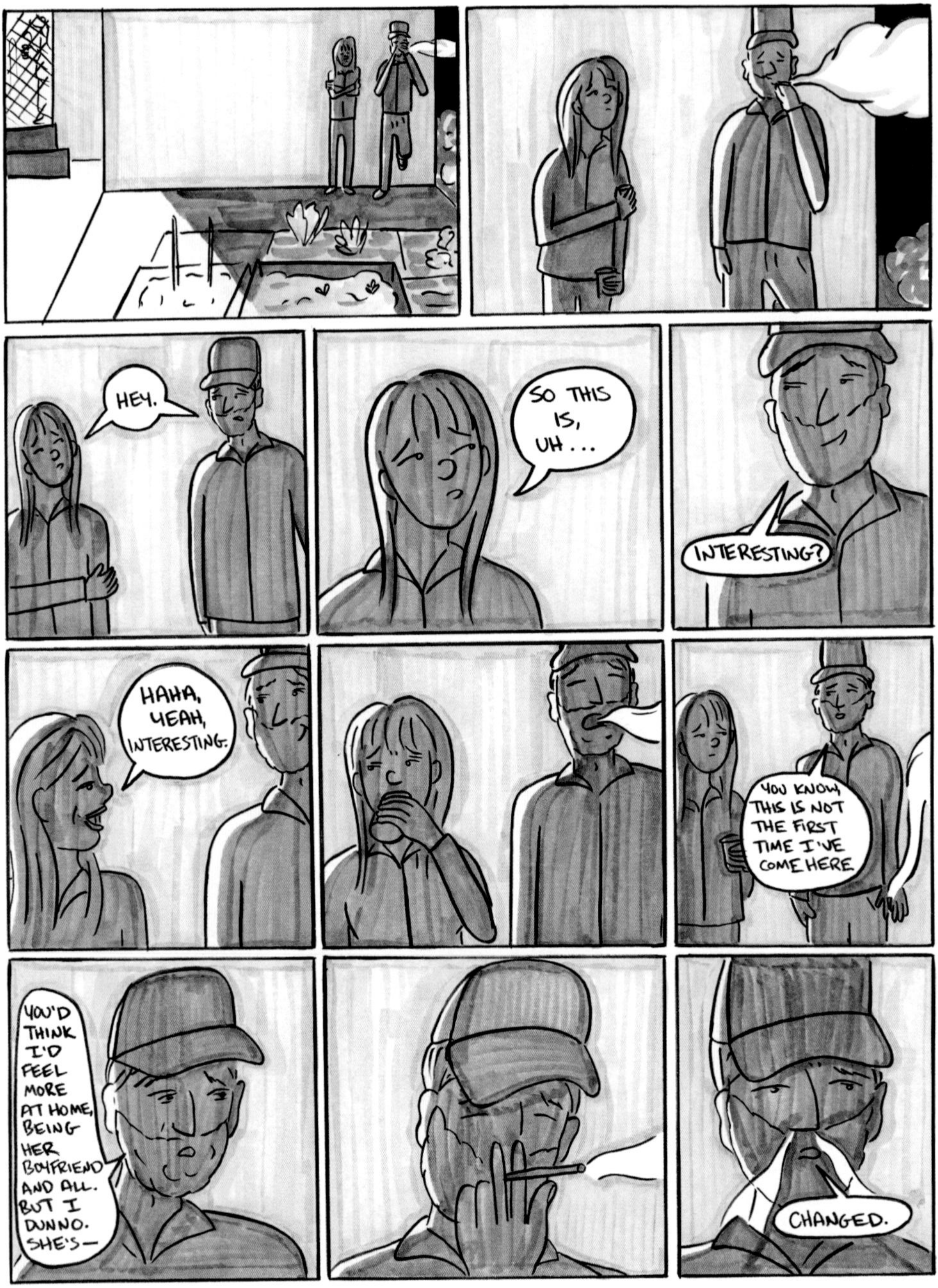
HEY.
SO THIS IS, UH...
INTERESTING?
HAHA, YEAH, INTERESTING.
YOU KNOW, THIS IS NOT THE FIRST TIME I'VE COME HERE.
YOU'D THINK I'D FEEL MORE AT HOME, BEING HER BOYFRIEND AND ALL. BUT I DUNNO. SHE'S—
CHANGED.

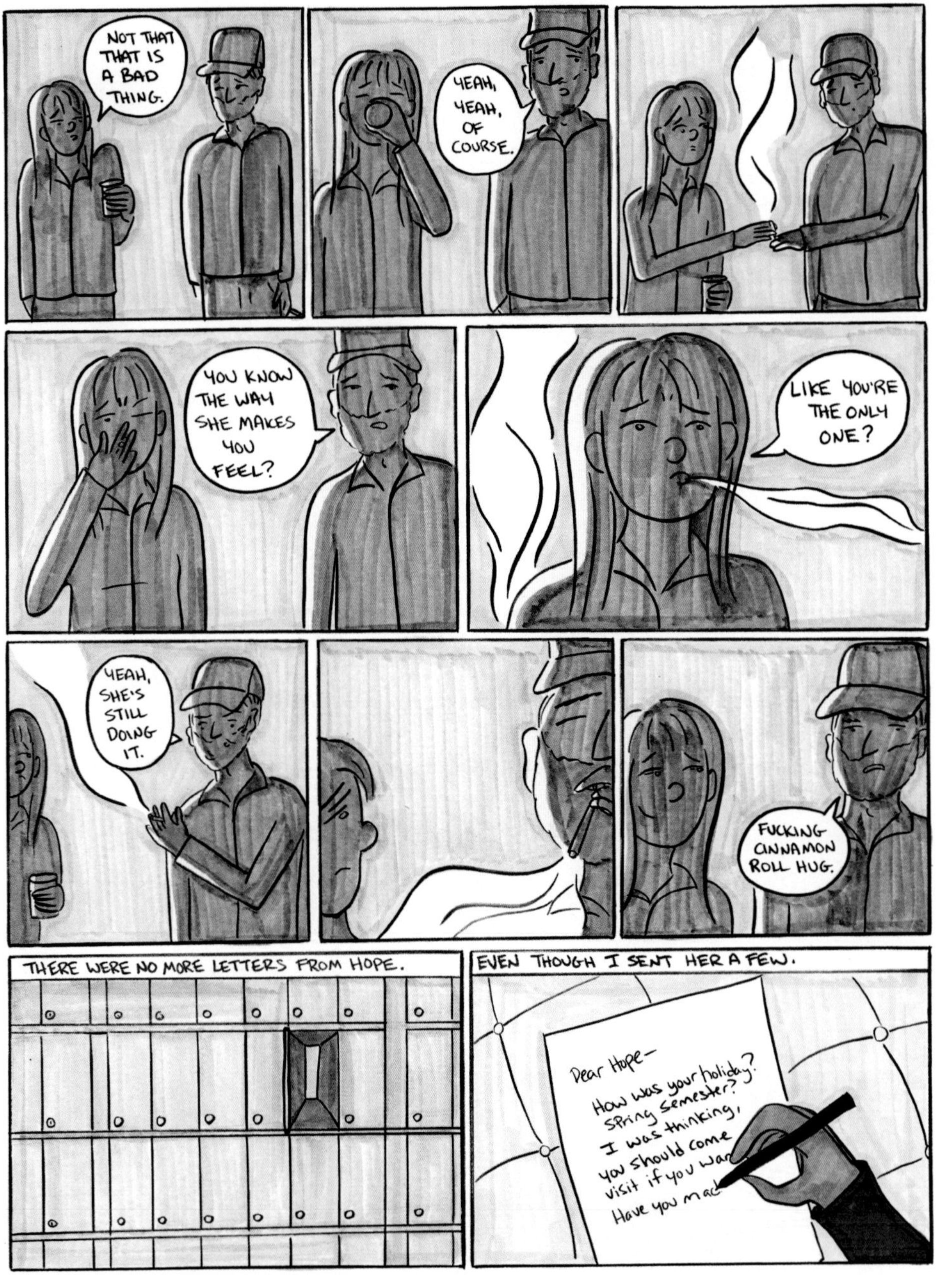
NOT THAT THAT IS A BAD THING.
YEAH, YEAH, OF COURSE.
YOU KNOW THE WAY SHE MAKES YOU FEEL?
LIKE YOU'RE THE ONLY ONE?
YEAH, SHE'S STILL DOING IT.
FUCKING CINNAMON ROLL HUG.
THERE WERE NO MORE LETTERS FROM HOPE.
EVEN THOUGH I SENT HER A FEW.
Dear Hope—
How was your holiday?
Spring Semester?
I was thinking,
you should come
visit if you wan
Have you mad

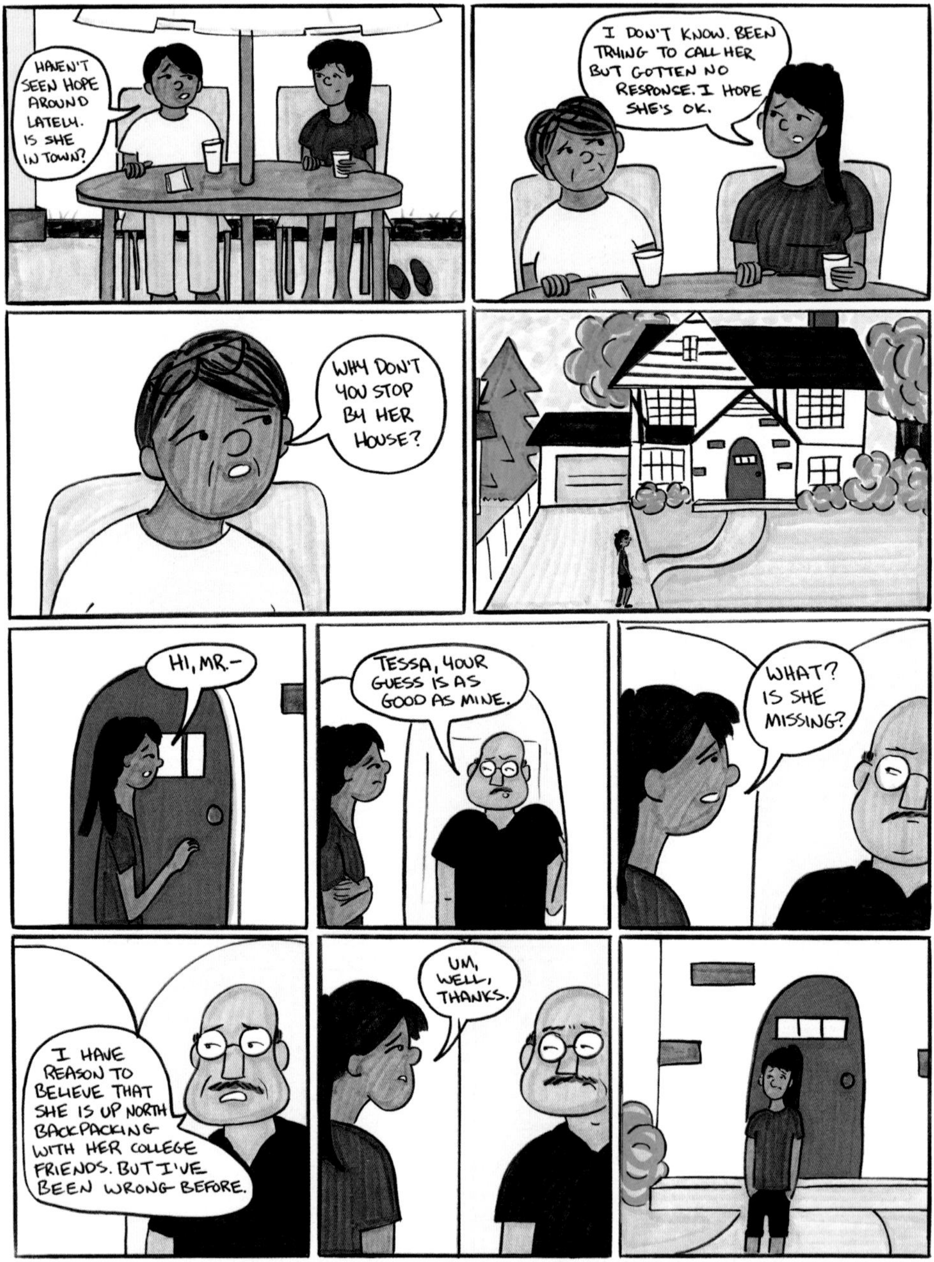
HAVEN'T SEEN HOPE AROUND LATELY. IS SHE IN TOWN?
I DON'T KNOW. BEEN TRYING TO CALL HER BUT GOTTEN NO RESPONSE. I HOPE SHE'S OK.
WHY DON'T YOU STOP BY HER HOUSE?
HI, MR.-
TESSA, YOUR GUESS IS AS GOOD AS MINE.
WHAT? IS SHE MISSING?
I HAVE REASON TO BELIEVE THAT SHE IS UP NORTH BACKPACKING WITH HER COLLEGE FRIENDS. BUT I'VE BEEN WRONG BEFORE.
UM, WELL, THANKS.

AUGUST:

Dear Tessa—
It's been a whirlwind of unforgettable experiences for me this summer. I just got back from the White Mountains with some of my co-op friends. I did get your correspondences so don't think I didn't. Consider it a sin of omission.

Best,
Hope

SIN OF OMISSION?!

Dear Hope—
Thanks for getting back to me. I've got to be honest, though. I'm a bit hurt, I guess, that you didn't take the time to let me know you weren't gonna be around this summer. I guess I was hoping to have a summer like the last one.

Tessa

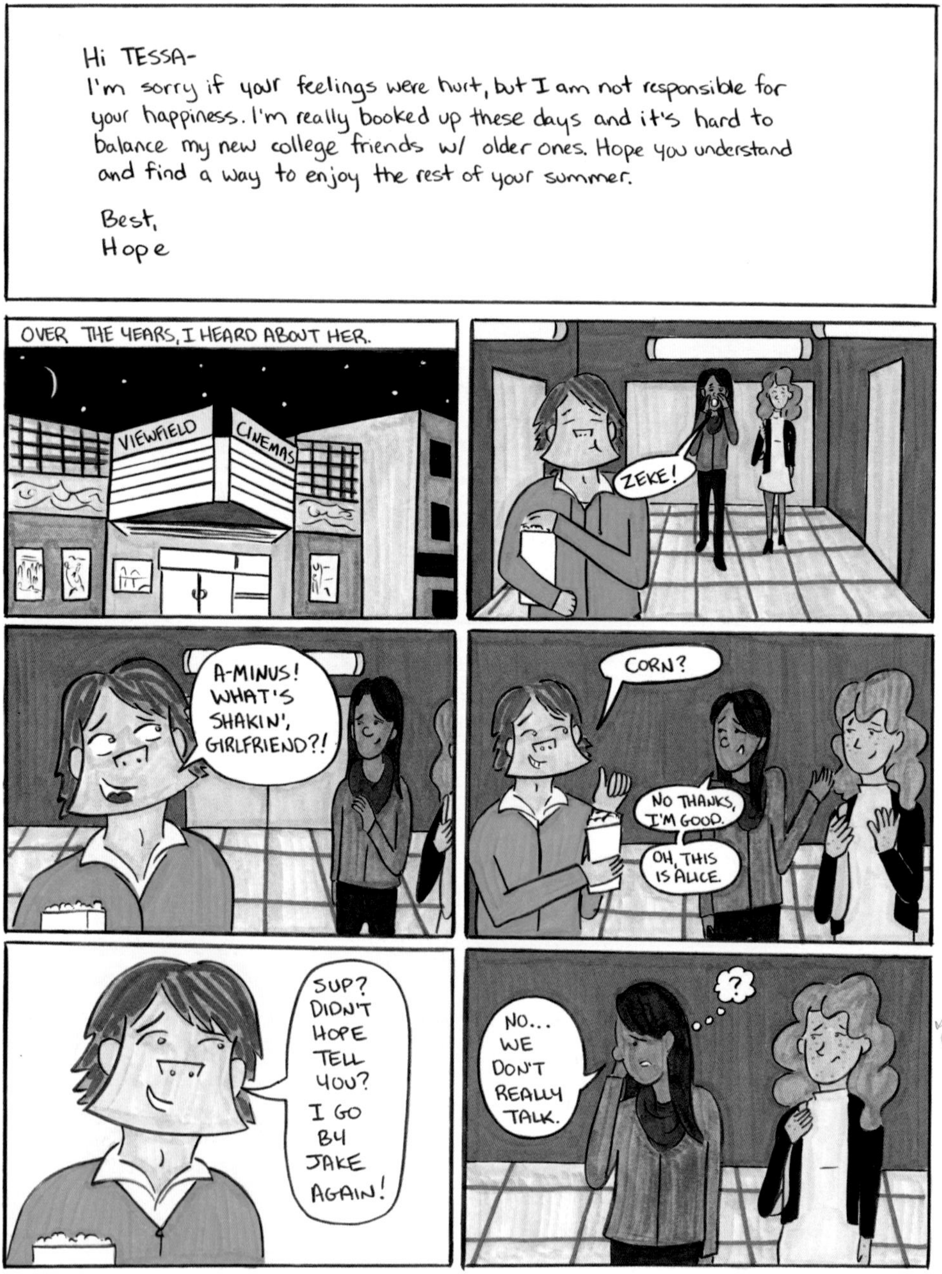
Hi TESSA-
I'm sorry if your feelings were hurt, but I am not responsible for your happiness. I'm really booked up these days and it's hard to balance my new college friends w/ older ones. Hope you understand and find a way to enjoy the rest of your summer.
Best,
Hope
OVER THE YEARS, I HEARD ABOUT HER.
VIEWFIELD
CINEMAS
ZEKE!
A-MINUS! WHAT'S SHAKIN', GIRLFRIEND?!
CORN?
NO THANKS, I'M GOOD.
OH, THIS IS ALICE.
SUP? DIDN'T HOPE TELL YOU? I GO BY JAKE AGAIN!
NO... WE DON'T REALLY TALK.
?

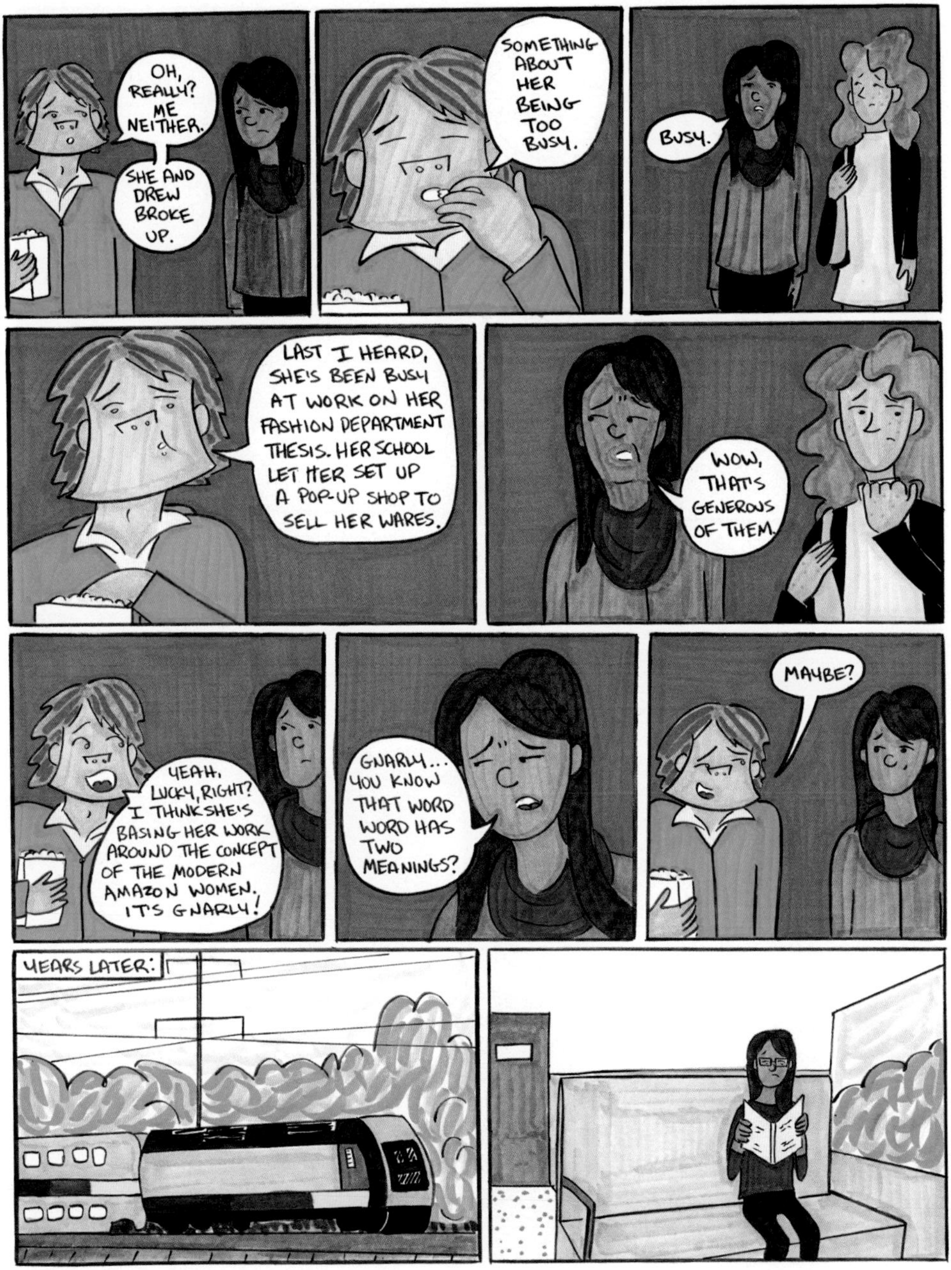
OH, REALLY? ME NEITHER.
SHE AND DREW BROKE UP.
SOMETHING ABOUT HER BEING TOO BUSY.
BUSY.
LAST I HEARD, SHE'S BEEN BUSY AT WORK ON HER FASHION DEPARTMENT THESIS. HER SCHOOL LET HER SET UP A POP-UP SHOP TO SELL HER WARES.
WOW, THAT'S GENEROUS OF THEM.
YEAH, LUCKY, RIGHT? I THINK SHE'S BASING HER WORK AROUND THE CONCEPT OF THE MODERN AMAZON WOMEN. IT'S GNARLY!
GNARLY... YOU KNOW THAT WORD WORD HAS TWO MEANINGS?
MAYBE?
YEARS LATER:

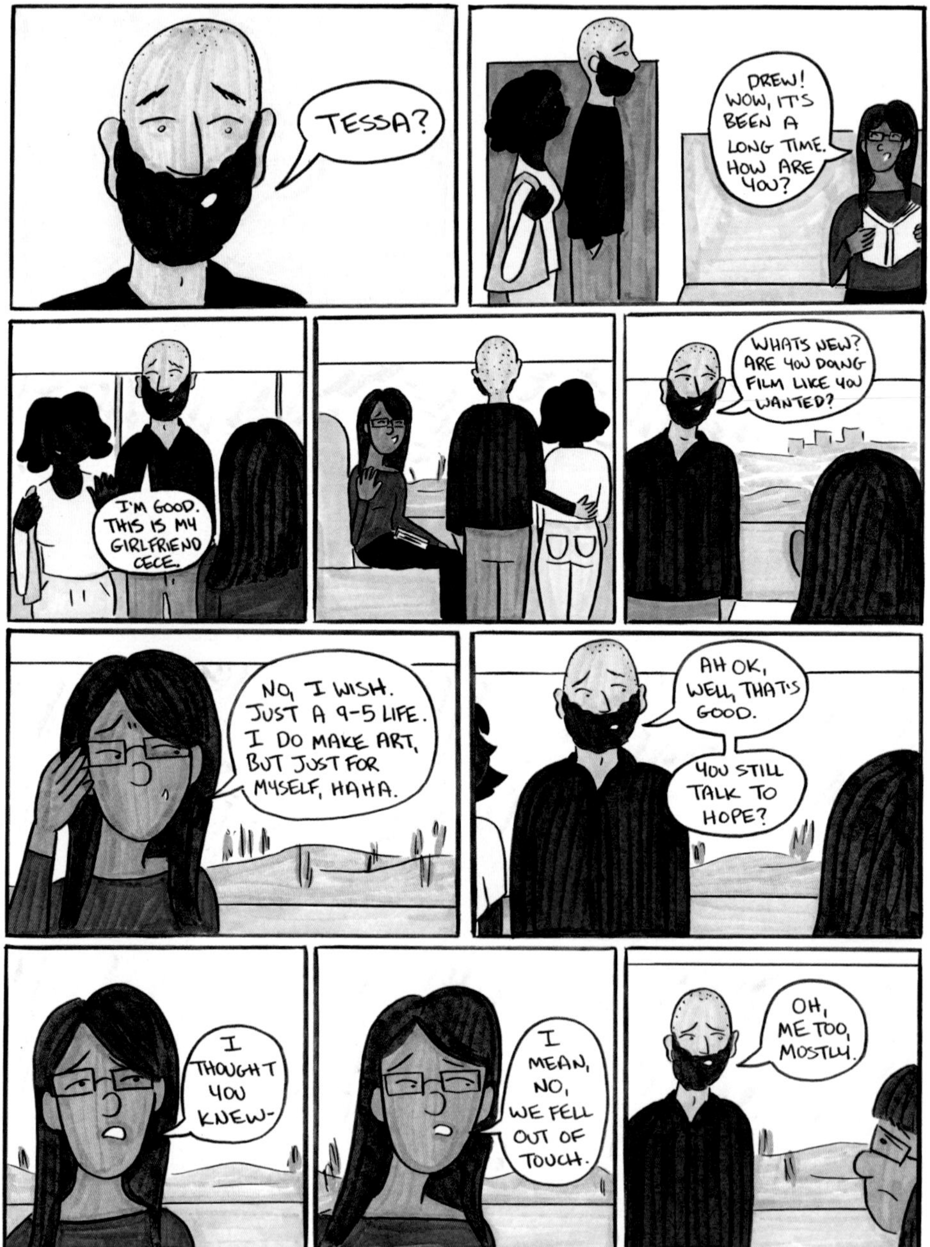
TESSA?
DREW! WOW, IT'S BEEN A LONG TIME. HOW ARE YOU?
I'M GOOD. THIS IS MY GIRLFRIEND CECE.
WHAT'S NEW? ARE YOU DOING FILM LIKE YOU WANTED?
NO, I WISH. JUST A 9-5 LIFE. I DO MAKE ART, BUT JUST FOR MYSELF, HAHA.
AH OK, WELL, THAT'S GOOD.
YOU STILL TALK TO HOPE?
I THOUGHT YOU KNEW-
I MEAN, NO, WE FELL OUT OF TOUCH.
OH, ME TOO, MOSTLY.

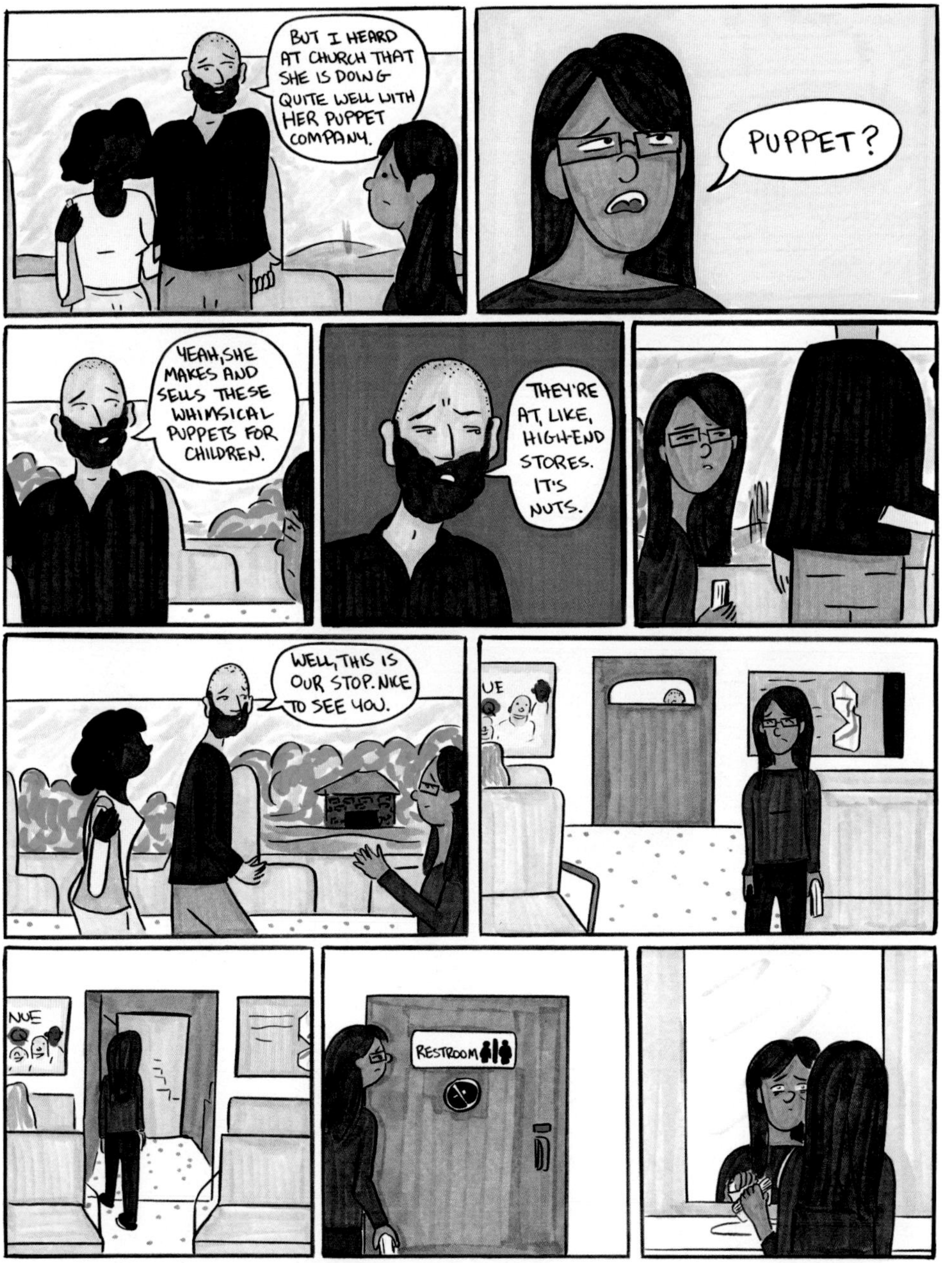
BUT I HEARD AT CHURCH THAT SHE IS DOING QUITE WELL WITH HER PUPPET COMPANY.
PUPPET?
YEAH, SHE MAKES AND SELLS THESE WHIMSICAL PUPPETS FOR CHILDREN.
THEY'RE AT, LIKE, HIGH-END STORES. IT'S NUTS.
WELL, THIS IS OUR STOP. NICE TO SEE YOU.
RESTROOM

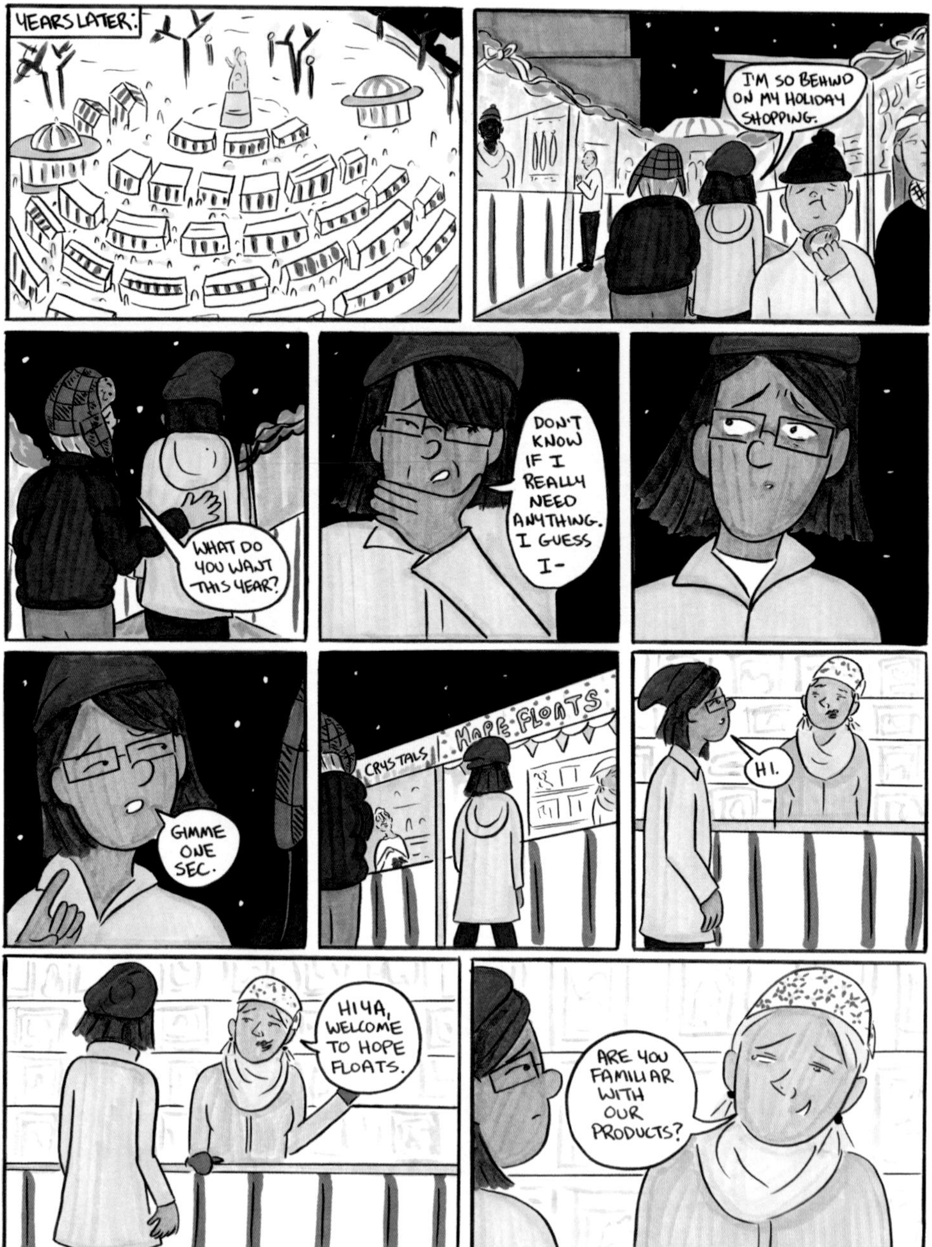
YEARS LATER:
I'M SO BEHIND ON MY HOLIDAY SHOPPING.
WHAT DO YOU WANT THIS YEAR?
DON'T KNOW IF I REALLY NEED ANYTHING. I GUESS I-
GIMME ONE SEC.
CRYSTALS
HOPE FLOATS
HI.
HIYA, WELCOME TO HOPE FLOATS.
ARE YOU FAMILIAR WITH OUR PRODUCTS?

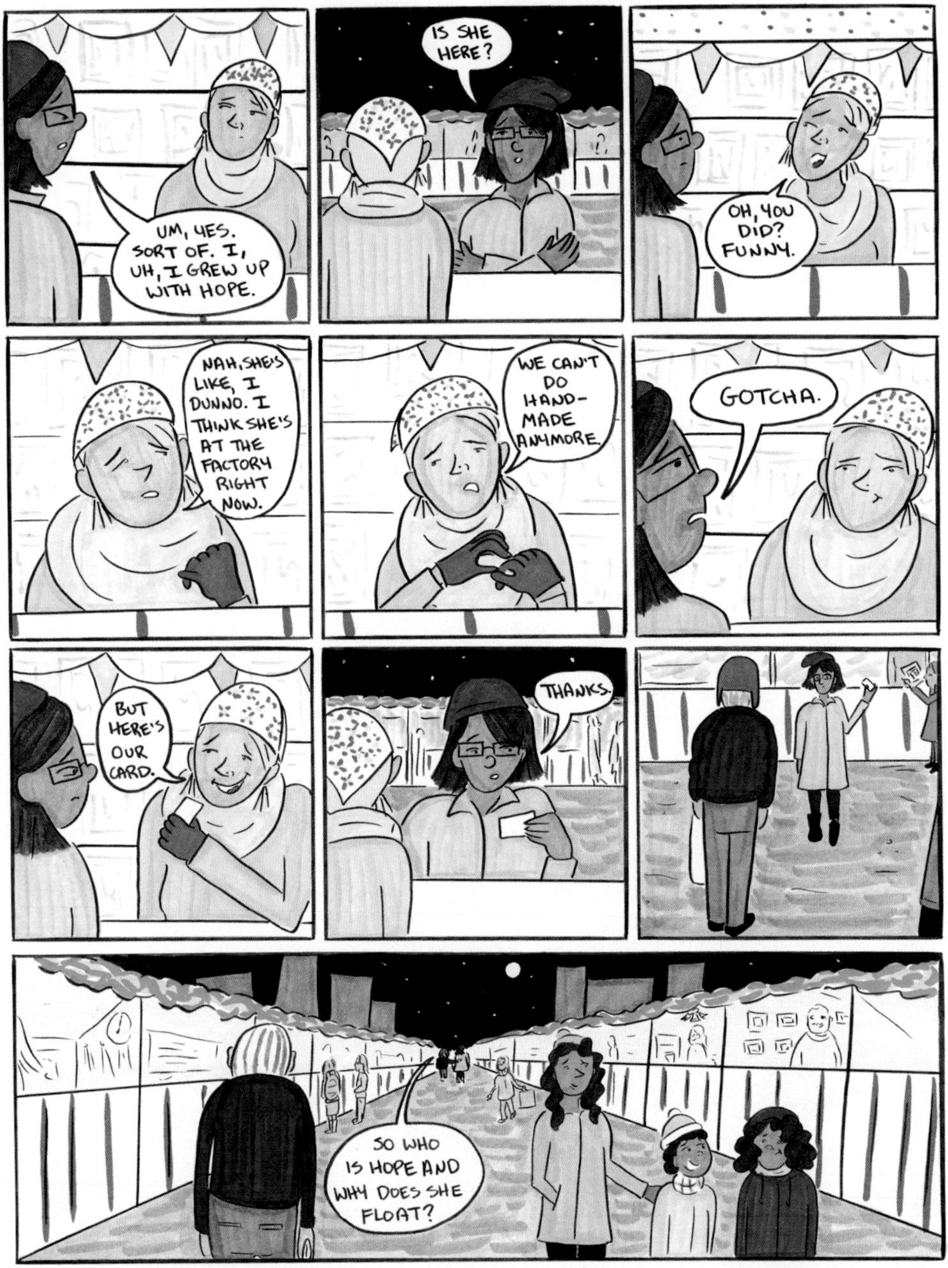
UM, YES. SORT OF. I, UH, I GREW UP WITH HOPE.
IS SHE HERE?
OH, YOU DID? FUNNY.
NAH, SHE'S LIKE, I DUNNO. I THINK SHE'S AT THE FACTORY RIGHT NOW.
WE CAN'T DO HAND-MADE ANYMORE.
GOTCHA.
BUT HERE'S OUR CARD.
THANKS.
SO WHO IS HOPE AND WHY DOES SHE FLOAT?

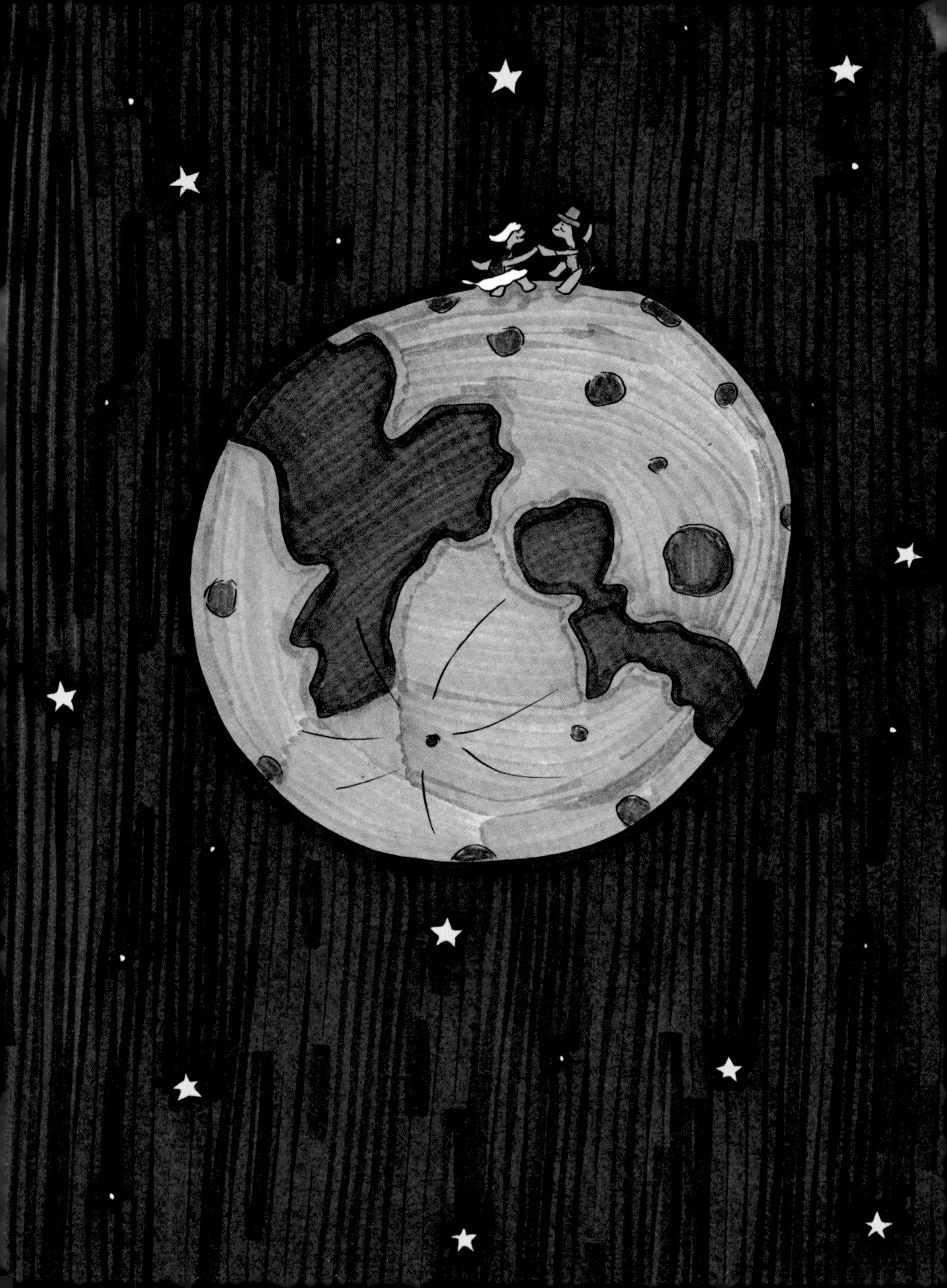

Whit Taylor is an award-winning cartoonist, writer, and editor from New Jersey. She has a bachelor of arts in anthropology from Brown University and a master of public health from Boston University. Her work has appeared on The Nib, Fusion, Illustrated PEN, The New Yorker, and other online publications.

A special thanks to Bill, Nora, Melissa, Sean, the Taylors, & Greg.